Praise for *The Gift: What tl*

Testimony from men and women of all ages and all stages of life compels the reader to consider a wide variety of Sabbath experiences. The short stories describe real experiences of people from around the world. It is a cultural and biblical feast, better than any church potluck.

—Edward Allen, dean and professor of religion, Union College

The Sabbath is God's gift to humanity, yet it is one that we do not always understand and appreciate. Drawing on the experiences of people from different nationalities, cultures, ages, and backgrounds, you see a common thread—the Sabbath is a blessing that expands and deepens our relationship with God. The more we engage with the Sabbath, the more we fully appreciate its beauty. It is like looking at different facets of a beautiful gem, and each story in this book gives the reader insights, inspiration, and encouragement.

—Audrey Andersson, executive secretary,
Trans-European Division of Seventh-day Adventists

The effort to prove the importance of the seventh-day Sabbath is pointless unless the Sabbath makes some difference in the experience of living. This story book makes clear the value of a change in the hustle and bustle of life on this day that is a sanctuary in time, an island of rest in the middle of the rushing river of time where stopping gives meaning to going.

—Gordon Bietz, associate director of higher education,
North American Division of Seventh-day Adventists

In this inspiring, thought-provoking collection of stories from around the world, the authors create a fantastic opportunity to rediscover one of God's greatest gifts to humanity, the Sabbath. This book is a gem that will keep you riveted from the first page.

—Ramón J. Canals, director of Sabbath School and Personal Ministries,
General Conference of Seventh-day Adventists

In a world of continuous activity where the pace of life is unprecedented, the Sabbath, and the respite it affords, is a blessing to all who experience it. The authentic stories provided by each writer in this book will be a blessing to all as readers will be able to see the life-changing experiences of the Sabbath through the lens of the authors. I count it an honor and privilege to be a part of this noteworthy project.

—Carlton P. Byrd, church administrator, pastor, evangelist, television speaker

God has given to each of us the special gift of the Sabbath. This book beautifully captures each writer's perception of this precious gift in a cogent, biblically sound manner. It is an inspiring read!

—Yvonne Shelton, cofounder and corporate consultant, 3ABN's Dare to Dream Network

So many studies show the importance of regular periods of rest and relaxation, with family and friends, away from the busyness of our daily life. And for millennia, the Bible has invited humanity to remember the Sabbath—a weekly day of rest. This book offers numerous stories of people who have been blessed by the Sabbath as such a day of rest. In themselves, these stories give personal evidence that this ancient practice is still very relevant today.

—Denis Fortin, professor of historical theology
and former dean of the Seventh-day Adventist Theological Seminary of Andrews University

The essays in this book are inspiring. Reading them not only gave me insight into verses in the Bible that address the Sabbath but made me think about the way I approach God's gift to us—the Sabbath. The essays also gave me ideas on how I can enhance my Sabbath experience.

—Jean Arthur, attorney, Maryland, United States

The Sabbath commandment is clear. But what does Spirit-led Sabbath keeping look like? Read this book and be enlightened, inspired, and blessed!

—*Derek Morris, president, Hope Channel International*

Warning: reading this book can change your life, eliminate stress, and show you a new day and a new horizon. It tells us about that golden thread in time that comes from eternity and is projected into eternity and shows what God does in the lives of those who accept one of the greatest gifts given to humanity, the Sabbath. He has given us not only that day but also the Manual—the Bible—that guides us in how to enjoy it and make it something special, a foretaste of the eternal rest that God has promised to give to His children. These are more than stories on paper; they are stories written by God in the hearts and minds of each author. This is a captivating book that is difficult to put down. You can be the protagonist of the next chapter and part of the glorious climax of the centuries.

—*Robert Costa, associate ministerial secretary, General Conference of Seventh-day Adventists*

The beauty and power of the Sabbath truth come to life in these inspiring and practical vignettes of Sabbath experiences.

—*Doug Batchelor, president, Amazing Facts International*

This book speaks to the heart, sharing special insights into one of God's great gifts. It is a much-needed book that should be on every bookshelf. Going beyond theology, it will help you discover—or rediscover—the joy, beauty, and power of the Sabbath day.

—*John Bradshaw, president, It Is Written*

This book helped me have a deeper appreciation for the holiness, purity, and generosity of God. From these inspirational stories about the gift of God's holy Sabbath, I have been strengthened to more earnestly seek to glorify His name.

—*Barry Black, 62nd chaplain of the United States Senate*

This much-needed and highly readable volume has brought us face-to-face with the what, why, and how of the Sabbath experience. I applaud the writers, whose unique and captivating stories will surely deepen our own appreciation of the Sabbath and lead us to a more meaningful Sabbath experience going forward.

—*Mansfield Edwards, president, Ontario Conference of Seventh-day Adventists*

This book has something for everyone, whether young or old, a scholar or not. It offers theological reflections and glimpses into the Sabbath on its weekly rotation in different contexts, even up through the COVID-19 pandemic. I enjoyed the peek into people's lives as Friday preparations were made to usher in the Sabbath. Cleaning the house, preparing special food to share with family and guests, laying out Sabbath clothes, the care of parents to make the Sabbath special for children, the sounds of song and praise, and then stepping into the wonder of the "temple in time" and into a fuller experience of what it is to be human, created in the image of an eternal God.

—*Lisa Beardsley-Hardy, director of education, General Conference of Seventh-day Adventists*

A wonderfully inspiring, touching, and eclectic collection of perspectives on the Sabbath. The diverse assemblage of authors and mix of personal stories with Scripture to frame the meaning of the Sabbath will certainly resonate with any reader.

—*Columbus Batiste, physician, California, United States*

This book effectively captures the unifying foundation that the Sabbath is for Seventh-day Adventists worldwide, brought to bear through real-life stories. At the same time, the individual anecdotes reflect diversity by featuring intergenerational and multicultural contributors with an experiential approach

to Sabbath observance. This book will evoke childhood memories for many and serve as a reminder of the Sabbath's divine origin.
—*Jakov Bibulović, executive secretary, Ontario Conference of Seventh-day Adventists*

This book is a beautiful mix of theological and personal reflections from all over the world. The different professional and cultural perspectives allow us to see the deep meaning of the Sabbath to people who have kept it all their lives, those who have just started keeping it, and those who needed to rethink how they have kept it. I was energized by the deep love of God's people around the world for this day of rest, liberation, and commemoration of Creation and salvation. There are so many suggestions for how to make the Sabbath meaningful—I cannot wait to share this book with those in my life who need to see Sabbath afresh and those learning to keep it.
—*Lisa Clark Diller, professor of history, Southern Adventist University*

This book is a refreshing exposé on how observing Sabbath weaves its blessings into the tapestry of our lives.
—*Lowell Cooper, former general vice president, General Conference of Seventh-day Adventists*

This is easily the most interesting and certainly the most refreshing book on the Sabbath that I have read. The authors write from their hearts, and the stories they narrate are bound to enrich anyone's Sabbath experience. I wish I'd had a book like this when our kids were growing up.
—*Gordon Christo, former secretary, Southern Asia Division of Seventh-day Adventists*

Thank God for this collection of Sabbath stories reminding us that the Sabbath is a gift from God to ensure that we have a life filled with jubilation, relaxation, and liberation. The variety of experiences that are shared highlights how God restores and energizes us during moments of intimate fellowship with him.
—*Ganim Hanna, president and CEO, Loma Linda Broadcasting Network*

These Sabbath stories are powerful. I have a renewed energy and conviction about the blessings of the Sabbath. This book is a must-read.
—*Trevor Stewart, pastor, Smyrna Seventh-day Adventist Church,*
Los Angeles, California, United States

What a wonderful book to remind us of how God has gifted us a day to focus on rest, recovery, and remembrance! This book helps us grow in our discovery and understanding of the health and wellness benefits of the Sabbath. A great read to remind us God still has a plan for humanity and deeply cares for each person.
—*Terry Forde, president and CEO, Adventist HealthCare, Inc.*

The Sabbath is unique in its origin and purpose. It is also unique in the way each person experiences its holy purpose. Its impact is as diverse as the individuals who embrace it. This book is captivating— unique stories and perspectives, each contributing to a fresh Sabbath enrichment.
—*Ivan and Elvera Blake, pastors, North Carolina, United States*

The editors have compiled stories from church leaders, professional people, students, and others who have found the Sabbath to be a life-changing reality. This is an excellent read that reminds us of the many benefits of a special day of rest, rejuvenation, and blessing—the Sabbath.
—*Kelly B. Bock, educator, California, United States*

This book is a gift from God, a timeless uplifting treasure. It reminds us that every Sabbath kept is a loving embrace of God's love, will, and character. "Great peace have they which love thy law" (Psalm 119:165, KJV).
—*Wintley Phipps, singer, songwriter, and pastor*

Packed with inspiring, insightful, and incredible stories and reflections, this book is a beautiful tapestry of how God puts His Sabbath idea into practice in the lives of people like you and me. You will delight in these bite-size thoughts for busy people. I highly recommend it to those seeking an easy yet deeper approach to Sabbath spirituality.

*—Martin Pröbstle, professor of Old Testament
and dean of the Department of Theology, Seminar Schloss Bogenhofen*

These experiences, so varied yet so similar, touched our lives. In many of the stories, we found a thread of either the events, the context, the time frame, or the overarching theme that was parallel to a stage or experience in each of our lives. We believe that each reader will also connect to these many authors' life situations in ways they may not expect. We see it as a profoundly rewarding and encouraging read.

—Peter and Jeanette Lewis, British Columbia, Canada

Interesting, insightful, and arresting! I am sure you will be blessed by the reflections, scholarship, and inspiration of each writer. The Sabbath, God's sanctuary in time, is a gift whose purpose and blessing we will continue to study, contemplate, and enjoy throughout eternity.

—Alvin M. Kibble, retired vice president, North American Division of Seventh-day Adventists

Timely, necessary, and important! The Sabbath is the banner of our Lord, under which His people stand. The Sabbath is an integral part of the eternal gospel.

—Mikhail F. Kaminskiy, president, Euro-Asia Division of Seventh-day Adventists

A powerful collection of personal reflections on the uniqueness and importance of the Sabbath, which is God's priceless gift to humanity, strengthening us on our journey through life and its struggles. These stories remind us that the Sabbath rest is about Him and not about us. Sabbath needs to be lived, and the Lord of the Sabbath celebrated. A refreshing must-read for everyone who wants to experience, as if for the first time, the relevance of the Sabbath.

—Jiří Moskala, dean, Seventh-day Adventist Theological Seminary, Andrews University

Sabbath is more than just time. It is time, *plus* the intimate, personal revelation of the Almighty God. Each writer here has managed to proffer the richness of Sabbath from his or her own experience. This is a packed suitcase filled with treasured revelations from around the globe.

—Carmela Monk Crawford, editor, Message *magazine*

This book focuses on the wonderful gift from God to the whole world: the Sabbath. Its presentation in the context of life stories from people of various backgrounds and cultures is simply exhilarating.

—G. Alexander Bryant, president, North American Division of Seventh-day Adventists

There are a few doctrines on which we, as Seventh-day Adventists, wholeheartedly agree without deviation. One of those is the Sabbath. It is so central to our being that it is ingrained in our name, Seventh-day Adventists. No matter one's age, station in life, or nationality, the Sabbath elicits stories of deep meaning, joy, rest, and blessing—everything that the Creator God wished for us as His creation. The authors of these short stories have captured the very essence of the Sabbath from their unique perspectives on what the Sabbath means to them. What is clear and consistent throughout this book is the centrality of that doctrine and the tie that binds us together. TGIS.

—Karnik Doukmetzian, general counsel, General Conference of Seventh-day Adventists

Seventh-day Adventists have studied the theological meaning of the Sabbath a lot. This book highlights the personal and practical meaning witnessed by many believers around the globe. It can be well used as a testimony in sermons and Bible studies and will also enrich our own Sabbath experience.

—Roland Fischer, president, Friedensau Adventist University

Calling all Seventh-day Adventists! This is a must-read and a much-needed (dare I say long overdue) book on the Sabbath. It reveals that the Sabbath is more than a commandment; it is about our relationship with God, ourselves, our family, and our community. More than just testimonials, this book causes one to reflect on what we might have missed out on, but what Sabbath can still be.

—*Ian Sweeney, field secretary, Trans-European Division of Seventh-day Adventists*

So many varied life experiences about the wonderful gift of the Sabbath enrich this book. The faith and trust in God under circumstances that placed people in a position where to obey and trust God would lead to loss of employment or education opportunities was inspiring to me. Each story is unique and inspiring. This great book will awaken some to the blessings of the Sabbath and others to reflect on the gift of time.

—*JoDee Bowen, certified public accountant, Georgia, United States*

Much appreciation for sharing these many experiences of the Sabbath. It made me think of what this special day means to me, working in the scientific community. And I have been able to pass on this thankfulness for a Sabbath rest to some of my geology colleagues.

—*Benjamin L. Clausen, Geoscience Research Institute, Loma Linda University*

This is a unique and beautiful book on the Sabbath that offers the reader a combination of personal experiences, memories, storytelling, theological reflections, and practical insights from a broad range of individuals. Their encounters with the Sabbath point us once again to the beautiful, joyful, and relational beauty of this special day provided as a gift to humanity from a loving, caring Creator.

—*Simon Martin, senior pastor, Betel Church, Oslo, Norway*

This book is a collection of great, inspiring, and thought-challenging personal stories that help the reader uncover the multifaceted meaning of one of the greatest gifts given to humanity. It is a delightful read for everyone—regardless of whether you are a curious observer, rookie, or veteran in enjoying the gift of Sabbath.

—*Zmago Godina, president, Slovenian Conference of Seventh-day Adventists*

These compelling personal stories from people of all walks of life will make you rethink what Sabbath is and why it was given. If you want to enjoy the blessings of the Sabbath, read this book.

—*Milan Bajic, Adventist-Muslim relations,*
Bosnia and Herzegovina Conference of Seventh-day Adventists

This is an immensely wonderful collection of memoirs on the Sabbath, a much-needed uplifting read! The authors eloquently and beautifully describe the joy of the Sabbath with such compelling conviction and delight that I find myself overcome with feelings of peace and happiness as I turn the pages. This is a book that leads all readers to appreciate the Sabbath all over again.

—*Lynette Mapp, lawyer–financial services, United Kingdom*

Our spiritual journeys should be centered on knowing Jesus intimately and experiencing all of His gifts fully, including the Sabbath. These authentic testimonies of so many diverse writers are an amazing help in our journey with Jesus. In these days of unrest, I hope you read this book. You will learn to enjoy our Lord and His deeper rest more fully as we wait for eternity coming very soon.

—*Jerry N. Page, ministerial secretary, General Conference of Seventh-day Adventists*

The Gift is a wealth of personal vignettes attesting to the miracle of the Sabbath in transforming our ordinary lives into extraordinary ones. Spanning the vast tapestry of our experiences, the Sabbath's peace and liberating power allows us to enjoy a foretaste of that greater celebration that awaits us in the new earth.

—*Leslie Hardware, physician, Maryland, United States*

Including thoughts from so many people of different ages and levels of spiritual maturity, this work reminds me of how I felt about Sabbath at different points in my experience.

—*Steven Sikora, attorney, Connecticut, United States*

Nothing represents love and caring for another like the commitment of time. And God, in His love for humankind, created an appointment on our calendar each week, an opportunity for rest and celebration. Enjoy these stories of the myriad ways committed Christians appreciate and enjoy this unique gift of time.

—*Robert Jepson, COO, Adventist HealthCare White Oak Medical Center*

I love a good story and this book is a heartwarming collection of personal experiences and perspectives about the Sabbath. Many of them resonate with my own background, reaffirming my faith journey. There are many insights shared that add a new dimension to my understanding and appreciation for the meaning of Sabbath rest. I encourage you to sit back and enjoy the delight of a wonderful story.

—*Rick Remmers, assistant to the president,*
North American Division of the Seventh-day Adventist Church

Inspirational and informational! This volume is a creative and innovative exploration of the role of the Sabbath in the lives of a diverse group of individuals. The varied perspectives and experiences of the authors are authentic and rich with spiritual nuggets that make this book a necessity and needed addition to our conversations about the uniqueness of the gift of the Sabbath.

—*Colwick Wilson, president, University of the Southern Caribbean*

What a great book about the experience of the Sabbath! People from different walks of life, ages, and cultures tell their personal story of what the Sabbath is to them. Some of the stories moved me deeply considering the great challenges many Adventist brothers and sisters must face to be faithful to God and to enjoy God's blessings on His holy day. As a family we decided to read one story each week during our Sabbath family worship! I commend Pacific Press and the editorial team for sharing these life experiences with all of us.

—*Sergio Becerra, dean of the School of Theology, Universidad Adventista del Plata*

This book beautifully illustrates how the Sabbath enriches our relationship with God in our lives and how it brings a global faith community together in terms of its collective spiritual journey. The readers will indeed be blessed to see the transformative blessings of the Sabbath experienced by many. Highly recommended!

—*Kyoshin Ahn, executive secretary, North American Division of the Seventh-day Adventist Church*

The writers have captured the essence of the Sabbath! Sabbath is not only a personal conviction but a way of witnessing when we keep it as the Lord asks. Fasten your seatbelt and be ready to enjoy your reading. Be ready to share your own story as you witness for God!

—*Magdiel Pérez Schulz, assistant to the president, General Conference of Seventh-day Adventists*

Sabbath is God's eternal gift of rest and peace to those who seek such solace, and we have the assurance that we can have that peace that passes all understanding through Jesus who remains our God and Lord of the Sabbath. Let us never fail to whisper that prayer of power and join God's people each Sabbath in raising our praises upward to His throne.

—*John M. Fowler, editor, Dialogue*

THE GIFT

WHAT THE SABBATH MEANS TO ME

Edited by
Nikolaus Satelmajer, Sheryl L. Beck, Steve D. Cassimy,
Abraham J. Jules, Ainsworth K. Morris, Ruth I. (Nutter) Satelmajer

Pacific Press®
Publishing Association
Nampa, Idaho | www.pacificpress.com

Cover design: Daniel Añez
Cover design resources: GettyImages.com
Interior design: Aaron Troia

The authors assume full responsibility for the accuracy of all facts and quotations as cited in this book.

You can obtain additional copies of this book by calling toll-free 1-800-765-6955 or by visiting http://www.adventistbookcenter.com.

ISBN 978-0-8163-6835-8

March 2022

Contents

Editors' Preface

How do six individuals coordinate the writing of a book by 168 writers? It was done with God's blessings and a lot of online video meetings, phone calls, text messages, and emails!

The idea for the project was first discussed a few years ago by several team members while they were at a small pizza parlor in New York. When work finally started, this book took shape in about two years, and now we are delighted to share it with you.

Our goal was to give each individual an opportunity to write their Sabbath story. How did they hear about the Sabbath? What does it mean to them? What challenges have they faced because of it? Why is it important to them? These are just some of the themes featured.

Those who were asked to write responded enthusiastically—young and old, experienced writers and individuals who had never been published before, all from various countries. The Sabbath is God's gift to the whole earth, and the writers represent the world family.

The book is organized into six sections. The opening chapter gives an introduction about God's gift of the Sabbath. If you want to study more about the Sabbath, we have listed some helpful resources in the last chapter.

We hope you will find the book encouraging for personal or group reading. Perhaps these stories will remind you of your own Sabbath moments, even though you may experience the Sabbath somewhat differently from the writers. For other readers, this may be an introduction to the Sabbath. While the focus of the book is not primarily doctrinal, we hope you will appreciate the many themes found in the stories. In any case, enjoy reading about this wonderful gift God has given us.

We want to thank each of the writers for their willingness to share their stories. We also owe special thanks to Janet Aldea, Shirley Evans, and Mary White for carefully reading the stories and offering helpful suggestions. A big thank-you to key team members of Pacific Press® Publishing Association, who enthusiastically supported the project. They are Miguel Valdivia, vice president of product development; Scott Cady, book acquisitions editor; Douglas Church, vice president of marketing; and Dale Galusha, president, who assembled the team with whom we worked.

This has been an exciting project for us. We hope you find in this book a renewed appreciation for God's gift—the Sabbath—and that you will be blessed as we have been. As you read, start thinking about your own Sabbath story.

Nikolaus Satelmajer, Silver Spring, Maryland   *Abraham J. Jules, Central Valley, New York*
Sheryl L. Beck, Laurel, Maryland   *Ainsworth K. Morris, Redlands, California*
Steve D. Cassimy, Elmont, New York   *Ruth I. (Nutter) Satelmajer, Silver Spring, Maryland*

About the Editors

Nikolaus Satelmajer started his ministry in New York, and he has served as a pastor, administrator, and lecturer. He retired as editor of *Ministry* and associate ministerial secretary of the General Conference of Seventh-day Adventists. He received his BA, MDiv, and DMin degrees from Andrews University and an STM in reformation studies, with distinction, from The Lutheran Theological Seminary at Philadelphia. He continues lecturing, editing, writing, and serving as an interim pastor and consultant. He and his wife, Ruth, are blessed with four children (Heidi, Ingrid, Marguerite Nikole, and John) and their families.

Sheryl L. Beck has enjoyed serving as editorial specialist of *Ministry, an* international journal for pastors and a publication of the General Conference Ministerial Association, for more than sixteen years. In addition to this book, she has been a member of editorial teams for several books and other publications. She holds a BS degree from Columbia Union College (now Washington Adventist University). In addition to her work, she enjoys reading, missions, and traveling with her husband, Jeff. They live in Laurel, Maryland, with their fur babies.

Steve D. Cassimy began his ministry in Canada, and his work has taken him to six continents. He has served as youth pastor, senior pastor, campus chaplain, television host, mentor, and director of various ministries. He received a BA degree from Burman University and MDiv and DMin degrees from Andrews University. He has contributed to several book projects. He is the pastor of the Co-op City Seventh-day Adventist Church in the Bronx, New York. He and his wife, Marilyn, are proud parents of David and Lavona.

Abraham J. Jules was born in Trinidad and Tobago and has pastored churches in various parts of New York. Currently, he is the president of the Northeastern Conference of Seventh-day Adventists, headquartered in Jamaica, New York. He received both a BA and BS from Oakwood University, an MDiv from Andrews University, and a DMin from United Theological Seminary. As part of his ministry, he has participated in several writing projects. He is married to Dr. Dominique (Juste) Jules, and they have two children, Raven and Dylan.

Ainsworth K. Morris was born in the beautiful island country of Jamaica. He graduated from Northern Caribbean University with degrees in business administration and religion and theology. He is also a graduate of the Seventh-day Adventist Theological Seminary at Andrews University, holding MDiv and DMin degrees focusing on urban ministries. For the past twenty-eight years, he has pastored churches across the West Indies and North America. Currently, he is the lead pastor of the Kansas Avenue Seventh-day Adventist Church in Riverside, California.

Ruth I. (Nutter) Satelmajer has received an AA degree from Andrews University, a BS from Atlantic Union College, and an MA from La Sierra University. She was born in Kelloggsville, Ohio. After graduating from Andrews University, she moved to New York City, where she worked for the *Faith for Today* broadcast and a Wall Street–headquartered corporation. After serving as a middle- and secondary-school teacher, she worked as principal of College Park Elementary School in Oshawa, Ontario, Canada, and Sligo Adventist School in Takoma Park, Maryland. She and her husband, Nikolaus, are blessed with four children (Heidi, Ingrid, Marguerite Nikole, and John) and their families.

A Gift From God

Nikolaus Satelmajer

What is the most important day of your life?

Is it your birthday? Perhaps your first day in school? Each of us has days we remember and cherish. There is another day that is more important than all of these days put together.

That day is the Sabbath. The *Sabbath*? Yes, that day, the seventh or last day of the week, according to the Bible. The Sabbath, as a day, is not the most important day unless we realize who gave it to us and understand its meaning.

The biblical Creation story tells us why the Sabbath stands above all other days. The Sabbath makes it clear that we are not the result of a cosmic accident but rather children of a personal God. After God created Adam and Eve on the sixth day, all was done—or so it seemed.

God saw all that he had made, and it was very good. And there was evening, and there was morning—the sixth day.

Thus the heavens and the earth were completed in all their vast array (Genesis 1:31–2:1, NIV).

This verse states, "The heavens and the earth were completed." Adam and Eve did not say, "God, You forgot something—a day is missing." Creation, so it seemed, was complete. What followed was unexpected.

"Then God blessed the seventh day and made it holy, because on it he rested from all the work of creating that he had done" (Genesis 2:3, NIV).

God's blessing of the seventh day is a surprise. But God is a God of surprises—*good* surprises!

Laurence A. Turner, a biblical scholar and preacher, puts it this way:

"This final day, unique in its content and narrative form, forms the apex and goal of God's creativity. . . . Here the seventh day, containing no recurring elements from other days, standing outside the two triads of preceding days, is blessed and sanctified like no other. It is separated from the preceding six; unique; blessed; holy."[1]

Unique—there is no other day like it. *Blessed*—by the Creator. *Holy*—so declared by God.

The Sabbath in the Bible

God is a gracious gift-giver and that is why He gave us the Sabbath. What we do with the gift is up to us. The Sabbath, according to biblical scholar Walter Brueggemann, reminds us of our special relationship with God.

"But because humankind is in the image of God, the rest of God is a promised rest for humankind (cf. Matt. 11:28–30). The rest to be granted is not a sleep which escapes history. It is the freedom and well-being of a new kind of history. As it is kept by the faithful week by week, sabbath is a disciplined reminder of how creation is intended."[2]

The Ten Commandments (Exodus 20) make it clear that the Sabbath was not a one-time gift to Adam and Eve. It is repeated weekly, even though, as New Testament scholar Sakae Kubo says, "The seventh day has no connection with any natural phenomena in the heavens or on the earth."[3] That fact is even more proof that the Sabbath is a unique and deliberate gift from God to all.

Yet, no matter how special and valuable the gift, some have not treasured it. In the Old Testament, Isaiah 58:13 admonishes God's people to "keep your feet from breaking the Sabbath" (NIV).[4] Old Testament scholar Franz Delitzsch states that the meaning is more dramatic than "breaking." He writes that this phrase means "If thou do not *tread* upon its holy ground with a foot occupied with its everyday work."[5] Thus, Sabbath holiness is emphasized.

In the New Testament, Jesus emphasizes the blessings of the Sabbath. John Brunt, a New Testament scholar and pastor, points out that "Jesus uses the Sabbath as a means to save life and to bring healing and wholeness through fellowship with Him."[6] And in the Gospel of Mark, Jesus asserts that the Sabbath is a blessing to all: "The Sabbath was made for man, not man for the Sabbath. So the Son of Man is Lord even of the Sabbath" (Mark 2:27, 28, NIV).

Challenged but still a blessing

After the New Testament period, arguments about the Sabbath arose. Some ignored it. Others proclaimed it was outdated. Eventually, some substituted Sunday for Saturday, while others saw no need for the Sabbath at all. Nowadays, there are those who claim that any day can be called the Sabbath. In other words, they claim the right to exchange it for any day even though God gifted the seventh day to us.

Our most cherished gifts speak of the special relationships we have with the gift-givers. Such is a gift I have from my parents. It is a suitcase—a rather plain suitcase made from the aluminum of an airplane. It was made by my father after World War II ended, while my parents and I were in a Communist concentration camp. During the imprisonment, my father was part of a work crew assigned to clear war rubble. Mother and I stayed in the camp. My father took the aluminum of a downed airplane and made suitcases and combs that he gave to the guards, hoping to receive better treatment. However, one suitcase he did not give away. It is the only item passed on to me. Others may not see anything special about it, but when I look at it, I think of my parents, who did everything possible to keep me alive in that camp. My parents are no longer alive, but that suitcase reminds me of how much they loved me. The value of the gift is not in the value of the aluminum. I value it because of who made it and gave it to me. Valued gifts come from those who love us. Likewise, the Sabbath is a gift from God who loves us.

Sabbath stories

This book is a collection of stories from those who value God's gift of the Sabbath. The writers are from many parts of the world, young and old. Some have never been published, while others are well-known writers. Some have experienced the Sabbath all their life, while others accepted the Sabbath later in life. Some tell the difficulties they have encountered receiving the gift of the Sabbath, but all thank God for the gift of the Sabbath. I believe each writer would agree with these words from former United States senator Joe Lieberman:

"I love the Sabbath and believe it is a gift from God that I want to share with everyone . . . in the hopes that they will grow to love it as much as I do."[7]

It is my hope that the stories in this book will help you appreciate the Sabbath as a gift from God.

---

1. Laurence A. Turner, *Genesis*, 2nd ed. (Sheffield, England: Sheffield Phoenix Press, 2009), 16.

2. Walter Brueggemann, *Genesis* (Louisville, KY: John Knox Press, 1982), 36.

3. Sakae Kubo, *God Meets Man: A Theology of the Sabbath and Second Advent* (Nashville: Southern Publishing, 1978), 41.

4. The Jerusalem Bible is even more dramatic: "If you refrain from *trampling* the sabbath"; emphasis added.

5. Franz Delitzsch, *Biblical Commentary on the Prophecies of Isaiah, trans.* James Martin, vol. 2 (Edinburgh: T and T Clark, 1884), 393, 394; emphasis added.

6. John C. Brunt, *A Day for Healing* (Nampa, ID: Pacific Press®, 2016), 68.

7. Joe Lieberman, with David Klinghoffer, *The Gift of Rest: Rediscovering the Beauty of the Sabbath* (New York: Howard Books, 2011), ix.

Sabbath Rest

Sabbath Came—and the Pressure Went Away

Roy Adams

In Grenada, the small Caribbean island where I grew up, the prejudice against Seventh-day Adventists was deep. We called them "seven devils" behind their backs. Many days, on the way home from elementary school, I would argue with a certain Adventist boy that the Anglican church was better than his church. "Look no further than Queen Elizabeth II," I would tell him. To my boyish mind, she was the epitome of insight and intelligence. And she was an Anglican.

Then came Hurricane Janet in September 1955. Severely damaging the small Adventist church on the island, it forced the Adventists to move their evangelistic meetings to a different venue—a tent pitched on the public recreation grounds. The move to a neutral place helped overcome the deep prejudice of the Adams family, and one of my sisters and I attended a meeting. The young evangelist, small in stature, captured our imagination, growing bigger every night he preached.

This all happened on the eve of my departure for boarding school in Saint George's, Grenada's capital. As Providence would have it, I found myself staying at the home of Mrs. Susana Davidson, an Adventist lady. One of the most powerful advertisements for the Sabbath I ever encountered was the mouthwatering aroma of fresh bread baking in her kitchen every Friday afternoon, whetting the appetite for supper following sundown worship.

But here I was, facing this new thing—the Sabbath. What was I to do with it? I was there to attend the Grenada Boys' Secondary School, perhaps the most prestigious educational institution in the country. The standards were high, and the competition was fierce. The first in my family to attend high school and college, I faced the opportunity with utter seriousness, determined to excel. I not only wanted to do well but also strived to be at or near the top in every class.

With that goal, I saw the Sabbath as an impediment. How could I clock out for a full twenty-four hours while the competition burned the midnight oil? No, Sabbath was not for me!

But being surrounded by the positive atmosphere at Sister Davidson's, the love and acceptance of the members of the capital church I attended with her family, and the winsome friendship of a bunch of caring young Adventist friends, I eventually said yes to Jesus Christ in a new way. And with Him came the Sabbath.

The high bar I had set for myself in my studies had come with a price. I remember feeling a persistent pressure in my head—not a headache but lingering, palpable congestion. Then as I began keeping Sabbath, something unexpected happened. I continued to excel in my studies, but the congestion went away and has not come back since.

How sweet upon this sacred day,

The best of all the sev'n,
To cast our earthly thoughts away,
And think of God and heav'n.[1]

_____

Roy Adams is a former associate editor of the *Adventist Review* and *Adventist World* in Silver Spring, Maryland, United States.

_____

1. Eliza Lee Follen, "How Sweet, Upon This Sacred Day" (n.d.).

Sabbath: An Invitation to Life

Jonas Arrais

The Sabbath was given to humanity in the Garden of Eden. And yet, even in the perfect world, God created the Sabbath as a reminder that life is not only about work and doing but about being and experiencing the gift.

Even after sin, the gift of the Sabbath remains true. The biblical record gives us fascinating insights into the nature of the Sabbath in a post-sin reality. This clearly appears later in the book of Exodus. There is a clear conflict between God and Pharaoh, who is behaving like an alternative god, putting pressure on people, forcing them to work, and eliminating freedom and rest. He embodies everything that subverts what we find in Eden: freedom, harmony, love, and rest. By enslaving people under the fake narrative that they are a threat to the nation, Pharaoh displays a complete lack of sensitivity to the things of God.

God, on the other hand, states that freedom is important and that rest is important. After the liberation of Israel, He invites whoever wants to help in the construction of the sanctuary to come. And then He talks about the Sabbath more than once, showing that He is not like Pharaoh. God focuses on freedom, choice, rest, existence, and life.

God's message about the Sabbath is important. Rest is needed, and the Sabbath provides it, for we are not robots or machines. The interesting thing is that, in Jesus, we also see this incorporation of the Sabbath and rest, bringing even more clarity to our modern dilemmas and passions. Jesus calls out those who are tired and burdened by religious and political oppression, and He offers rest and relief (Matthew 11:28).

The Sabbath helps us celebrate life. God created it for our benefit. The Sabbath is a gift from God—we do not earn it. It is a weekly reminder that we are humans, created in the image of a God who brought the work of Creation to completion through rest.

The Sabbath is a reminder of what it means to be human. We were made for work and play—service and life. So it becomes a radical countercultural principle. Our society experiences emotional and physical exhaustion—the body and soul have no time to breathe. The Sabbath comes as an oasis in the modern world.

Today, in our society and culture, Sabbath continues as a sign of hope. It reminds us that even in the midst of all this turmoil, we can remember Eden again. We can also look forward to the day when the Garden of Eden will be restored in the new earth.

Jonas Arrais is a ministerial secretary at the Northern Asia-Pacific Division of Seventh-day Adventists in Paju-si, Gyeonggi-do, Republic of Korea.

Bring Sabbath Joy Into Others' Lives

Sheryl L. Beck

Although I was blessed with parents who did not have a critical "do and don't" list of activities for the Sabbath, there were others in the church who not only had lists but attempted to force their lists on others.

One extremely hot and humid Sabbath day, I overheard a church member expressing "concern" that a single mother of five took her children to the public swimming pool one Sabbath afternoon to cool off. Even at a young age, I was upset by the conversation, and even now, many years later, it still irritates me. Were the mother's circumstances taken into consideration—single income, no air conditioning in their small apartment, cranky young children, and other factors? My young heart was annoyed because two of those children were my classmates in our small school operated by the church. While I appreciate and love the sanctity of the Sabbath, was judging this mother and talking behind her back the best course of action? Why not offer to help her instead?

We need to ask God to open our eyes to those around us and give us a compassionate heart to see if we can help others have a more joyful Sabbath. Is there a teenager who may be stuck in a bedroom playing video games whom you can take with you on your family hike? Is there an elderly person lying in a bed watching television whom you can visit instead? Is there a recently widowed father who doesn't have a clue what to do with his children whom you can invite over for lunch and then a walk? What about that university student many miles away from home who has no way to get to church and would love to go to church with you and then go to your house for a home-cooked meal? What can we do to make the Sabbath a memorable experience in the lives of others?

God has many children, and He has placed some in our path so we can be His hands and feet to them. Let's look at those with various needs and say, "God, I will help!" God just may use us to help make their Sabbaths a wonderful experience. If the Sabbath is a blessing in our life, we can help others experience that blessing also. Let's share the joy of the Sabbath.

Sheryl L. Beck is an editorial specialist for *Ministry*, an international journal for pastors produced by the General Conference of Seventh-day Adventists in Silver Spring, Maryland, United States.

Sabbath: An Invitation to Spiritual Rest

Clarence Brown

Ever since I learned about the Sabbath during an evangelistic series in the 1960s, the Sabbath has been a special time for me, with profound sacred significance. In fact, it was the discovery of the Sabbath message that convinced me to become a Seventh-day Adventist. As a new believer, I zealously discussed the verity of the Sabbath with Sunday keepers, drawing from my arsenal of compelling proof texts that I had memorized.

Through adolescence, I savored the Sabbath and looked forward to its weekly arrival. I vowed to "keep the Sabbath Day holy," dutifully preparing for it well before sunset on Friday. I diligently guarded my words, thoughts, and activities during the sacred hours—lest I "break" the Sabbath. In fact, some friends and I used to have "contests" as to who could keep the day most holy.

For me, Sabbath was hardly a day of rest but rather a day of exhaustion. Back then, we stayed at church all day long, engaging in Sabbath School, worship, neighborhood witnessing, choir rehearsal, youth service, and often a fun game night. There was very little downtime to connect intimately with God, but I easily justified that in the name of doing the Lord's work.

Over the decades, I have remained a faithful Sabbath keeper, along with my wife. We have passed down the Sabbath tradition to our children and now to our grandchildren. However, one major change has occurred. I now keep the Sabbath differently. While still an active church member, my focus now is less on *observing* the day and more on *experiencing* the day more intimately with God.

Rest was the missing component in my Sabbath keeping. My inner spirit needed to enter a more personal state of spiritual rest and refreshment. So now Sabbath has become my prime time for intimacy with my Savior—a kind of "date night" with my God. It is my time to commune and meditate without distraction. It is my time to reflect on the reality that the Lord of the Sabbath rested on *His holy day* from His completed works of Creation (in Eden) and redemption (in the tomb), all out of love for me. It is into this sacred state of spiritual rest that I enter at sunset on Friday and carry into corporate worship the next day. It is this mindset and attitude of gratitude that inspire me to serve and minister to others throughout the day with greater purpose.

What a joy it is now to authentically enter God's rest on His holy day!

_____

Clarence Brown is a retired journalist and corporate communication executive from Lake Elsinore, California, United States.

Sabbath Afternoon—September 15, 2001

Nathan Brown

I have a strong memory of Sabbath afternoon, September 15, 2001, the Sabbath after the world had been shaken by the terrorist attacks in New York and Washington, DC, and the downing of an airplane over Pennsylvania. I was living in Townsville, northern Queensland, Australia, but even half a planet away, we felt the shockwaves, fear, and uncertainty created by the tragic events of that week.

That balmy Sabbath afternoon found a group of our family and friends sitting together on a nearby beach. We talked, reflected, and simply spent time together, looking across to a nearby island with only a gentle breeze to ruffle the clear blue water.

The beach was not crowded, but many people came past us—walking, running, or throwing a ball for their dog. Then I noticed another group farther down the beach who were seemingly less hurried or anxious about getting somewhere. I recognized them as another group of Seventh-day Adventist families from another church simply being together after church that morning.

It seemed significant to me, perhaps more symbolically, that the only two groups of people who were together and seemed unhurried that afternoon were the two groups who were sharing Sabbath. Even more than just the activities of our fellow beachgoers that day, the stress and fear of the world around us contrasted with the pause for peace that we are offered week by week.

Amid the ceaseless swirl of headlines, the pressures of our always-on culture, and the feelings of tumult in our own lives, we are regularly invited to switch it off and to simply stop.

We stop because there are forces larger than we that take care of the universe, and while our efforts are important, necessary, and useful, they are not (nor are we) indispensable. The galaxy will somehow manage without us for this hour, this day, and so we are invited—nay, commanded—to relax and enjoy our relative unimportance, our humble place at a table in a very large world.[1]

The memory of that Sabbath afternoon, September 15, 2001, reminds me how Sabbath gives us a different perspective on the troubles and fears of the world around us, an opportunity to catch our breath, and a way to practice the peace that God can bring to each of our lives.

Nathan Brown is a writer and book editor at Signs Publishing in Melbourne, Australia.

1. Wayne Muller, *Sabbath: Finding Rest, Renewal, and Delight in Our Busy Lives* (New York: Bantam Books, 2000), 83.

The Sabbath and Rest

Alejandro Bullón

In 1998, Rede '98, a satellite evangelistic series in Spanish, was broadcast from São Paulo, Brazil, for the three Americas—South, Inter, and North America. Exactly six days before the start of the meeting, I was taken to the hospital for emergency gallbladder surgery. One day before the start of the evangelistic meetings, I got out, still convalescing.

On Friday, the organizers' apprehension was visible, and I was worried myself. I was not in any physical or emotional condition to preach for fifty minutes. I thought about giving up. From my point of view, I did not know what to do. The meeting could not be suspended because the Hispanic world of the three Americas was ready for the broadcast: the churches were mobilized, and the members had distributed the invitations to their friends, family, and colleagues. What should we do? Or, what *could* we do?

At sunset, alone in my hotel room, I poured out all my anxiety to God. Up to that point, I had done what I could to prepare for the evangelistic series, but from a human point of view, the situation was grim. Then, when the blessed hours of Sabbath arrived, I said to God, "Lord, this day is the Sabbath, but my heart is heavy over this situation. Give me your rest, oh God, and put peace in my heart."

At that moment, I felt a gentle breeze coming through the window and blowing on my face. I cried. And when I got up, I felt as if a heavy load had come off my back. I went to the bathroom and looked at my face in the mirror. My eyes reflected peace and joy; God's Sabbath had come into my life.

The next night, I was in the pulpit, preaching the Word of God to thousands of Hispanics in the three Americas. The Sabbath is not just a doctrine but a real and trans-formative experience.

Alejandro Bullón is a former ministerial secretary at the South American Division of Seventh-day Adventists in Brasilia, Brazil.

My Sabbath Resolution

Mauvette Cuevas

The Sabbath is very important in my life. It is something I have always known, having grown up as a Seventh-day Adventist. My entire family on my mom's side is Adventist, and that fact has taught me a lot about how to live my life and what things are most important to me. The Sabbath is when we can rest and really have a day to ourselves to praise and learn more about God.

When I was younger, I often went to church on Saturdays with my family. Before COVID-19, I always tried my best to go. Since my church is closed, I do not go at all, which is kind of frustrating. Actually, it is really hard for me. It feels as if I am pulling away from God.

My grandparents have always inspired me and continue to inspire me. They go to church via Zoom every Sabbath. They do not wash the dishes or wash clothes or anything like that, but rest on the Sabbath. They resume their regular activities when the sun goes down and it is no longer Sabbath. I think it is really cool that, after all these years, they still follow the same routine. I hope to be that passionate one day and that God is included in my life.

I think the Sabbath is also a way to refocus my week on God. We have the entire week to do things we need or want to do, and they sometimes distract us from God, so the Sabbath is there for us to refocus on Him. Fortunately, since I go to a Seventh-day Adventist school, we have religion classes to learn more about God and the Bible. The school helps me keep my eyes on the important things in life.

I am grateful to be a part of the Seventh-day Adventist community. It has been amazing growing up and learning different Bible stories. As I have grown older, it feels like I have become more distant from God. Some terrible things have happened in my life, and it is hard not to blame Him for them. The things that have gone wrong in my life are obviously not God's fault, but I often seem to blame Him anyway. I just do not know where else to direct my anger. I feel bad, turning against the One who loves me unconditionally. I use the Sabbath to help me with this problem. Every day we learn more and more about God's love and how much He cares for us. The Sabbath reminds me that I have to put my faith in what God does because He wants only what is best for me.

A resolution of mine is to try not to blame God for problems in my life. I need to remember that God has a plan for me, and He knows what is best for me. I must learn to put all my trust in God. Even without knowing what will or what could happen in my life, I should always trust what God is doing.

Mauvette Cuevas is a twelfth-grade student at La Sierra Academy in Riverside, California, United States.

What Sabbath Means to Me as a Hospital Administrator

Lyndon C. Edwards

A hospital never shuts down completely. At all times, there are many professionals on duty prepared to care for existing and prospective patients. In a variety of ways, Sabbath in a hospital is not significantly different from any other day. We do not empty our patient beds on Friday afternoon and welcome them back at sunset on Saturday evening. Our emergency department operates at full capacity and is often busiest on Friday evenings. Many medical roles fit neatly into our concept of healing like Jesus often did on the Sabbath. But a hospital also requires a host of others, such as admission clerks, receptionists, and security personnel—just to name a few. Other professionals—attorneys, communication specialists, and even administrators—are also "on call" on Sabbaths.

My guide has been Jesus' words in Mark 3:4, when He healed the man with the deformed hand in the synagogue on the Sabbath. He challenged the religious leaders, who watched this act of healing with legalistic condemnation, with these words, "Which is lawful on the Sabbath: to do good or to do evil, to save life or to kill?" (NIV). The answer was simple from Jesus' perspective but theologically confounding to those who saw Sabbath observance as a yoke versus a delight, as described in Isaiah 58. While we need to do these good things on the Sabbath, can we call it Sabbath rest? How do we reconcile these seemingly competing concepts?

When I came to Loma Linda from a secular organization, I noticed something different on my first Friday. I called one of our administrative departments Friday afternoon, and the recorded phone message stated that the department was closed. I asked my assistant what was going on, and she reminded me that pretty much everything shut down at 2:00 p.m. on Friday at Loma Linda. My entire career, I had worked pretty much up to sunset on Friday before leaving the office. After spending a few weeks at Loma Linda, I realized that administrative workers were determined to be nonessential for Sabbath work and that midday Friday was acceptable for leaving. Patient-care personnel, on the other hand, continued their roles.

As an administrator of a Seventh-day Adventist hospital, I realize the Sabbath is essential, and I will do everything I can to make the environment one that is respectful of the day's holiness. I am more concerned, though, about how our faith informs our actions the other days. Ellen White writes, "In times past, some in the sanitarium have felt it their duty to introduce the Sabbath question in all places. They have urged it upon the patients with earnestness and persistency. To such the angels of God would say, Not *words*, but *deeds*. The daily life tells much more than any number of words."[1]

Our mission to those who are not of our faith is to treat them in such a way that they will choose to follow the Creator of the Sabbath. In our hospital, we have that opportunity every day, every hour—seven days a week.

Lyndon C. Edwards is senior vice president and administrator of adult hospital services at Loma Linda University Health in Loma Linda, California, United States

1. Ellen G. White, *Evangelism* (Washington, DC: Review and Herald®, 1946), 543; emphasis in the original.

Sabbath: A Temple Made of Time

Prema Gaikwad

"Sabbath is almost here; let's get ready!"

The excited call of my mother during my early childhood in India still rings in my memory. The reminder to leave my play or outdoor activities was typically not so welcome, but it was different Friday evenings. I had much to look forward to as Sabbath set in: the neat and tidied home, the appetizing aroma of special Sabbath meals, soft gospel music, and family worship to welcome the Sabbath. Father, a musician and busy school administrator, always looked relaxed that evening; he usually had a new Bible song to teach us. Family worship was special on Friday evenings.

After that came corporate spiritual activities—vespers service, Sabbath morning services, and afternoon story time and nature activities—for rejuvenation and fellowship. I realize that these early experiences were ways God helped me understand that Sabbath is different from other days of the week. Everything felt special on Sabbath—intentional, resembling a celebration. I was blessed.

The Bible verses in Exodus and Hebrews—"Remember the Sabbath day, to keep it holy" (Exodus 20:8, ESV) and "So then, there remains a Sabbath rest for the people of God, for whoever has entered God's rest has also rested from his works as God did from His" (Hebrews 4:9, 10, ESV)—had, indeed, come alive in those formative years of my life. Sabbath as a holy day was etched in my mind as a "temple made of time." This was a day set aside to focus on worshiping God, on family bonding, and for "restful" interactions.

Later, when I had my own family, many of these Sabbath practices continued. My husband and I decided that our Sabbath activities needed to be deliberate and meaningful. We intentionally tried to make Sabbath enjoyable for all—a weekly celebration. As our two boys are now settled and have their own families, our prayer is that the beautiful Sabbath celebration will continue in their respective families. We also pray that their example, in turn, will be an inspiration to their children and to countless others.

So, what does Sabbath mean to me? The song title "Temple Made of Time" says it all. God has set aside and blessed a recurring sacred day of the week—the seventh day, the Sabbath—and promised to bless all those who keep it holy: "God blessed the seventh day" (Genesis 2:3, ESV). It makes a great deal of sense to me. It is my prayer that the Bible-based seventh-day Sabbath find fulfillment as a temple made of time in your life too.

Prema Gaikwad is a professor of education at the Adventist International Institute of Advanced Studies in Silang, Cavite, Philippines.

Rediscovering Freedom—The Danger of Being Too Busy on the Sabbath

Laszlo Gallusz

Sabbath is the busiest day of the week for pastors—even in the former Yugoslavia, where I was born and I ministered for twenty years. It is a day of blessings and joy, but it is also a day that can drain your energy. I was expected to preach at least two sermons every Sabbath (for the morning and the afternoon services), teach a Sabbath School class, attend a Sabbath School teachers meeting, conduct board meetings, and be present at other church meetings. I looked forward to the Sabbath, enjoying the ministry, but I also welcomed Sunday as a day of recuperation and refreshing.

After twenty years of working as a pastor or working with pastors, I moved to a full-time teaching position. This shift in vocation brought a number of challenges but also many blessings. One of the most surprising things that happened to me was a rediscovery of the beauty and joy of the Sabbath.

A week in a higher-education institution can be very demanding mentally, so Sabbath comes as an invitation to freedom. It is an opportunity to slow down, stop, and distance myself from the pressures of life while tuning in to the frequency on which God can be heard and experienced. Sabbath also provides me with the opportunity to spend quality time with my family and friends, bringing me great joy. I rediscovered Sabbath as a day of refreshing, a day that, according to Jesus, "was made for humankind, and not humankind for the sabbath" (Mark 2:27, NRSV).

In light of my recent personal discovery, I began wondering: To what extent are we crowding out the blessings of the Sabbath that the Creator intends to give us each week? Being too busy on the Sabbath day robs us of the shalom that the Sabbath, as a divine institution, is meant to provide. Sabbath, a sign of freedom in Christ, is given as a gift that we receive every seventh day, but what are we doing with this gift? Do we take time to receive the Sabbath and be blessed?

Laszlo Gallusz is a senior lecturer in New Testament studies at Newbold College of Higher Education in Binfield, Bracknell, United Kingdom.

Rest: The Sabbath for a Millennial

Kerrian Hayman

Our bodies and our minds are crying out for replenishment. Can we rest? I have heard from Seventh-day Adventists and other friends that there needs to be an extra day on the weekend. As Adventists, we often get recruited into participating in church activities that are enjoyable but at times tiring. Before the COVID-19 quarantine, it almost felt like Sabbath had turned into a checklist of services that I had to participate in throughout the day. Often, I have been told, "Oh, but you're young! You should be able to teach the lesson without any problem!"

My non-Adventist friends work all week and try to squeeze in time for errands, socializing, and just plain relaxing between life and jobs, but sometimes it just does not happen. One friend recently asked me, "Why isn't there a day when we all just stay home and do nothing but rest?" Wow! What an opportunity to share our faith and the Sabbath. I shared with my friend that Jesus created the Sabbath for *us*.

That is true, isn't it? Mark 2:27 reminds us of this. The Sabbath is the Lord's gift to us—to all of us. Old and young—the Lord created this day of rest for us, a day to delight in Him and His Word. As the week goes on, I find myself yearning not only to enjoy the rest that my mind and body so desperately crave but also to delight in the presence of the One who knows me best. We, all of us, deserve this rest in the same way we deserve His love—not because we have earned it but because that is who He is. He loves us enough to care about every detail of our experiences, understands us enough to know that we need this time with Him, and wants us to enjoy every aspect of our lives. The Sabbath does not require a certain level of experience or an exhaustive list of what we have done throughout the week to prove that we have earned it. Our God does not do that. He simply offers His love and His time—always, but especially on His designated day of rest.

Our need for rest and our desire for closeness with God help us appreciate why He gave us the Sabbath.

Kerrian Hayman is an administrative assistant in Long Island, New York, United States.

A Palace in Time

Andrea Moskalova Jakobsons

Abraham Heschel, in his book *The Sabbath,* states, "The Sabbath is the presence of God in the world."[1] He also maintains that God is in moments of time. In other words,

Sabbath is a moment in time. As such, he calls it "a palace in time." When I think of a palace, I think of a king and queen, princes and princesses, a coat of armor, knights, nobility, land, stables, lots of servants, and tons of luxury, activity, and riches. So when I first thought of the Sabbath as a palace in time, I was not sure it fit the picture. Now let's be honest—there have definitely been Sabbaths in my life that did not feel like palaces but days of boredom. It took me a while to see the Sabbath as a palace, as a luxurious moment in time.

It finally occurred to me when I saw how God designed the Creation week that Sabbath is different. The six days of the Creation week are similar to each other, but the Sabbath day stands out. In creation, God reverses the "formless and empty" (Genesis 1:2, NIV) earth by forming and filling it. However, He forms on the first three days and then fills on the following three days. God intentionally fills each space that He formed in the first three days.

Forming		Filling	
Day 1	Light and darkness	Day 4	Sun, moon, and stars
Day 2	Separation of waters (sky and water)	Day 5	Birds and fish
Day 3	Land and vegetation	Day 6	Animals and humans
	Day 7	Sabbath	

Day seven is different. On that day, God forms and fills at the same time. He forms the space (the day) and fills it with His presence. It is a holy day because God is in it.

God gave us the seventh day as a moment for relationships. It was a day for Adam and Eve to enjoy each other and delight in God. The vertical relationship with God and horizontal relationship with other people was to be cultivated on the Sabbath day. God did not rest because He needed to but because He wanted to spend time with the couple He had just created.

He also gave us the seventh day as a moment for re-creation. In order for us to be different from the animals and not ruled by passions and instinct, we need to come to God and be re-created, renewed by Him each Sabbath.

The Sabbath is also a moment of celebration. I realized that the Sabbath is a celebration when I went to Jerusalem. On Friday evening, the Jews gather at the wailing wall (the only standing part of the Jerusalem temple) and sing, dance, pray, and read Scripture together. They welcome the Sabbath and celebrate it. Then they go home and invite friends and family over to celebrate some more. God has given us an incredible gift in the Sabbath. When I take the time to celebrate it, focusing on God and others, God changes my perspective. Instead of being stressed and anxious about what is going on in my life, I can focus on the big God who takes care of everything because He is my Creator.

The Sabbath is a palace in time. It is filled with the greatest luxury—God with us.

Andrea Moskalova Jakobsons is the lead pastor of the Kettering Seventh-day Adventist Church in Kettering, Ohio, United States.

1. Abraham Heschel, *The Sabbath* (New York: Farrar, Straus and Giroux, 2005), 21.

My Sabbath Experience

Stacey P. Knight

As a self-confessed workaholic and perfectionist, I struggle with knowing when to let go. I have been accused of arguing too much, taking things too literally, trying too hard to make a point. Being also indecisive and dithering, I spend too much time trying to make up my mind about details that often do not really matter to anyone but me.

Because I set standards of personal performance that are difficult to attain, I used to work until I was exhausted. I often pushed myself right up to a given deadline, and then, because I was still not satisfied with my work, I invariably ended up being late.

Several years ago, while writing my graduate thesis, I learned that the Sabbath was made for *me*. I needed a break. I was working hard every day. There was so much to do that I thought I had to use every possible minute to make the project perfect. It never seemed right to spend any of my time socializing, playing, or doing anything for myself. There was no such thing as spare time. I felt guilt pangs whenever I was not working—until I learned the purpose of God's day of rest.

It was there to give me a break, to make me rest in Him. There was no need to feel guilty, because this was not slacking off; this was being obedient to His Word. I was taking a break because *God* said I should. I had the permission of the Creator of the universe to rest from my labor. This was a refreshing thought to me. Instantly, I felt unburdened and released from the bondage of work.

I still struggle with perfectionism and a tendency to work too many hours. But no matter how hard I push myself during the week, I am guaranteed a day of rest from my toils.

Through the Sabbath message, I am learning to practice balance, ensuring that I get enough daily rest. I have committed my time to God, and He blesses me with more time. I have been able to accomplish so much in a day that it could only be through His grace.

Over the years, I have found that there's never been a good or compelling reason for me to give up my Sabbath rest. Although I have been asked on so many occasions—"Just this one time"—I realize that if I did it for one meeting, one birthday party, or one appointment at the salon, then I would do it for another and another. The sacredness of the Sabbath has taught me to be more decisive. I have a sense of resolve. I'm able to demonstrate my commitment to serve the Creator above all else by saying, "I'm not available on Saturdays, because I have already dedicated that time to God." But most of all, keeping Sabbath keeps me from overburdening myself.

Stacey P. Knight is an attorney in Kingston, Jamaica.

Sabbath Rest: A Pandemic Discovery in the Wilderness Leading to the Promised Land

Ruth Koilpillai

By March 2020, when a virus had shut down much of the world, many Sabbath activities had shut down too. Knowing a pandemic could not break the Sabbath God created, I asked Him for new understanding about Sabbath rest, taking comfort in His promise, "The LORD himself goes before you and will be with you; he will never leave you nor forsake you. Do not be afraid; do not be discouraged" (Deuteronomy 31:8, NIV).

One Sabbath morning in May, as part of my family's new normal, I logged on to Zoom for Sabbath School. As I was sitting with my family, God's promise, "See, I am doing a new thing" (Isaiah 43:19, NIV), came to mind. I saw God's blessing in providing technology that allowed many of us to gather with Him despite shuttered churches. I saw God changing me, along with my fellow sojourners, as we feasted on His Word (John 6:35) and united in sincere prayer through the Holy Spirit, journeying from the wilderness into Sabbath rest (Hebrews 3 and 4).

As 2020 ended, Sabbaths had grown more joyful, peaceful, and restful than at any time of my life, even as the devastating effects of the pandemic raged on, wreaking havoc for me, my loved ones, and millions around the world. How did my Sabbath rest grow? Jesus! Jesus was my blessing. Jesus proved trustworthy, freeing me from my sins so I could return to Him and rest (Matthew 28:20; 2 Peter 3:9).

Jesus, through the Holy Spirit, used His Word to open my eyes and ears to the pain sin inflicted on me and the pain that through me was inflicted on others whenever I chose myself over Him. He gave me joyful freedom from sin each time I repented and returned to Him (Isaiah 30:15, 18). Abundantly loved, abundantly forgiven by Jesus, I can love, forgive, and see my wilderness restlessness become rest in Jesus (Joshua 21:44, 45; John 14 and 15).

Sabbath rest comes *to* me from Jesus, *for* me. I am able to exchange my filthy self-righteousness for Jesus' pure robe of righteousness, arming my heart in love every day of the week, culminating in Sabbath delight. Sabbath rest is worth living, sharing, and celebrating!

God gave us the Sabbath at Creation as His seal of love. We, the people of Sabbath and Advent, believe we are called to return to this Sabbath rest (Isaiah 58). Let's show and tell others the trustworthiness of God's good promises (2 Corinthians 1:20–22). As we are being restored to God's image, let's abide in His love. That is how light defeats darkness so we can enter our rest in His promised land—together with Jesus.

Ruth Koilpillai is a clinical psychologist in Frederick, Maryland, United States.

You Need to Rest Today

Ainsworth K. Morris

It is not surprising that when I became a pastor, I had a checklist of things that I needed to accomplish each week. Even the Sabbath was evaluated by the tasks I completed. Whenever I failed to complete my responsibilities, I was disappointed and criticized myself. This accomplishment-based Sabbath keeping continued until my fourth year of ministry, when I learned a precious lesson about Sabbath rest.

This particular Sabbath was a sunny day. I had prepared my sermon, gone through my usual checklist, and prepared to visit all five churches under my care. I started driving to my first church when, fewer than ten minutes into the journey, I felt sudden fatigue. As I drove, the fatigue was more intense. I was caught off guard. I tried to ignore it, but the longer I drove, the more intense the exhaustion became. I could not understand the fatigue. I was in good health and had slept well Friday night.

What is going on? I thought. Then suddenly, I heard a clear voice telling me: "You need to rest today."

I immediately pulled over and parked the car on a hillside from which I could view picturesque Kingston, Jamaica. I hoped that by doing this, my mind would be quieted and my energy recovered so I could continue driving to the church.

"Keith, you *need* to rest today," I heard the voice again.

Guilt ridden and frustrated that I could not accomplish my pastoral duties, I exited the car and stood looking across the vast scenic landscape. I had no mobile phone to call the church leaders who, no doubt, were wondering where I was. I reminded myself that I had told the elders to be prepared in case of emergencies.

"Keith, *you* need to rest today." That voice again!

I cannot tell you the precise moment when frustration and annoyance gave way to reflection and worship, but my thoughts shifted to the incredible blessings of God I had witnessed in my life. Before I knew it, I started to see the sun disappear behind the orange horizon. I had spent an entire day alone with God without regard for time. My curious bout of exhaustion was replaced with a sense of renewed energy and hopefulness.

As expected, that evening several church members inquired about my well-being. I explained my absence and set everyone's heart at ease.

That day, I learned that the Sabbath is never about how well I keep up with my checklist of activities. Instead, I realized that it is always about how well my awesome God checks up on me!

Almost twenty-four years later, on each Sabbath, I still hear that unmistakable voice saying, "Keith, you need to rest today." Yes, I preach and do other ministries on the Sabbath, but that voice reminds me to reflect on God's beautiful blessings and serve Him and His people with gladness.

Ainsworth K. Morris is the pastor of the Kansas Avenue Seventh-day Adventist Church in Riverside, California, United States.

Developing a Sabbath Rest Cycle

Emil Dean Peeler

Growing up in Sacramento, California, the rhythm of my spiritual life was largely shaped by the cycle of activities that began at sundown each Friday evening. I vividly recall, prior to the sun hiding its face in the sky, performing a variety of chores, preparing our home for the Sabbath—a day for people to realign with their Creator. I was taught that the Sabbath was a special time, deserving careful preparation and reverential focus unlike any other day of the week. Thus, my brothers and I alternately shared the tasks of dusting the furniture, vacuuming the floors, and washing the dishes. We then showered, ironed our Sabbath clothes, and even polished our church shoes to make sure that everything was in proper order for the twenty-four hours of rest, reflection, and renewal.

In my early years, I did not always appreciate the value of the Sabbath. Sometimes I thought the Sabbath was an unnecessary inconvenience that took the joy out of life. Since that time, however, my desperate need for a break from life's unrelenting challenges has changed my perspective regarding God's day of rest. Now I see the wisdom and beauty of embracing this weekly respite. I have adopted a Sabbath that brings peace to me.

Each Sabbath, I:

Stop: I purposely take time to pause in the midst of all life's busyness and demands to still my spirit and silence all the deafening noise that envelops me.

33

Switch: I intentionally turn off any device that might cause any distraction and turn my gaze away from God, who deserves my undivided focus.

Sing: I deliberately take the time to lift my voice to God in songs that commemorate His goodness and challenge me to live in a way that pleases and honors Him.

Study: I consciously read and study His Word and other inspired materials that help me understand His character, discover His will, and show me ways to successfully live life in the Spirit.

Socialize: I intentionally make quality time to enjoy worship and fellowship with family, friends, and fellow believers in order for me to grow in my faith.

Share: I determine to faithfully share the good news of the gospel to others by helping, praying, teaching, and cheerfully giving to others so that Jesus may be seen and felt in practical ways.

Surrender: I unabashedly take the opportunity to cry out for the grace that provides forgiveness and the strength I need to navigate another week that will end in repeating this cycle of resting in Jesus.

I invite you to join me each Sabbath in implementing these seven ways of connecting to God as we prepare for eternity. _____

Emil Dean Peeler is the senior pastor at the Capitol Hill Seventh-day Adventist Church in Washington, DC, United States.

The Sabbath and Time

Timothy G. Standish

I am lying with eyes closed on my backyard's soft grass, feeling the cool breeze and the sun's warmth. It is the sensory equivalent of eating a tree-ripened orange, perfectly balancing citric acid tartness with the sweetness of natural sugar. Birds fly in on the breeze, and occasionally the sound of their wings rises above leaves rustling. The smell of earth and grass contributes to this sensory feast, even before I open my eyes to an overwhelmingly blue sky and my white dog named Jill, who just flopped down beside me. When shared with her, the experience is even better.

My life is not always like this. I can sit for hours in front of a computer screen or jammed aboard an aircraft. There's the slow torture of droning presentations or encounters with difficult personalities spouting incoherent arguments about science, philosophy, theology, or—worst of all—politics. Sometimes modern life feels like a giant conspiracy to separate us from all that is beautiful through ever more frenetic, complex, and pointless activity.

When I am not consumed with meetings, paperwork, and other futilities, I enjoy the functional aspect of being a biologist. I study connections between processes within organisms and their environment. That means that I spend a lot of time working with, reading about, and thinking through how DNA and other molecules function.

If that sounds complicated, it is; but it is also fascinating. However, sublime beauty is only glimpsed during times when we reflect on the relationships that make all this happen. That time is God's gift. Time differs from other dimensions. We travel in lockstep with time, moving only forward through it. Time must be used in the moment, or it is gone. When God gave the Sabbath to all creation, He made it out of this unique dimension.

The Sabbath connects us in time as we remember our Creator's acts in the past and look forward to His promised new creation. It anchors our understanding of who and where we are at the moment by emphasizing our relationship with our Creator, our fellow humans made in His image, and the rest of creation made to sustain, fascinate, thrill, teach, and occupy us.

On Sabbaths, I lie in my backyard paradise. The breeze is moving air, most of which is nitrogen. Plants harvest sunlight energy to grow while sharing some with microorganisms that use information stored in DNA to make protein machines. These machines join nitrogen to organic molecules that are made into more DNA and proteins. The thousands of relationships we call life necessarily came together in a moment when God spoke and it was done. Sabbath time in my backyard with Jill provides the opportunity to open my eyes, breathe in the air, and look up at that remarkably blue sky. Jill appreciates the firmament in her own way, but only I know that it is blue because God made air mostly of nitrogen.

Timothy G. Standish is a senior scientist at the Geoscience Research Institute in Loma Linda, California, United States.

I Started Reading the Bible and . . .

Vladimir Stefanović

I live in Serbia, a beautiful country at the crossroads of central and southeast Europe. The dominant religion in Serbia is the Serbian Orthodox Church, and it is traditionally considered the "state religion."

I was born into an Orthodox family. My neighbors and friends were Orthodox. I attended Orthodox churches; lit candles; kissed the icons; and, if I had money, left some for the church. In our home, we had two Bibles, but reading them was not encouraged. The priests told us that the Bible was not for ordinary people.

My parents knew a Protestant pastor, even though all the Protestants in Serbia comprised only about 1 percent of the population. Most of the population considered Protestants to be a religious cult. This Protestant pastor, in fact, was a Seventh-day Adventist. He visited our family often and, since my parents were interested in religion, they talked to him about it regularly. I listened to the conversations, and he impressed me because he always used the Bible to make his points. I had never seen or heard anyone use the Bible that way. Religion finally made some sense and began to hold a deeper meaning for me.

During those conversations with the pastor, one of the topics we discussed was the seventh-day Sabbath. As an Orthodox, I was taught that Sunday was the seventh day. But this pastor read passages from the Bible showing that Saturday was the seventh day of the week and that it was the Sabbath. I was shocked!

I started reading the Bible. I wanted to know its message and find God's will for me. The pastor was right. Sabbath *is* the seventh day of the week. This revelation changed my life. The message of the Sabbath helped me develop a stronger relationship with God. Eventually, I became a Seventh-day Adventist, a significant decision in my country and culture. When I was a young person, the idea of Sabbath rest was not all that important. But, as an adult, I welcome the opportunity to rest. And, most of all, I experience the blessing of the Sabbath. Nothing can replace that.

Vladimir Stefanović is a ministerial student at the Belgrade Theological Seminary in Belgrade, Serbia.

The Sabbath as Rest in Jesus

Elizabeth Talbot

I have always been interested in the well-known passage in which Jesus offers His rest: "Come to Me, all who are weary and burdened, and I will give you *rest*. Take My yoke upon you and learn from Me, for I am gentle and humble in heart, and YOU WILL FIND REST FOR YOUR SOULS. For My yoke is comfortable, and My burden is light" (Matthew 11:28–30, NASB; emphasis added).

We all need rest, especially for our souls.

I was particularly intrigued by the fact that these three verses are immediately followed by the only two stories in Matthew's Gospel that take place on the Sabbath (Matthew 12:1–8 and 9–14). In these few verses, Jesus declares Himself to be both the *Provider of Rest* (Matthew 11:28–30) and the *Lord of the Sabbath* (Matthew 12:8). I wondered how these two declarations were related to each other, and that is how the topic of my doctoral dissertation was chosen. Continuous examination of this theme changed my life and my understanding of what the Sabbath day means.[1]

I discovered that the word Jesus used for *rest* (*anapausis*) in His invitation occurs 137 times in the Greek Old Testament (Septuagint version) and that in the *Law*—the first five books of the Bible—the term predominantly relates to a *sabbatical rest to the Lord*. Therefore, when Jesus invited the weary to come to Him for rest (*anapausis*), His audience understood that, in Him, they could find the *real sabbatical rest for their souls*. Isn't that amazing? But wait! There's more.

In the *historical and prophetic* books of the Greek Old Testament (Septuagint), the most prominent use of the same word relates to the promise of a "peaceful dwelling" given to Israel through David, Solomon, and the future Davidic ruler (Jesus), who was to come (see 2 Samuel 7:11; 1 Chronicles 22:9; Ezekiel 34:15, 23, 24). A peaceful and restful dwelling. Who does not want and need that?

Josephus, the ancient Jewish historian, attests that in Matthew's time, the word *anapausis* (rest) had become normative for "Sabbath day of rest." Furthermore, the people believed their weekly *sabbatical rest* was pointing to the Messianic age, which we call eternal life or heaven. Therefore, their weekly Sabbath was a celebratory "appetizer" of heaven. I love it!

It dawned on me that we enter into the *Sabbath* rest in its fullest sense by heeding Jesus' invitation, extended to all of us who are weary, to *rest* in Him. And we can start experiencing heaven right now in our souls, because Jesus offers and guarantees eternal life through His sacrifice on the cross on our behalf. That is what I commemorate every week on the Sabbath day: my Creator is also my Redeemer, and that on the cross He has guaranteed my eternal life. *He is my complete rest!* This understanding has brought incredible joy and assurance to my own walk with Jesus Christ, and I hope it will yours as well.

Elizabeth Talbot is the speaker and director of Jesus101.TV; the Jesus 101 Biblical Institute; learn more at https://jesus101.tv/.

1. For an easy read on what I found, see Elizabeth Talbot, *I Will Give You Rest* (Nampa, ID: Pacific Press®, 2015).

A Nature Sabbath

Diane Thurber

My parents helped me see the value of the Sabbath as a day of rest to reflect on God's blessings. The Sabbath was always more than a church worship experience. Wherever we were, from sundown Friday to sundown Saturday, there seemed to be an atmosphere that enveloped our family during the Sabbath hours, or perhaps a closeness that I later identified as coming into the presence of God in more meaningful ways.

Fast-forward to my adult life and my pastor husband and our two children. Sabbaths were an entirely different experience than in my childhood. A pastor is often pulled in many different directions as soon as he or she opens the church door, so the family regularly experiences Sabbaths alone. The atmosphere I grew to love as a child seemed to nearly disappear, and I did not know how to recapture it.

One Sabbath, my husband was away. I wanted my sons to experience what I had felt as a child. But how? I thought back to some of my most meaningful Sabbath childhood memories that included times in nature with God. I decided we would have a "Nature Sabbath."

Early Sabbath morning, while the boys slept, I packed a picnic lunch and researched parks where we could experience the beauty of God's creation in a quiet environment. I then planned a worship service.

When my oldest awoke, I told him my plan for Nature Sabbath and asked if he would prepare a message to share with me and his little brother. I think I even called it "the sermon." He seemed excited and asked for a pen and paper. That seven-year-old boy wrote and wrote, soon filling four or five pages, front and back. He beamed as he tucked it into his pocket to share later.

I next asked my younger son to plan which songs we would sing and if he would have prayer. He was only three, but I could tell both he and his brother were excited about the new adventure that awaited.

At the park, we found a picnic table beside a beautiful cove. There was no one in sight. As we sat and worshiped together by the lake, my heart was full of joy, and tears filled my eyes as I listened to the Holy Spirit bless me through my sons.

To me, Sabbath is not about a place, ritual, or tradition. It is about clearing space in my life for God to draw near and then waiting expectantly for His arrival and blessings. One of the richest blessings is finding rest and peace in Him.

"There remains, then, a Sabbath-rest for the people of God" (Hebrews 4:9, NIV).

Diane Thurber is the president of Christian Record Services, Inc., in Lincoln, Nebraska, United States.

The Sabbath—My Sanctuary in Time

Kern Tobias

I was born into a Seventh-day Adventist family and was familiar with the Sabbath through our family traditions and Scripture. I enjoyed repeating the fourth commandment: "Remember the Sabbath day, to keep it holy. Six days you shall labor and do all your work, but the seventh day is the Sabbath of the LORD your God. In it you shall do no work. . . . For in six days the Lord made the heavens and the earth, the sea, and all that is in them, and rested the seventh day. Therefore the LORD blessed the Sabbath day and hallowed it" (Exodus 20:8–11).

The Sabbath became, for me, a sanctuary in time. It was special, separated, and sacred. It was my first exposure to holy time. Abraham Heschel points out, "When history began, there was only one holiness in the world, holiness in time."[1] I was excited whenever this special time came, because it afforded me some privileges and benefits.

Early in life, I was exposed to the necessity of work. The Sabbath provided relief from the demands of my toil. I wished that the day of rest could have been more frequent in the week, but nevertheless, I was accustomed to the weekly routine. Because of the demands of family chores, I was delighted when the Sabbath, my sanctuary in time, came to the rescue.

Another benefit derived from the Sabbath was the opportunity to worship our Creator. Our home became like a sanctuary, and we were involved in unhurried moments of singing, reading the Bible, sharing experiences of the week, and prayer. It was a joy to listen, learn, and participate in the singing with my large family of twelve to fourteen people. The singing was melodious and harmonious. I learned to sing the tenor part, the same sung by my father, and it made me feel more closely connected to him.

Mealtime was a very important feature of the Sabbath. Meals including sweet and savory delicacies were prepared on Friday. Because we were involved in subsistence agriculture, there was an almost unlimited supply of produce to make a variety of delicious meals. Working tirelessly during the week gave me a large appetite, so I enjoyed the nutritious meals that were prepared.

Most of the scriptures I know as an adult I learned as a child during the sacred Sabbath hours. I also learned of my Creator as I enjoyed Sabbath nature walks that enabled me to become attuned to Him. These experiences empowered me to become a better husband, father, and pastor and have enabled me to effectively teach my congregation the importance of the Sabbath as a sanctuary in time.

Kern Tobias is the president of the Caribbean Union Conference of Seventh-day Adventists in Trinidad and Tobago, West Indies.

---

1. Abraham Heschel, *The Sabbath: Its Meaning for Modern Man* (New York: Farrar, Straus, and Giroux, 1951), 29.

Sabbath Rest

Mike Tucker

For me, growing up in the Seventh-day Adventist Church was not the best way to develop a positive relationship with the Sabbath. While I learned to demonstrate from Scripture that the true Sabbath was the seventh day of the week, I also realized that there existed a long list of extrabiblical Sabbath prohibitions designed to "protect" the day.

As a young person, this experience left me with a very narrow picture of the Sabbath. I dreaded the beginning of the Sabbath hours as a period of enforced inactivity that left me with little to do but endure the boredom. I welcomed the end of the Sabbath hours much as a prisoner welcomed release from confinement.

It was not until someone shared the gospel with me that my relationship with the Sabbath changed. I was nineteen years old and yet had never understood the basic teaching of righteousness by faith in Christ alone. This was world-altering for me.

As a college student preparing for ministry, I struggled to reconcile the importance of a day, Sabbath, with the larger concept of the gospel. It was then that Exodus 31:13 challenged my thinking: "Now as for you, speak to the sons of Israel, saying, 'You must keep My sabbaths; for this is *a sign* between Me and you throughout your generations, so that you may know that I am the LORD *who sanctifies* you' " (NASB; emphasis added).

Sanctification, the growth of the redeemed, is a part of the gospel and every bit as much a gift from God as is justification. Therefore, the Sabbath is a sign of our salvation.

Further studies in Hebrews linked for me the rest of God with the Sabbath and, of course, salvation. It was then that the Sabbath became a weekly reminder that the part I was to play in my salvation was to rest in the One who had already secured my eternity.

The Sabbath assures me that the work of saving humanity was completed at the cross. By faith, believers enter into the rest of God, as we confidently trust that the One who freely justifies (forgives) us will also freely sanctify (perfect) us and eventually glorify us when He takes us to heaven after the Second Coming. The Sabbath is the assurance that we are freed from sin's penalty, power, and, eventually, its very presence. The Sabbath is the surety of salvation.

This understanding dramatically altered my relationship with the Sabbath. Instead of a time that must be endured, it is a time of joyous celebration. The Sabbath is an oasis from the drudgery of everyday labor. It eases my feelings of inadequacy and failure as I trust in the gift provided on my behalf at Calvary.

When the sun sets on Fridays, I sigh a sigh of relief. I repeat to myself: "I am redeemed! I can rest confidently in the work of the One who died to save me. As I abide in Him, He will replicate His perfect character in me. And one day soon, He will return to remove me from the very presence of sin. I am at rest."

That which demanded begrudging adherence is now a joyous release from worry, fear, work, and useless labor. The Sabbath is my delight!

Mike Tucker is the speaker emeritus for *Faith for Today*.

The Sabbath From the Perspective of a High School Student

Adara Walker

The Sabbath is a special day for me. Between Sunday and Thursday, my days are pretty regular, and I do all of the work that needs to be done. Friday, however, is the day I prepare for Sabbath. I look forward to Friday evenings, not only because I know that it is time to honor God and rest but also because I also know it is a time when I can reflect on the past week. The Sabbath is a day to meditate on what I have done, worship God, fellowship with Him and others, and prepare to make the best of the coming week.

My preparation for the Sabbath typically goes like this: Friday morning, I attend chapel worship at my school, Greater Atlanta Adventist Academy. I make sure that my home is clean and my errands are all done. I also set the alarm for sunset, so I know when I should refrain from working. Once the Sabbath has begun, the television is either turned off or tuned to a program that contains something with biblical content and meaning. Similarly, the music in the house is changed. I like to welcome the Sabbath with a devotional reading, prayer, and song. I often read my Bible on Sabbath, and I read Bible stories to my little brother. On Sabbath mornings (before the COVID-19 pandemic), I would get ready to attend church. After church, I would (and still do) join my family for Sabbath dinner at my relatives' home. We stay there afterward until the Sabbath ends, and we close the Sabbath together.

The Sabbath is more meaningful to Sabbath keepers than what society portrays. Most of society views Sabbath as people going to church on Sundays, then going about their business like any other day. In reality, the Sabbath has always been on the seventh day of the week—Saturday. And for Sabbath keepers, it is more than just the seventh day of the week. It is the day of rest, meditation, reflection, worship, and preparation for the following week. The Sabbath changes life for the better. It assures twenty-four hours of guaranteed rest.

Each week I thank God for the gift of the Sabbath. It brings me closer to God and produces positive changes in me.

Adara Walker is an eleventh-grade student at Greater Atlanta Adventist Academy in Atlanta, Georgia, United States.

The Sabbath in the Military

Charles Zacharias

I was inducted into the United States Army on June 23, 1969. I had taken deferments through five years of college and two years of graduate school. At the age of 25, I received notice from the draft board and began my military service.

Like most Seventh-day Adventist young men at the time, I entered service as a conscientious objector and was sent to Fort Sam Houston in Texas for basic training and advanced individual training as a medic. In my first class, I discovered that about 90 percent of my classmates were also Seventh-day Adventists. Our training classes were only Monday through Friday, leaving us free on Sabbath and Sunday. However, we could not leave the base. There was a chapel nearby retained for Seventh-day Adventist use, and all the Adventists on the base attended worship services there. On Sabbath afternoons, most of us stayed at the chapel writing letters, playing music, or talking.

After completing the ten weeks of advanced training, I was relieved to be sent to Letterman Army Hospital in San Francisco, California, rather than to Vietnam. At Letterman, I, and several others holding college degrees, was given the opportunity to work in the psychiatric ward rather than in the general hospital. My wife and I were able to rent an apartment off-base. I was free of duty most Friday nights and Sabbaths, and we were free to worship at the San Francisco Central Seventh-day Adventist Church.

Unexpectedly, after nine months of duty at Letterman and with only nine months left to serve, I was transferred to Vietnam. Upon my arrival in Vietnam, I was assigned as a medic in a heavy artillery unit at the battalion headquarters aid station located in Tuy Hoa. I was later moved to a large airbase in Phan Rang.

As it turned out, I served only six months in Vietnam. The war was winding down, and I was granted an early release to return to school. In all my time in Vietnam, I never came across another Seventh-day Adventist.

Thanks to the example and work of soldiers before me, like Desmond Doss, I never had any problems with Sabbath observance while in the army. Sure, I had to be on call for medical duty sometimes, but my superiors never gave me any hassle. The army provided chapels for religious services on every base, so I spent most of my Sabbaths in the chapel alone, reading my Bible, praying, playing the organ, or writing letters.

During my military training and in Vietnam, the Sabbath was a particularly special time for me. It was a time to commune with God and gain strength to endure the challenges ahead of me.

Charles Zacharias is a musician and educator in Calhoun, Georgia, United States.

Sabbath Worship

How Great Thou Art

Julius Abanise

One of the indelible impressions I have about the Sabbath is the hymns sung at church. I must confess that, as a child, I did not always grasp the full meaning of the songs. But I have found that the rhythm and sounds are so imprinted in my mind that, even on a non-Sabbath day many years later, they provide comfort in sorrow and triumph in joy.

My grandmother loved to sing hymns. As a child, I heard her sing them while she sewed clothes, swept the floor, and even when she was just walking around the house. One hymn that she often sang was "How Great Thou Art." Grandma had seven children, six boys and one girl. My mom was that girl. Grandma passed away in 2007.

Years later, when my wife and I were expecting our first child, we decided to give the baby my grandmother's name. My daughter—Mom's first grandchild—was born early on a Thursday morning. After the initial burst of activity related to the delivery, my wife and baby fell asleep in the hospital room. My mom began to sing "How Great Thou Art" softly as she watched over them.

My body was physically present as I listened, but my mind was teleported back to the innumerable times when my grandmother sang that same song and when I sang that precious hymn as a child during Sabbath worship at church. When my mom began the chorus, I began to weep. The full significance of what had transpired hit me like a brick. I finally understood. God truly is great!

Julius Abanise is an attorney in Los Angeles, California, United States.

Ancient Stories About the Sabbath

Jonas Kojo Apau-Baidoo II

Even though I grew up in a home where the Sabbath was not kept, I heard stories about it.

My parents were born into Ghanaian royal families. Many of the African customs and traditional practices mirrored, in several ways, the biblical Sabbath. Even as a little boy, I heard numerous stories, as oral history was and still is a very important aspect of our lives, and observed many practices that imitated the biblical Sabbath that I embraced many years later.

I witnessed my mother's faction—the Breman people of the Fante tribe—and my father's—the Akim (Akyem) tribe—observe the seventh day as a sacred day.

One custom that was observed was the gonging on Friday evenings. It was a reminder of the Saturday morning worship. Saturday is referred to as *Memeneda* or *Mene Mene Da*, meaning "I AM's day" or "I AM THAT I AM's day." It was said that anyone who dared visit the farm on Saturday desecrated that day and would suffer dire consequences, possibly even death. The Akan people of Ghana still refer to the day as *Memeneda Dapaa*, meaning "Good Saturday," signifying blessing for those who regard it as sacred.

I came to the United States forty years ago, accepted Jesus as my Savior, and became a member of the Seventh-day Adventist Church. I was pleasantly surprised as I experienced the joys of the biblical Sabbath, especially since it reflected some of the beloved customs and traditions of my tribal communities.

Now, for me, the Sabbath is far more than custom and tradition. It is about Jesus and the rest I find in Him. It is about twenty-four hours of fellowship, rest, joy, gladness, and growing closer to Jesus.

The stories of my ancestors exposed me to a sacred day called Sabbath. After I accepted Jesus and developed a relationship with Him, I discovered the biblical Sabbath and the rest and fellowship it offers. Today I am blessed to have a more complete understanding of I AM's day—the Sabbath.

Jonas Kojo Apau-Baidoo II is the head elder at the Co-op City Seventh-day Adventist Church in the Bronx, New York, United States.

I Love to Sing on Sabbaths

Noris A. Campbell

The most energizing thing for me is using the God-given gift of singing and playing the guitar during worship service on Sabbath. I have had the privilege of doing so for close to fifty years, and it gets sweeter as the days go by.

I grew up in the parish of Saint Andrew, Jamaica, mentored by staunch Christian parents. Some of the fondest memories of my early years occurred on Sabbaths. My siblings, friends, and I were given opportunities to participate in the church worship services and use our talents to glorify God. Those experiences propelled me into a ministry of music. My first musical accompaniment was a guitar that I made out of bamboo. The bamboo guitar was replaced by a small guitar that my father presented to me as a surprise gift. I quickly learned how to play my new instrument and continued to grow in my singing ministry.

Although I sang solo pieces at my home church in Cavaliers, Jamaica, I also sang in a small six-person group. Our group was often invited to sing in neighboring churches throughout the region.

I also had the honor of singing throughout my homeland and at a number of places in the United States. These opportunities allowed me to meet many people who, like myself, worship on the Sabbath. The Sabbath was indeed the high point of my week.

Every week, when the sun sets on Friday evening, I think back to the times when my parents gathered my siblings and me to sing songs from the hymnal to welcome the Sabbath and praise God for the blessings of another week. Those moments prepared me for the ministry I now cherish.

I praise God for the Sabbath and the energizing strength I receive on His special day. I thank Him for the gift of music—a gift that blesses me and others. I am committed to using music to proclaim the gospel for the rest of my life, and I look forward to Sabbaths on the new earth, where I will sing the redemption story forever.

Noris A. Campbell is a music minister in Kingston, Jamaica.

Friday Evening Sunset Worship on the Hilltop

Steve D. Cassimy

Living on a hilltop in Carenage, Trinidad and Tobago, placed our Seventh-day Adventist family prominently in the eyes of the public. We were seen and heard very easily. At that time, our family consisted of four boys and three girls along with our parents, making us a family of nine.

My parents were devout Seventh-day Adventists. My father did the duties of church elder along with a few other responsibilities. My mother was one of the sweetest singers in the church and volunteered her time in several church ministries.

Friday evenings, about an hour before sunset, Father always reminded us to be ready for the Sabbath. He wanted us to avoid rushing and "breaking the edges of the Sabbath," he said. On Friday afternoons, at least half an hour before sunset, my father was always sitting in his favorite chair surrounded by books. These included his Bible, Sabbath School lesson, daily devotional books, hymnals, and other spiritual books. It was a regular practice for our family to memorize the daily readings from the devotional book. As the sun faded in the west, my father started our family singing. That was our signal that the toil and labor of the week were over and that it was time for us to assemble for Friday evening sundown worship.

My mother led out in singing songs that were favorites of the children. We sang songs such as, "Jesus Loves the Little Ones Like Me, Me, Me," "Jesus Loves the Little Children," and "Heavenly Sunshine." She then led us in singing, "The Seventh Is for Jesus," a favorite of the children.

We were not the only ones who enjoyed the singing. Usually, neighborhood children came and stood on the steps and joined us. Many of those children enthusiastically looked forward to singing with us on Friday evenings. They also looked forward to the little pastries and treats that my mother gave them at the end of the (sometimes long) worship services. Parents in the neighborhood knew that if their children were not at home, they were most likely welcoming the Sabbath with our family. Some of those children even convinced their parents to allow them to accompany us to Sabbath worship services.

Friday evening sunset worship on the hilltop was a joyful reminder that the Sabbath was coming. And what a blessing it was to know that we not only welcomed the Sabbath with the local neighbors but were also united with Sabbath keepers around the world in praising God.

Steve D. Cassimy is a pastor in the Greater New York Conference of Seventh-day Adventists in Manhasset, New York, United States.

The Sabbath: The Sense of Power

Jerome C. Crichton

As Sabbath approaches, it is not unusual for me to anticipate a sense of power, the power to turn off and shut down. The Sabbath follows six consecutive evenings and mornings. These two components of the day that span from one evening to the next often seem to overlap and blend into one busy day after another. However, when the Sabbath comes, my expectation escalates, and, with a sense of relief, I anticipate the power that enables me to turn off and shut down. I turn off and shut down because I can.

I can shut down because I am able to exercise my power of choice, unhindered by civil authorities impinging on the one gateway that literally leads from time into eternity. Unlike its predecessors, the seventh day is not circumscribed by the limitations of evening and morning. It is the only day of the seven upon which such limitations were not imposed at Creation; hence, it is the gateway that leads us from time into eternity. I exercise my power of choice by turning off the cares and shutting down the preoccupations that might otherwise encroach on my Sabbath repose. This speaks of connection, liberation, and peace but also of sovereignty. It reminds us that when God finished His creation, He stopped and opened the access way between time and eternity because He could. Ever since then, the Sabbath has been a symbol of His sovereignty through which connection, liberation, and peace are mediated.

Fridays have become associated with practices and habits designed to make a clean break between the first six days and the seventh. Whether it is washing the car, closing textbooks, or cutting the lawn, these defining activities, once completed, signal my retreat into the Sabbath. They are fitting reminders that once my work is done, I am empowered to give my undivided attention to connecting with God.

That connection became most salient to me once I understood that the purpose of Christ's passion was to restore to humanity what rightfully belonged to us. In His act of justification, the Father demonstrated His steadfast love for us and forever settled the question, Is the power of love greater than the power of sin? The consequent grace of my connection to Him rests as a poignant reminder of my liberation from sin and death and helps explain my anticipation of power.

Oppressed people yearn for liberation, which once experienced is not concealable. The transition from the powerlessness of oppression to the empowerment of liberation breathes new life into the liberated; such has been my Sabbath experience. The fatigue of six days of labor gives way to the seventh day of renewal because, unhindered by common cares, I am able to reflect on the "mighty hand and . . . outstretched arm" (Deuteronomy 5:15) that secured my freedom. With this liberation comes a new consciousness of the many obligations, commitments, and preoccupations to which I am bound. It causes me to relish the anticipation of the power to turn off and to shut down that the Sabbath brings.

Jerome C. Crichton is a professor of psychology in San Francisco, California, United States.

Original Love

Des Cummings

In six days, God created life; on the seventh day, He created love. That sentence led Mary Lou and me to a whole new Sabbath experience. As new parents, we had committed to studying the Sabbath more deeply so we could help our children experience it more fully. We realized that Genesis 1 and 2 is a love story that enchants us with six fantastic days of dazzling creation. Everything that God was doing during the first six days of Creation was made meaningful on the seventh day as He gave us *Himself*.

Life without love is mere existence, but life filled with love is Sabbath. We concluded that the Sabbath was the day on which God breathed original love into our world. Imagine God taking the perfect day to teach His children of perfect love. We realized that we had spent more time studying original sin than learning original love.

If we could teach our children to live Sabbath in love, we reasoned, they would experience an abundant life. Love is the image of God that He has placed in each person. This is why Sabbath is the seal of God; because we behold Him and are transformed. God is love in person, Sabbath is love in time, and church is love in a place.

Sabbath is a love story filled with romance. It is love in three dimensions: rest/security, blessing/worth, and holiness/unity. We found that Jesus practiced these principles in His Sabbath observance, and we decided to pattern our Sabbaths after His example.

So began our study of "Sabbaths With Jesus." The result was engaging in acts of God—reaching out to the sick in visitation, lifting others' burdens with a helping hand, sharing the hope of His promises, and talking about our mission as Jesus did in His home church. He was not passive or boring on Sabbath, and that inspired us to be active as well.

Mary Lou built the children's anticipation of the Sabbath with a sunset tradition that engaged all the senses. It included inspirational music, lighting scented candles, a Sabbath surprise gift, repeating the Sabbath commandment with gestures, blessing each member of the family, and then sharing a Sabbath meal that delighted the taste buds. After the meal, we engaged in Friday night games like "Where did you see Jesus this week?" These goodness games teach us to complete the week by remembering the good. In six days, we major in work; on the seventh day, we major in love. Happy Sabbath!

Des Cummings is the former president of the Creation Development Foundation in Celebration, Florida, United States.

The Misunderstood Sabbath

Nicceta Davis

Have you ever been misunderstood, or have you ever misunderstood someone? Maybe it was about a meeting time or location resulting in a missed flight. Or a misunderstanding in what was intended to be a casual conversation that led to hurt feelings and distrust. The consequences of misunderstanding can have far-reaching effects and result in missed opportunities, frustrated plans, fractured relationships, and worse. For decades, I misunderstood the Sabbath and what God wanted me to learn and experience through His special institution.

Growing up in a relatively conservative Seventh-day Adventist home in New Jersey, I learned the 1950s and 1960s version of Sabbath keeping. On Thursday, we would prepare the house, clothes, and meals for Sabbath. Friday evening, we would open the Sabbath. Sabbath, you went to church for Sabbath School, worship service, home for lunch, and then back to church for "MV"—the young people's meeting.

As a child, the Sabbath hours were excruciatingly long, particularly in the summer when the sun did not set until after 8:00 P.M. Winter Sabbaths were much better because the sun set at a more reasonable time for children—around 4:30 in the afternoon. As far as I was concerned, Sabbath time was no substitute for riding bikes, playing outside, or watching TV. I did not call the Sabbath a delight.

What was it that I misunderstood about the Sabbath? Pretty much everything. I misunderstood that the "In the beginning" God, who "spoke, and it was done," who "commanded and it stood fast," was inviting me to remember that He is the Creator and when He finishes His work, it is "very good" (Genesis 1:1; Psalm 33:9; Genesis 1:31). I misunderstood that the Sabbath is a reminder that any and all things I lack in the spiritual, mental, physical, social, financial, and professional areas of my life can be spoken into existence by the "In the beginning" God. I misunderstood that the Sabbath is a time to rest, refresh, recalibrate, and reset after a challenging week. I misunderstood God's love of beauty as seen in nature. But more than anything, I misunderstood that through the Sabbath, the "In the beginning" God is constantly reassuring me that *I am His and He is mine.*

I see now the consequences of my misunderstandings of the Sabbath and, consequently, the God of the Sabbath. For years, I did not personally know the love and care of the "In the beginning" God. Now I know it is by design that the Sabbath is a sign between God and me. His desire for us is "that where I am, there you may be also" (John 14:3). I can now rest in my relationship with the "In the beginning" God—the Creator and Sustainer. And guess what! Just as He said in the beginning, it still is "very good."

Nicceta Davis is a professor at Loma Linda University in Loma Linda, California, United States.

Sabbath Influence

Charles N. Drechsel

"Charly, I need to speak with you," my supervisor said to me one day.
"Sure, Bob," I replied.
"I've got a problem, Charly," he said.
"How can I help?"
Bob told me his dilemma.
"You know it's Memorial Day next weekend. We are not planning any operations that weekend, and most of the staff is anticipating the extra days off. Only a standby crew will be on duty. You are scheduled for the evening shift—4:00 P.M. to midnight."
"I was planning to cover your shift myself, but my kids and wife reminded me a few days ago that I had promised them to go visit the grandparents."
I realized immediately that the problem was I would have to work on the Sabbath. We operated the country's highest neutron flux–density nuclear reactor, and whenever our reactor core was loaded with reactive fuel, a licensed operator had to be present on-site. There were only five licensed operators. One was already gone for the weekend; two

others were scheduled to leave. That left my boss and me.

One of my colleagues spoke up. "Charly, you could just come in, sit, and read your Bible." It was no big problem in his mind.

I was praying silently for the Lord's guidance. My employer had always been very kind and considerate in accommodating my religious beliefs and practices. But it was getting close to the time for me to sign in to take over responsibility for the facility. What was God telling me to do?

My phone rang.

"This is Al, your branch chief. How long can you stay this afternoon?"

"Well, Al, sundown is about 9:00," I said. "I'd like to get off about an hour before then."

"Can you stay until about 6:00?" Al asked.

"What happens then?" I responded.

"I'll come in and relieve you," he replied.

"But Al, you don't have a reactor operator license," I protested.

"Listen, that's my problem," Al responded. "I'm your boss. What about it?"

My God had come through for me again. He solved my dilemma.

A few days after Memorial Day weekend, I was sitting and chatting in Al's office. He told me that he had been brought up as a Quaker. He related to me how he, as a conscientious objector, had often spent time in a military brig (jail) with Seventh-day Adventists and Sabbath keepers. He said that he knew how important those beliefs were to practicing Adventists.

"I knew you were a practicing Adventist by your actions around the facility," he stated.

God had been working on my problem long before it became an issue for me. He had influenced someone by putting him in contact with faithful believers many years before.

Charles N. Drechsel is an engineer, an overseas development director, and an educator in Bonners Ferry, Idaho, United States.

Angels Join the Choir

Jason Max Ferdinand

It was my first year as choir director of the well-known Pine Forge Academy choir from Pine Forge, Pennsylvania. We were on a grueling spring tour, and toward the end, students began getting ill. The last leg of the tour took us to Massachusetts. On that Sabbath, at the afternoon concert, about six students could not participate, voices of soloists were cracking, and the choir was not singing in tune. By the standards of the choir, it was an absolutely inferior concert.

After that concert, we jumped on the bus and headed to what was to be the grand finale of the tour. As a young conductor, I was shaken by the fact that the choir was in shambles. How were we going to perform with so many choir members sick? I prayed during the entire drive to the last church. We arrived there, and the church was packed. One sensed the anticipatory energy of the audience. As we were about to enter the choir loft, the students who were too sick for the earlier performance joined the choir one by one. One student said, "I'm not sure how, but we have to rally for this last one!" We prayed and went into the choir loft.

The repertoire was difficult and demanded a lot from the singers. They did the first song, and it went well. The second song was even better. It was going so well that I refused to stop the momentum to address the audience or introduce songs. We just kept singing. I looked at the accompanists and mouthed over to them while shrugging my shoulders, "Do you hear this?"

It was right at that point, on that Sabbath day, that I heard a clarion voice that said, "There are angels mixed in with your students. Enjoy and keep going." It was the same voice I had heard five years earlier, convincing me to choose music as my life's work. That concert, on that Sabbath day, represents some of the best music-making I have ever heard in my life. Tears flowed down my face as I looked up to that elevated choir loft. I knew the sound of my choir very well, and I assure you that it was not just them singing that day. The sweet voices of angels rescued us, and it proved to be a blessing to all.

Jason Max Ferdinand is the director of the Aeolians at Oakwood University in Huntsville, Alabama, United States.

Keeping the Sabbath as a Professional Musician

Nadja Floder

I was practicing the harp at the university when my professor suddenly entered the room.

"I have good news for you! I have received an email that you have been invited to take part in a recording for a radio channel," she exclaimed.

Oh, I hope it is not on a Sabbath, I thought privately.

Even though my professor knew I did not perform on Saturdays, except when I played for God in church, I did not know whether she would understand. Besides, I had declined offers so many times, and yet, this year was a very decisive one for my musical future. Nevertheless, I concluded that I would not play on the Sabbath.

The professor continued: "Because the second round of Austria's music competition has been canceled, all the winners of the first round are invited to participate in a radio broadcast. The date for the recording is October 24 . . ." Her voice trailed off. Then she turned toward me and finally said, "A Saturday."

Just as I feared, I thought, knowing most of these recordings were on Saturdays.

"You will have to talk with your parents and decide whether you can play or what is possible," my professor answered, somewhat frustrated with my nonenthusiastic look.

"But we have to know soon if you are going to participate," the professor continued. "The recording is in two weeks."

Not knowing what else to say, I replied, "I will tell you by the end of the week."

After the lesson, on my way back home, I called my mother and told her about my dilemma.

"I know it is very unrealistic," I told my mother, "but I would so love to play. Couldn't we write an email to the lady who is responsible for the recordings, asking if I could do it another day? Let's at least give it a try, and if God wants me to play, He will make it possible. If not, I will not have to feel bad for not having tried to find a solution for my professor."

My mother agreed, and we wrote an email explaining the reason why I would not play on a Saturday.

Unexpectedly, the institute answered back just two days later, telling me it would be no problem at all to find an alternative date for me. They later notified me that I was scheduled to play on a Sunday. Although this was exactly what I had hoped and prayed for, I was really surprised! In the past, my sister (who is also a musician) and I had often been refused alternative dates from the same institute. And this time, they had no trouble at all! I praised the Lord for that opportunity and am happy to honor and worship Him every Sabbath.

Nadja Floder is a harpist who was born in Austria, is a student at Seminar Schloss Bogenhofen, and is also studying music at Vienna University in Austria.

The Sabbath and Nature

Lisa Froelich

As I was growing up, my family and I spent many Sabbaths in nature. One of my favorite Sabbath spots, when I was about nine years old, was Patapsco Valley State Park, located west of Baltimore, Maryland. We often walked its trails, but on this particular Sabbath, we decided to do a little additional exploring. We found a narrow pathway that took us up a very steep hill to some railroad tracks. We decided to check it out and walk the tracks for a little while for a change of scenery.

A favorite family activity while walking was to look for a "Sabbath deer." Anytime we walked in or near the woods, we would see one! It is as if God, too, enjoyed the little game we played. In this particular park, deer are a rare sight because the area is heavily populated. But the most remarkable thing happened while we were walking the tracks. We did not just see more deer than we could count; we saw an *albino* deer! I had never seen anything like it before, and haven't even to this day. It made our Sabbath trek along the tracks even more special.

We walked for quite some time, expecting to see another pathway down to the main trail, but it never came. While my sister and I thought it was a fun adventure, my parents began to get worried. The sun was starting to set. The farther we walked, the longer it would take us to get back to our car, and there was a greater chance of us having to walk the trail back in the dark.

After several minutes of searching, we finally found a pathway down the hill that was safe enough to try. As soon as we reached the main path, we raced the sun as we made our way back to our car. We did walk part of it in the dark, but it only created the perfect ending to an awesome adventure that still remains one of my fondest Sabbath memories.

Ellen White wrote, "The Sabbath calls our thoughts to nature, and brings us into communion with the Creator. In the song of the bird, the sighing of the trees, and the music of the sea, we still may hear His voice who talked with Adam in Eden in the cool of the day. And as we behold His power in nature we find comfort, for the word that created all things is that which speaks life to the soul."[1]

Spending time in nature is one of the easiest ways to connect with our Creator. Next time a beautiful Sabbath day comes along, take a walk in the woods. Perhaps you will find a Sabbath deer or two. But one piece of advice if you decide to go exploring—always carry a flashlight!

Lisa Froelich is a music teacher at Spencerville Adventist Academy in Spencerville, Maryland, United States.

---

1. Ellen G. White, *The Desire of Ages* (Mountain View, CA: Pacific Press®, 1940), 281.

Sabbath Under Quarantine

Kevin Jenkins

As was our custom at the Genesis Seventh-day Adventist Church (in Plainfield, New Jersey), we were preparing for Communion on the first Sabbath of the New Year—2020. The church leaders and I were monitoring updates concerning COVID-19 to determine whether we should have a live worship service or shut things down. As a precautionary measure, we decided that Communion service would be conducted differently.

I asked church leaders to purchase a box of prefilled Communion cups and wafer sets. This was a preemptive measure taken in the context of the new reality. And then it happened. The state issued an emergency shutdown of all business and worship gatherings. The leadership of the Alleghany East Conference of Seventh-day Adventists concurred.

As a result of the shutdown, streets were empty—no people or car traffic, and churches were closed across the state. There would be no worship in the church building.

And yet, for me, this was the greatest Sabbath-keeping season I'd ever experienced! As a pastor, I got used to Sabbath being the busiest time for my calling. On Sabbath, I preached, taught, counseled, and greeted the members. After sunset, I usually had other church meetings. That was my typical busy Sabbath.

When the quarantine lockdown was mandated, I wondered what I was to do. God's message to me was, "Use this time to rest, My son!" And I did. This is not to say that I did not continue to preach and teach. Our church used technology for both our worship and prayer meeting services. We even conducted virtual church board meetings.

But for me, Sabbath was a very special experience. I was in the comfort of my home, and I knew that I did not have to spend all day at the church. Things were finished earlier, and I could spend more time with the Lord in prayer and study.

And guess what? I could even take a Sabbath nap for rest and cognitive repair and not be anxious about it. As a result of this Sabbath experience, I have become more energetic than ever before. I sincerely believe that Sabbath under quarantine added more years to my ministry and has given me a tremendous appreciation for the gift God has given to us.

In spite of the devastation caused by COVID-19, I am reminded of this scripture: "And we know that for those who love God all things work together for good, for those who are called according to his purpose" (Romans 8:28, ESV).

As it relates to Sabbath under quarantine, I can say this worked for my good, and I will be ever thankful to our Lord Jesus Christ for the experience.

Kevin Jenkins is the pastor of the Genesis and University Heights Seventh-day Adventist Churches in New Jersey, United States.

What the Sabbath Means to Me

Michael Jenkins Jr.

From my earliest memory, the Sabbath has been meaningful because of its sacredness. Genesis 2:1–3 tells us that God blessed the seventh day and made it holy. This very passage is the most meaningful to me when it comes to the Sabbath. At an early age, my understanding of the Sabbath was shaped by these texts. At a very young age, I recognized that it predated sin and the need for a Savior. I recognized as well that it predated the tradition of Sunday sacredness practiced by many.

Basketball has been a part of my life since I was a child. I still play as often as I can. In high school, I wanted to play on the school team. In those days, the Denver, Colorado, public school system had three male teams in each school. During my freshman year, most of the games were on Thursdays. I tried out for the team and earned a spot. I played in every game except the two games on the Sabbath. It was a sacrifice, but it was only two games. I wanted to play, but it was a compromise that was easy to make. I had no internal struggle. I did not have to talk it through with anyone. No one—not my mother, grandparents, pastor, or anyone else who was a close influencer in my life—had a conversation with me about Sabbath observance and choices. To me, it was a given—I was not going to play on the Sabbath.

My sophomore through senior years of high school were different. I had to play on the junior varsity or the varsity team to earn a roster spot. And most of those games were on the Sabbath.

When tryouts were completed, the head coach placed the list of those who made the cut. My name just had to be on that list. I needed everyone in the school to know that I had the skills to make the team. This meant bragging rights, a specific standing among my peers and the girls. No self-respecting girl would want to date a guy who tried out for the team and got cut! At least that is what I thought then.

Mind you, my commitment to the Sabbath had not changed from what it was my freshman year. I was still resolved not to play on the Sabbath. So, sophomore through senior years, I tried out and made the team but chose not to play. My name was on the list, and that is all that mattered.

When I look back over the years, I am a bit surprised at my understanding and overall mindset regarding the Sabbath. Even today, nothing has changed, and it all stems from Genesis 2:1–3. No matter what anyone else says, does, endorses, or encourages, nothing can change the fact that the seventh day was made special by God, and it remains so today. That is why the Sabbath has such significant meaning for me.

Michael Jenkins Jr. is the administrative pastor at the Kansas Avenue Seventh-day Adventist Church in Riverside, California, United States.

The Saturday I Heard About Jesus

Bledi Leno

CHARACTER ONE: "There has only been one who has risen from the dead, Jesus Christ!"
CHARACTER TWO: "Don't be ridiculous, only the ignorant believe that."

That was the dialogue between two characters in a theater play I was watching with my parents one Saturday morning. It was the first time in my life I had ever heard of Jesus Christ and that He had risen from the dead. "Who was this Jesus?" I asked my parents.

"You'll learn about Him in school," they responded.

We were a household of atheists living in Albania, the only constitutionally atheist country in the world. The nation's 1967 constitution banned all religious practices. Churches, mosques, and synagogues were either destroyed or transformed into cultural centers, museums, or public halls. Clergy and staunch believers were persecuted, imprisoned, and killed. Proudly, the Communist government declared Albania to be the world's only atheist nation.

In school, I did indeed learn about Jesus Christ. We were told that He was a Jewish philosopher, like the ancient Greek philosophers Socrates, Plato, and Aristotle. And what about God? He did not exist, we were told. God was an invention, a mirage of the hopeless poor living under evil capitalism.

Yet, in the midst of spiritual darkness, God was reaching out to me—even through that theatrical play. I never forgot that phrase from the play: "Jesus Christ, the only one to have risen from the dead."

A few years later, after Communism collapsed in many Eastern European countries, I was on my way one Saturday to an international book expo at the public library. I was looking for car magazines. Our country had very few cars but many bicycles. To my dismay, the expo was closed, so my friends and I headed over to the next large open hall in the library building. Standing at the door was a kind lady who invited us to come in and listen to a Bible story. "What is a Bible?" I asked. "And who are those people in the auditorium?" That was my first introduction to the Bible and a church group. I still remember the experience. I met Jesus and started reading the Bible.

Today I am a pastor in New York. I look back and realize that God had a plan for me. Interestingly, both of my first two encounters with Him took place on the Sabbath. How special the Sabbath is! To me, it is a monument in time to God's omniscience, omnipotence, and His power of deliverance, salvation, and liberation. Every Friday evening, as I sit down with my family to reflect on the Sabbath, I am reminded of my secret first encounter with God, of His care, loving-kindness, and mercy, and I thank Him for making Himself known to me. I would not have it any other way.

Bledi Leno is the multiethnic ministries director of the Greater New York Conference of Seventh-day Adventists in Manhasset, New York, United States.

Lockdown Sabbath

Trudy Morgan-Cole

In the spring of 2020, when, like many people around the world, I found myself working from home because of the COVID-19 lockdown, I noticed a frequent complaint circulating on social media. "I can't tell the days apart anymore," people would post. "Is it Thursday? Tuesday? Sunday? Time has no meaning anymore!"

With parents working from home; children doing online schooling; and few, if any, outside activities to mark the days of the week, people worried that time was becoming meaningless. One day slid seamlessly into the next, work and home life all tangled together in a kind of chaos that offered no real rest or respite.

I had some complaints about living in lockdown—as well as many pleasures—but losing track of time was never one of them. While I worked from home, my weeks, just as they had done for the fifty-five years before that, swung back and forth on the hinge of Sabbath.

True, lockdown Sabbaths were different from "normal" Sabbaths. Church was on Zoom; we watched from our couch, dressed in our comfortable clothes instead of our best, sometimes finishing off our brunch in front of the computer as we listened to the sermon. But regular responsibilities were still laid aside, and setting the Away message on my work team's account became a new way to mark the beginning of the Sabbath hours each Friday afternoon.

A friend of mine, who is a life coach, says that one of the reasons we find modern life stressful is that we lack the predetermined rhythms of daily life that governed past generations. I wake up to a pile of laundry in the corner of the bedroom and think, *Do I have time to wash that today?* My great-grandmother never had to ask this question: Monday was always wash day, just as other days of the week were set aside for other specific chores. Such routines, although we might not want to be bound by them, offered structure that would make much of our constant modern decision making unnecessary.

I am grateful for the Sabbath as the unchanging marker of weekly time. When I have a pile of student papers to grade and book edits to complete, Sabbath is the one day I don't wake up and ask myself, *Which of these tasks will I tackle today?* The answer is predetermined: *None of them!* I have only one item on my to-do list: rest in the presence of my Creator.

Whether I am working from home or going to the classroom five days a week, Sabbath is the fixed point in my routine. Sabbath keeping not only tells me what day it is, but it also tells me who I am and who God is—seven days a week.

Trudy Morgan-Cole is a writer and educator in Saint John's, Newfoundland and Labrador, Canada.

The Sabbath: After My Life-Changing Issue

Floyd Morris

Becoming blind is one of the most traumatic experiences that any human being can endure. It is even more debilitating for an individual in the prime of his or her life. The process brings frustration, fury, and forlornness.

In 1983, just two years after entering high school, I discovered that I had the dreaded eye disease glaucoma. It was the first time that doctors in Jamaica learned of this obscure eye disease in a teenager. Glaucoma, one of the leading causes of blindness, damages the optic nerves and ultimately destroys eyesight if the optic pressure is not controlled. Glaucoma had a deleterious effect on my education because I could not see to read and write. I was confined to my home in the rustic community of Bailey's Vale, Saint Mary, Jamaica.

When an individual is ill in my community, it is customary for people from various denominations to offer prayer for healing. During one such prayer, an individual uttered that I must have committed a terrible sin for all of this to have happened to me. The statement infuriated me, and I said that I would never accommodate any of these individuals at my home again.

One of my sisters was a health professional working at the local hospital. She had encountered a Seventh-day Adventist nurse and shared my situation with her. This nurse indicated that she would come and visit me. We had a wonderful conversation. She told me that in spite of my blindness, she wanted me to know that God still loves me. This statement was reassuring and transforming for me. She asked a church leader to study with me and, within two weeks, I started attending the Port Maria Seventh-day Adventist Church.

My experience at the church was transformational. The care and attention that the members displayed were heartwarming. The support was overwhelming and increased my desire for a relationship with Jesus Christ. I learned that the Sabbath is an extraordinary day established for us to commune with our Creator. God promised that "if thou turn away thy foot from the sabbath, from doing thy pleasure on my holy day; and call the sabbath a delight, the holy of the LORD, honourable; and shalt honour him, not doing thine own ways, nor finding thine own pleasure, nor speaking thine own words: Then shalt thou delight thyself in the LORD; and I will cause thee to ride upon the high places of the earth, and feed thee with the heritage of Jacob thy father: for the mouth of the LORD hath spoken it" (Isaiah 58:13, 14, KJV).

Indeed, the Lord honors His promises. Thirty-five years after high school, the Lord helped me complete a doctorate. I am honored to be a minister in the government of Jamaica; the president of the Jamaican Senate; Caribbean Community Special Rapporteur on disability; the first individual from the Caribbean to be elected to the United

Nations Committee on the Convention on the Rights of Persons with Disabilities; and, most importantly, a happily married man.

It is a wonderful experience to honor God's Word and keep the Sabbath holy.

Floyd Morris is a senator in Kingston, Jamaica.

The Holiness of Sabbath as Experienced by a Child

Jan Paulsen

Contemplating the Sabbath takes me back to the time when we lived as a young family in Tübingen, Germany, where I was studying. The university there made Tübingen the city it was—students from abroad made for a very diverse, international, and complex community. All kinds of religious traditions found their way into the environment. Some were better understood and accepted than others. Seventh-day Adventists were a strange sect in the eyes of most, yet there was an amazing openness toward those who were viewed as nontraditional and different.

Across the road from where we lived was a Roman Catholic family whose children often played with ours. Laila and Jan Rune (ages 10 and 8) would be in and out of their house, or we invited them over to ours.

Here is my wife, Kari's, account:

For one reason or another, I never had the chance to properly get to know the children's mother. One day I was walking to the local store, pushing Rein Andre (our youngest) in his pram. My neighbor was coming the other way, holding her youngest child by the hand.

She introduced herself in German and said, "Mrs. Paulsen, I have wanted to talk to you for a long time. I have a question."

"Yes, of course," I said. "What is it?"

"Your children always leave our house late Friday afternoon and don't come back until Sunday. I asked Jan Rune why, and he said, 'That's when Sabbath starts.' So I asked him, 'What do you do on Sabbath?' And he said, 'We eat fruit and pray.'"

"Mrs. Paulsen," she added, "I can't even take my children to Mass because they won't sit quietly, and yet it seems yours pray all day."

I laughed. "Well, it is not as holy as it sounds," I said. I explained our living on a tight student budget that included two pieces of fruit each weekday but that on Friday evening, as a special Sabbath treat, they were allowed to eat all the fruit they wanted. And as for praying, yes, there was extra worship time on Sabbath, but it was far from being a twenty-four-hour prayer vigil, I assured her.

"Oh, thank God," she said, "you're normal." And from then on, our friendship grew.

My reflections on Kari's account

I ask myself, How do our children experience Sabbath? Is "holiness" a description that makes sense to them? What does our list of what we do and don't do with our children on Sabbath look like? Is Sabbath, to my children, the most boring day of the week because they can see only the long list of dos and don'ts? Maybe it would be a good idea to scratch that list completely? The danger is that the proverbial "If you enjoyed doing it, it was wrong to do on Sabbath" is allowed to cloud their minds to the notion of embracing happiness and enjoyment without compromising "holiness."

I go back to my own childhood in Northern Norway. I have good memories of a loving Adventist home. But we were kids growing up 200 miles north of the Arctic Circle. In winter, the days are short, and the Sabbath begins in the early afternoon on Friday. What do we do?

The trusted counsel "Take your kids for a walk in the woods and enjoy the beauty of nature" comes to mind. Wonderful! The challenge is that there is snow on the ground, and it will be there for the next five to six months. You can only "walk" if you put skis on. Go skiing on the Sabbath? Why not? Fresh air. Nature. The family enjoying time together.

Holiness is what you bring to the moment of enjoying the beauty of God's handiwork and doing it with your kids. That moment fills the child's mind with memories of love and happiness.

And God is honored.

———————————

Jan Paulsen is a former president of the General Conference of Seventh-day Adventists in Silver Spring, Maryland, United States.

Singing on the Sabbath

Tracey-Ann Richardson

I grew up attending church on Sundays with my grandma. At sixteen, I was baptized into her church. I really enjoyed the long walk to church on the country roads and meeting up with friends along the way.

The year after my baptism, I immigrated to the United States from Jamaica and lived with a Seventh-day Adventist family who treated me as their own child. I began attending church with them. Going to church on Saturdays was a real treat. We would get ready early in the morning, pack food for the day, and leave home at 8:30 A.M. We stayed at church all day and into the evening. After a year, I realized the importance of the Sabbath and became a member of the Grand Concourse Seventh-day Adventist Church in the Bronx, New York.

Now I cannot wait for Sabbath to come. I am very active in my church. Our worship services are well organized and power-packed. Each Sabbath is filled with activities to enhance the spiritual growth of every member.

I have the awesome privilege of working as the minister of music in my church. I work closely with the pastoral staff and other church leaders. My team consists of the musicians as well as the praise and worship team. We invite church members to share their gift of singing with our congregation. It brings me much joy when someone comes to me and says, "I really appreciated the music today."

I can truly say there is always a song that speaks to me. I appreciate songs with meaningful lyrics. There are some hymns that, when sung by the congregation, give me a glimpse of heaven. Those songs include: "This Is My Father's World," "Rejoice, Ye Pure in Heart," "The Old Rugged Cross," and "When We All Get to Heaven."

On Sabbath, I enjoy hearing the worshipers shouting praises to God. Some stand or raise their hands while others close their eyes and rock in their seats, each signifying in their own way that a particular song is speaking to them. Through music, I believe I am able to make Sabbath a more enjoyable day for those who come to worship.

The family that I lived with when I immigrated to the United States is still very close to me. In fact, I am happy to say that they are my in-laws. We still worship and fellowship together. They are a blessing to my husband and me.

There have been changes due to the COVID-19 pandemic. I am a health-care worker, and the pandemic has changed my life. Worship has changed. I remain home and watch our services online. Although we miss physically being in church, we still have scheduled programs throughout the Sabbath day, either through livestream or conference calls. And through these, Sabbaths are still a blessing.

Tracey-Ann Richardson is a nurse in Elmhurst, New York, United States.

The Day My Sabbath Experience Changed

Eli Rojas

My father had gotten a temporary contract in Costa Rica in a location that has the best beaches in the country. Our family took advantage of his location and spent time with him there. It was great.

One of those visits extended over the weekend. *That's no problem,* I thought. *I'll just be careful to plan my Sabbath.* Sabbath morning came, and I started my adventure.

My plan was to go to church, hope that someone would invite me over for lunch, and then read by the pool in the afternoon. But that church family was not too friendly. No one talked to me, and no one invited me for lunch. That is when my day started going wrong.

I made my way back to the hotel. When I arrived, there were some young ladies with a small band playing popular music. It was enticing, but, just like the proverbial ostrich buries its head in the sand, I locked myself in my room. It was a hot and humid day. The hotel room was small and had no air conditioner.

Hot, sweating, and frustrated, I started to read *Path to the Heart* by Glenn A. Coon. As I read, my frustrations started to dissipate. I was reading things that I had never heard before. I gained new insight into my condition as a sinner and saw that sin separated me from God. Then my heart broke as I learned about God's solution to my problem: out of love for me (and for humanity), God gave His Son, Jesus, to pay for my sins by dying on the cross. My heart burst as it was filled with God's love. I cried as I accepted Jesus Christ as my personal Savior and surrendered my life to Him.

I was thirteen years old and had gone to church my entire life, but this was the first time the gospel message penetrated my mind and heart. I was overwhelmed by God's amazing love.

I left the room. Hunger left me, and the sight of the girls or the band playing did not bother me anymore. The cool breeze refreshed my face, the joy and love of God filled my heart, and all I wanted to do was tell someone about Jesus. A Sabbath of frustration became a Sabbath of delight.

Sabbath is not a day about rules, what to do or not to do. It is a day to focus on God's love, a day to meditate on His Word and His creation. From that day forward, I learned to focus on the many wonderful things I can do to enjoy the Sabbath.

Eli Rojas is ministerial secretary for the Chesapeake Conference of Seventh-day Adventists in Columbia, Maryland, United States.

Sabbath and Justification by Faith

Pavle Runić

Have you ever been told that keeping the Sabbath is legalism? I have heard it a number of times. However, no one would call it legalism if a person does not steal or commit adultery. Why then would Sabbath keeping be called legalism?

As a theologian, I was delighted to realize that in the Word of God, the Sabbath is the most antilegalistic commandment. As a matter of fact, the Sabbath is the celebration of justification by faith in Jesus Christ—resting in Jesus while denouncing human attempts to earn salvation by our works.

In Hebrews 3:7–4:11, the main word is "rest" (Greek, *katapausis*). It is repeated eight times, and the corresponding verb "resting" is used an additional three times. The passage is all about entering God's rest. The beauty of the Promised Land was a representation of God's rest. But strangely, after the Hebrews entered the land, they still did not enter the rest because of unbelief (Hebrews 4:2–8). In other words, entering the Promised Land was only a symbol of God's rest, not the rest itself. There is a higher concept of rest, connected to the gospel of Jesus Christ (Hebrews 4:2).

Paul is trying to explain God's rest by associating it with the seventh day. "For He has spoken in a certain place of the seventh day in this way: 'And God rested on the seventh day from all His works' " (Hebrews 4:4). God is resting and enjoying quality time with His creation. It is an example of how we should rest.

Paul draws this conclusion: "There remains therefore a rest for the people of God" (Hebrews 4:9). But, unexpectedly, in verse 9, he changes the word for rest, from *katapausis* to a completely new word, *Sabbatismos*—"Sabbath rest." "For he who has entered His rest has himself also ceased from his works as God did from His" (Hebrews 4:10). This ceasing from works is a clear allusion to Romans 4:1–5.

From this, we can understand the central point of the Sabbath. It is all about resting in Jesus, not trying to earn salvation by works but believing in His merits and being justified by faith. That is why those who did not believe could not enter God's rest. And what a better picture of justification by faith than Sabbath rest? On Sabbath, we do not work, just as we do not work in order to earn salvation. The purpose of the Sabbath is to deepen our relationship with God, and that is the core of justification by faith.

Hence, the Sabbath is a monument of justification of faith, a weekly celebration of receiving salvation through faith in Jesus, not earning it by works. Hallelujah! Learning this has been a blessed experience for me. I see Jesus in the Sabbath as never before, and thus I experience more love and joy.

————————

Pavle Runić is the academic dean of the Belgrade Theological Seminary in Belgrade, Serbia.

Preparing for a Guest

Ardis Stenbakken

It was Friday afternoon when I ran down to the basement, which we shared with seven other army chaplain families in our chaplain course row house. I needed something from the freezer. The rabbi's wife was there, so I said something to her about both of us hurrying to get ready for Sabbath. She seemed a little surprised that I was preparing for Sabbath and asked a question or two, but after a few comments, she left.

I thought about our conversation as I headed back to our quarters. We were both following the Ten Commandments, but, from what I knew, our reason for preparing and keeping the Sabbath was somewhat different. My focus was on preparing for a guest: Jesus.

When I was a child, Sabbath breakfast had generally been the only time we had hot chocolate and homemade cinnamon rolls. How we looked forward to Sabbath and our Sabbath Guest! Now, as an adult in the chaplain's quarters, my house would be clean before Sabbath's arrival. I would do my shopping during the week. I did not want to be so busy in the kitchen that Jesus and I would not have time to visit, so I prepared what I could ahead of time for the hot Sabbath dinner. I might even invite some guests over to share the afternoon with us. Some Sabbaths, we would go out for a walk to enjoy what God had created. If the kids wanted to, we might play some Bible charades or other Bible games or even watch a nature video. I think Jesus would have enjoyed the fun and would have wanted to join in.

During Jesus' Sabbath visit, I would not be reading things that would take my attention away from Him. I would wait until later to read the newspaper, catch up on the mail, and check whatever social media I might be following. And I would keep the TV off too—I certainly would not want anything to interrupt our short time together.

How much better can it get than to spend twenty-four hours with our Creator and Savior!

Ardis Stenbakken is an editor and writer in Loveland, Colorado, United States.

Sabbath Through the Eyes of a Child

Evelyn Sullivan

My first memories of Sabbath go back to my early childhood years. Sabbath was a day I looked forward to, and preparing for the Sabbath was a six-day experience in our home.

The anticipation of the Sabbath was a key element of the weekly celebration. Every day we heard my mother say, "Six days we work and play, but the Sabbath day is for Jesus." In simple words, this was the day when we did not do any work; instead, it was time to connect and enjoy spending time with God, family, and friends.

As soon as the Sabbath ended, we began preparing for the next Sabbath. After sundown worship, we chose the clothing we would wear the next Sabbath and shined our shoes. Each morning when we opened our closet door, we saw our Sabbath clothes and shiny shoes waiting to be worn. The countdown to Sabbath continued.

During the remainder of the week, we prepared our home to welcome the beloved day of rest; each day involved a different task. We cleaned and cooked a little as the evenings and mornings passed, but we left a few important chores for Friday. These included placing clean sheets on our beds, dusting, and vacuuming. Setting the table and making final preparations for our Sabbath meals signaled that the Sabbath was only a few hours away.

I fondly remember Friday evenings as the crown jewel of the week. That is when we bathed, put on our Sabbath pajamas, and, with our wet hair combed in place, we gathered in the living room ready to welcome the day of rest. As an adult, I continue similar practices to prepare for the Sabbath, and in our home, I have added some new traditions that help us anticipate and welcome our beloved day of rest. The older I get, the more my soul longs for the Sabbath hours.

I am so glad my parents modeled how to prepare for the Sabbath. More important, I am grateful that they taught me at an early age that Sabbath was a day when we spend quality time with our heavenly Father and His Son, Jesus, our family, and our dear friends. I cannot wait until we celebrate our first Sabbath in heaven!

Evelyn Sullivan is the director of early childhood education for the North American Division of Seventh-day Adventists in Columbia, Maryland, United States.

The Sabbath After . . .

Gary B. Swanson

On the Sabbath morning following the September 11, 2001, attack, it was my scheduled responsibility to serve at the door of the Spencerville (Maryland) Seventh-day Adventist Church to welcome members and any visitors to the worship service. On this particular morning, though, it was plainly evident that more than the usual number were showing up. The act of terror had brought religion to the minds of many.

This phenomenon has become a focus in the study of social science. For example, research on religious activity before and after a major earthquake in Christchurch, New

Zealand, in 2011 reported what researchers, in their study of computer models, have described as

> an uptick in religious service attendance . . . after a large and deadly earthquake. . . .
> Both individual characteristics and environmental events affected the strength of an agent's [computer-controlled character's] religious conviction.[1]

To put it more bluntly—and certainly less clinically—those who experience disasters often get religion. And it could be added that the disaster could be of human origin, such as a terrorist act. Or it could be, as it is often described, "an act of God," such as an earthquake.

But then the research on the event in New Zealand goes on to add that "people living near the earthquake, whether religious or not before the event, became more religious in the wake of the tragedy, *at least for a while*."[2] And here arises an almost tiresome theme that is all too evident in observing the behavior of God's people throughout the Old Testament. Over and over again, God allows adversity to draw His people back to Him.

This is not to say that, in this modern age, the collapse of the twin towers or the earthquake in Christchurch are direct visitations of God. But the all-too-common human response to such disasters seems rooted in the DNA of human behavior. Suddenly, in such circumstances, there is among many a kind of return to a belief in something transcendent, or at least a willingness to reconsider the possibility of it. But, too often, it is a short-lived experience.

Sabbath keepers, on the other hand, experience an ongoing relationship with God. Each Sabbath is an opportunity to worship God and to remember that God never leaves us—even when terrible events take place in the world.

———

Gary B. Swanson is a writer in Silver Spring, Maryland, United States.

———

1. Wesley Wildman, "How Computer Scientists Model the Role of Religion in Society," *Smithsonian* magazine, June 11, 2018, https://www.smithsonianmag.com/science-nature/human-computer-simulations-may-help-us-understand-religious-behavior-180969296.

2. Wildman, "How Computer Scientists Model," https://www.smithsonianmag.com/science-nature/human-computer-simulations-may-help-us-understand-religious-behavior-180969296; emphasis added.

Sabbath Community

The Sabbath and Family Fellowship

Keith A. Albury

My appreciation for the Sabbath developed during my college years. I grew up in a Seventh-day Adventist home, and my father was a minister. Yet, my initial understanding of this scripturally prescribed day of rest primarily focused on prohibitions. I knew more about the activities I was expected to avoid than the liberty this day meant for me and those I loved.

That eventually changed once I started attending West Indies College in Mandeville, Jamaica. As I often fondly recall, most days on the campus meant bustling traffic as students, faculty, and staff commuted to their respective classrooms or undertook their operational duties. But each Friday morning, something remarkable happened. The bustling almost ceased with fewer classes and reduced operation. By sunset, all was so quiet that one heard the music of the wind on the city's mountainside. And for the duration of the Sabbath, students gathered in informal settings for spiritual reflection and fellowship. Whether it was to share God's work in my life or to express gratitude for a much-needed recharge, I looked forward to those special gatherings. And for me, it was then that the Sabbath experience changed from being action-prohibitive to a day marked by fellowship and reflection.

After my time at the college on the hill, I replicated this newfound joy in weekly gatherings with my immediate and extended family members. Sabbath afternoons meant gourmet cuisine, family fellowship, and deep reflection on the things of God. I looked forward to the Sabbath each week.

Now, with a family of my own, the tradition continues. And although I am a minister myself, it is a tradition I protect. We look forward to what blessings each seventh day might bring while gathered without distraction from daily cares, whether outdoors or around our family's dinner table. In a personal and peculiar sense, I have found the joy that the Sabbath affords (Mark 2:27). And I am happy that I am able to share it each week with my loved ones.

Keith A. Albury is the senior pastor at the Linden Seventh-day Adventist Church in Queens, New York, United States.

Sabbath in My Hometown

John Bradshaw

Hoping to find out where I could worship on the coming Sabbath, I called the pastor of the church nearest my parents' home. I was newly back in New Zealand after a year of living in England, and I had just been baptized the previous Sabbath.

"I think I could get you a ride to church if you'd like," the pastor said. "We have a family living in your town who comes to church every week."

I was astonished! Could it be possible that an entire family from my hardscrabble, blue-collar hometown were attending the Seventh-day Adventist Church? "Maybe you know them," the pastor suggested. "Mike and Colleen Smith." *No, that could not be,* I thought. *It is simply not possible!*

Mike was from a prominent Catholic family. Like my father, his parents were pillars of the church in which we grew up. Our families had been well acquainted for many years.

"John?" the pastor said, unsure if I was still on the phone.

"Uh, I know a Mike Smith," I stammered, "but it can't possibly be the same guy." The last time I saw Mike, he had an important leadership role in my former church.

The pastor called Mike and got a similar reaction. "Sure, Pastor, I know the Bradshaws, but—it couldn't possibly be the John Bradshaw I know. Maybe there's someone else with that name?"

On Sabbath morning, Mike's white Toyota van pulled into my parents' driveway. I stared in disbelief as he got out of the van to greet me.

"It's *you!*" I stammered.

Mike laughed. "It's *you!*" he said in return.

Neither of us knew where to begin. How had this happened? How in the world could rock-solid Catholics from our town become Sabbath-keeping Christians? We had a lot of catching up to do.

It was one of the most unforgettable Sabbaths I have ever experienced. Here were Mike, Colleen, and their four young children. We shared our testimonies, marveling at how God had worked. Mike's daughter went on to marry a pastor, and today they form a powerful ministry team. One son became a nurse and a preacher of powerful sermons. Another son did mission service.

Over the years, still others from my hometown started attending my church. Another friend, Jody, and I played on the same rugby team from the time we were six years old. And now *he* was in church, along with his wife, Turu, who had been in my class in high school. Later, yet another high school classmate began attending church on Sabbath.

These experiences are clear evidence to me that the gospel is going to the world. Even those whom I never would have dreamed of observing the Sabbath have become Bible-believing Christians. I have to believe God is still not done.

Sabbaths spent in my hometown remind me that God has called me to surrender my life to Him. And what He has done in my life, He does in the lives of others.

John Bradshaw is the president of It Is Written in Chattanooga, Tennessee, United States.

The Sabbath and My Non-Sabbatarian Friend

Balvin B. Braham

We were the best of friends. We grew up attending the same schools and the same church on Sunday mornings. One day, I accepted the Sabbath as the weekly day of worship as a memorial of Creation, sanctified by God to be observed by all humanity.

My friend questioned my decision, stating, "The Sabbath is for Jews, and Scripture does not instruct that it is a day of worship for non-Jews." He was an altar server in his church and was interested in becoming a priest.

I wanted my friend to experience the joys of learning about the Sabbath because he loved the Lord, was very intelligent, loved to study, and enjoyed engaging discussions. My weekly "friendship evangelism outreach" took place on Sabbath afternoons, between the worship hour and the Bible class at my church. In those conversations at his house, I shared with my friend nuggets from the Sabbath services.

As we conversed, I presented scriptural evidence to show that the Sabbath is a day of worship or holy convocation for all. "Six days shall work be done, but the seventh day is a Sabbath of solemn rest, a holy convocation. You shall do no work on it; it is the Sabbath of the Lord in all your dwellings" (Leviticus 23:3). I explained that the word "convocation" is from the Hebrew word *miqrâ*, meaning "a public meeting, assembly, or gathering." It is also a time for holy assemblies (i.e., worship services). I regularly emphasized Isaiah 66:23, which speaks of Sabbath worship in eternity:

"It shall come to pass
That from one New Moon to another,
And from one Sabbath to another,
All flesh shall come to worship before Me," says the Lord.

I highlighted that Jesus participated in corporate worship on the Sabbath while here on earth (see Mark 1:21; 6:2; Luke 4:16).

My friend and I separated to pursue higher education, yet we maintained our friendship. The Sabbath conversations continued. Influenced by our Sabbath conversations and a Seventh-day Adventist young lady whom he married, he became a Seventh-day

Adventist. For almost two decades now, he has been serving as an elder in the Seventh-day Adventist Church.

Like the apostle Paul, who reasoned with people from Scripture on consecutive Sabbaths (Acts 17:1–4; 18:1–11), it is for me a day to abstain from secular work, participate in worship services, reason with people from Scripture, and inspire non-Sabbatarian friends to become disciples of Christ. I am delighted that my friend is also experiencing the blessings of the Sabbath.

Balvin B. Braham is a vice president for the Inter-American Division of Seventh-day Adventists in Miami, Florida, United States.

Spending the Sabbath With Those Who Do Not Know the Sabbath

Marcia Coombs

Once, while vacationing in New York City, I stayed with relatives who were not Seventh-day Adventists. A weekend trip to Hartford, Connecticut, was planned to visit some of our in-laws.

At that time, I was a new Adventist bubbling over with spiritual energy. Everyone was kind to me and showed me great respect. They were careful with their language, and when they slipped up, they would apologize by saying, "Pardon my French." Life was good.

Friday morning and afternoon were spent connecting with the relatives in Connecticut. We had a really great time. Sabbath morning was also very quiet. I did not attend church, but I spent the time in solitary worship. The relatives moved about the house quietly, trying not to disturb me. I appreciated their care and concern, considering they were not Sabbath keepers.

Everything was going well until late Sabbath afternoon. One of my sisters-in-law approached me. "Marcia, we are going to the mall. Would you like to join us?"

"I am sorry, but I won't be able to," I said.

"Why not?" she queried.

"The sun has not yet set. I am still on holy hours," I remarked.

"What? Why can't you go shopping? You will not be doing anything bad," she countered.

I tried to explain why I could not go shopping during the Sabbath, but the explanation sounded empty.

"I don't know why you can't go shopping. It is not like you are going to a party or something like that. Get dressed and come with us. You do not have to purchase anything.

Just tell us what you need, and we will purchase it for you," she pressed.

I then realized that as a new Sabbath keeper, I was not equipped to answer questions related to why I was or was not doing certain things. I retired to my room and resorted to tears of frustration because I could not explain my practices.

I then prayed as I had never prayed before. The Bible tells us to "draw nigh to God, and he will draw nigh to you" (James 4:8, KJV). I asked God to give me the answer to the question I was asked. The answer came swiftly. *You are a member of the Seventh-day Adventist Church. One of the founding principles is the Sabbath. The Sabbath is special, and you choose not to go to the mall.*

I sought out my sister-in-law and shared my thought with her. She listened attentively then said, "You won't go, so we won't go."

I was very happy that she respected my decision and enjoyed the rest of the Sabbath. I learned a very valuable lesson that day. The church had done its part in preparing me for baptism, but after baptism, I did not follow through with my promise to study God's Word as well as other books available to me. I joyfully vowed to change my ways.

Marcia Coombs is a professor at York Early College Academy in Queens, New York, United States.

Sabbath Date Night

Robert Cundiff

In a recent sermon, I told a humorous but fake story to help illustrate how the Sabbath brings good things to our lives. The story goes like this: I took my wife out to dinner for our weekly date. Once seated, I promptly pulled out my phone and began to endlessly scroll Twitter. After a few minutes, she reminded me it was date night and politely asked me to put my phone away. I conceded, but just then, an important call came in that I absolutely had to take. A brief glance across the table let me know that it would be best if I tried not to look her way again until I got off the phone.

I concluded the call quickly, but the conversation required a few follow-up texts to wrap up the business at hand. A temperature check across the table let me know that the thermostat was falling rapidly and that it was time to store my device. Tucking my phone in my pocket, I folded my hands and flashed a smile across the table in an attempt to thaw out the growing iceberg.

Just then, the waitress stopped by for our drink order. As she was walked away, I offhandedly asked if she could tilt the wall-mounted TV my direction so I could watch the football game. Needless to say, this request brought a cold, wintry atmosphere to our date night.

Now, what is the point of this fictitious story? Although I could technically argue that I had taken my wife on a date, the truth is that such a date would have done more harm than good to our marriage. The purpose of date night is to foster closeness and nurture your relationship. Just keeping the appointment is not sufficient. The appointment must be kept in a way that actually accomplishes the goal of marital bonding rather than just scratching an item off one's to-do list.

For me, this illustrates the beauty of the Sabbath. The Sabbath is like our weekly date with God. Its purpose is to foster closeness, intimacy, and a strong relationship with God. We do not just keep Sabbath because the Bible teaches us to do it. We do not keep it as part of religious duty or religious ritual. Rather, God gives us the Sabbath to help us guard regular, unhurried times in His presence.

This truth becomes even more precious when I realize that the Sabbath was God's idea. He is the one who created the Sabbath and invites me into His Sabbath rest. Why would He do that? Because He is good, and He longs to bring that goodness into my life. He created the Sabbath as a venue through which He can access my heart and fill me with the good things that come from a vibrant relationship with Him. That is why I love the Sabbath. That is why I keep it and invite others to also experience the joy of Sabbath rest.

Robert Cundiff is president of the Ohio Conference of Seventh-day Adventists in Dayton, Ohio, United States.

The Sabbath: A Teacher in the Art of Sharing and an Exhibition of Miracles

Cloreth Greene

During my childhood, Sabbath celebrations were special events at home. The saying "Thank God it is Friday" took on new meaning as preparations went into high gear, especially in the kitchen. A variety of items not served during the week would be on the menu for the Sabbath meal. Best of all, there was usually a baked treat! As I recall, someone was always invited to our home for lunch. I enjoyed serving the guests their meals, and the cleanup afterward was fun.

What amazed and impressed me the most was how the food seemed to multiply, no matter how many were present for the meal. Everyone had enough to eat! On one memorable weekend, my mother was exhausted Friday evening, and the grocery list had been shortened. She prepared just enough food for Sabbath lunch for our family—her, my father, and me—and told my father that we could not host any guests. Instead, according to his usual practice, he invited over some visitors without warning my mother. Imagine her surprise when four guests arrived home with him! She was not happy with this development, but extending hospitality to our guests was the only available option.

In addition to the prepared meal, we made a few sandwiches and some lemonade. We held hands at the table, and my father said grace to bless the food. In my childhood fascination, I could not help staring at everyone's plate during the meal. People were having second servings (one person even had thirds), and it seemed like they ate more than usual. Except for me, that is. I was so busy watching the plates of others in total disbelief, wondering where the food came from, that I was not eating. I had to be encouraged a few times by my mother to "eat up."

Meal-sharing in my home was a practice that extended beyond Sabbath days. This instilled in me a desire to share meals with others, even when I was not at home. School became my primary "mission field." Without even realizing it at first, I found myself checking to see which of my classmates did not seem to have something to eat at lunchtime. I enjoyed going over to them and offering some of my food. Some accepted and some did not, but I enjoyed making the offer.

Sharing meals has become a natural part of my life, mainly because of my childhood Sabbath experiences. As for the food being multiplied? It seems to happen all the time. God blessed and reserved for His children a special day to fellowship, share, worship, and praise Him—and maybe even see food multiply before their very eyes!

Cloreth Greene is a communication specialist in Hamilton, Ontario, Canada.

The Sabbath in Our Family

Omar E. Grieve

I remember the happiness I experienced with my family at my grandparents' home. On Friday, we joyfully prepared for the Sabbath. Everyone had something important to do—clean the house, prepare the special meals, iron our clothes, shine our shoes. It was important for my grandmother to carefully choose the newer bills of paper money and even iron them, making sure they were crisp and clean to place them in our Bibles, ready for tithes and offerings. Then the special Sabbath hours came. Singing with my family during Sabbath vespers, studying the Bible, going to church, and enjoying nature—all beautiful activities that were part of our Sabbath experience.

The small town of Villa Ocampo, in the province of Santa Fe, Argentina, was the place I learned the foundational concept of what I grew to cherish and respect: honor the Creator of all on His holy day, the Sabbath.

The Sabbath is an external sign of an internal experience with God. The holiness of the Sabbath day can be a blissful experience in our lives if we honor it by not going our own way and not doing as we please or speaking idle words. And to fully participate in the blessings and refreshment that result from the observance of the Lord's Day, careful and thorough preparation is essential. With the sunset on Friday, all the secular work, secular reading, and cares of this life must be put aside. Then we will be able to "call the Sabbath a delight, and the holy day of the LORD honorable" (Isaiah 58:13).

The world is not the same as it was in the days of my childhood, but one thing is unwavering: "God blessed the seventh day and made it holy" (Genesis 2:3, NIV). And as I continue to observe the Sabbath with my family, we remember that it is the sign that God gave us, that we are accepted and beloved, and that one day we will enter the City of God and partake of the fruit of the tree of life.

Omar E. Grieve is the speaker and director for *La Voz de la Esperanza* in Riverside, California, United States.

My Sabbath Experience

Joshua Jara

God created the earth in six days. On the seventh day, God saw that what He had made was good, and He rested that day. This is why Seventh-day Adventists believe that the week starts on Sunday and ends on the Sabbath—the seventh day.

Sabbath is a special day. It gives us an opportunity to grow our relationship with God. This growth can happen by going to church, studying the Bible, or going outside to enjoy God's creation. Some individuals are extreme in how they spend the Sabbath, while others just spend most of the day sleeping and not doing much else.

I grew up in a church where the people were serious about their religion. For instance, the kids were told how to spend the Sabbath. My dad was the pastor, so I was (and still am) held to a higher standard. As a kid, I wanted to play and run around until my legs fell off. The church had a big grassy field with trees everywhere. The church was gated, and my parents were fine with me running around as long as I did not go outside the gate. When there was a church service happening, though, I was expected to be in the sanctuary.

According to the Bible, once the sun goes down, it is the next day. So once the sun went down on Sabbath, we were allowed to go out and play various games, including soccer and volleyball. Some church members had different ideas about what we should do after the Sabbath was over. They wanted us inside, not doing anything and being quiet. None of the kids liked that, so we played outside anyway. There was one lady who would always yell at us and get our parents. So we had to go back inside the church.

For me, Sabbath was always a two-sided coin. It was a day of fun with my friends. It was also a day of strict rules and watchful eyes that seemed to be waiting for me to step over a line so they could pull me back onto the path of the righteous. As I have grown older, I have had to define what the Sabbath is beyond the rules and the fun. I have been able to grow spiritually and understand why some people are so strict. I understand that observing the Sabbath is a holy ritual. Sabbath is about spending time with God and growing in that relationship. It is disrespectful to play or do something that does not bring you closer to God. Now I have learned how to be closer to God. Every Sabbath, I try to grow with Him by worshiping with my family and studying the Bible.

Joshua Jara is an eleventh-grade student at La Sierra Academy in Riverside, California, United States.

Sabbath in India, Shabbat in Israel

Jim Jeffery

Several years ago, I found myself welcoming the Sabbath in Pune, India. Two weeks later, while staying at a bed-and-breakfast in Jerusalem, I was invited to welcome in the Shabbat at an Orthodox Jewish synagogue, led by a woman rabbi. Here is what I experienced.

After traveling for more than twenty-four hours, I eagerly looked forward to a peaceful Sabbath in India. The beginning of the Sabbath at Spicer Adventist University began with a robust song service followed by a devotional. The coziness of their brand-new church sanctuary was a God-given blessing to my soul. While honking cars, motorized rickshaws, taxis, and trucks roared past on the congested street outside, the sanctuary kept the noise in abeyance. This quiet beginning to Sabbath was a balm to my weary soul as old and young, students and faculty joined in worship.

Two weeks later, on my way back to the United States, I found myself on my first trip to Jerusalem. After fifteen hours of travel, I arrived in Jerusalem at 3:00 Friday morning and settled into a small bed-and-breakfast.

I ventured out into the city Friday afternoon, but as the Sabbath approached, everything began to shut down. The market stalls stopped selling, and the buses and taxis stopped running. The city became quiet.

Walking back to the bed-and-breakfast, I noticed on the dining room table a large amount of food under a linen cloth. The Swiss German lady who was also staying there mentioned to me that all the guests were going to visit a synagogue for the beginning of the Shabbat. She asked if I would like to join, and I readily agreed, even though I was exhausted.

A group of about fifteen of us walked more than a mile to the Shira Hadasha, an Orthodox synagogue in the German colony neighborhood. As we entered, a cantor was reciting prayers. His back was to us at all times, and the congregation responded on occasion. After forty-five minutes of recitations and prayers, the service ended, and we made the long journey back uphill.

The Friday night "family" dinner began with candles and blessings over the challah bread. The meal was abundant with fish, soup, side dishes, and lots of fresh fruit. We began our dinner as fifteen strangers, all pilgrims from around the globe who found ourselves in a foreign land. Each participated in the conversation—a Jewish lawyer from Australia, a Black Jew newly immigrated from North Africa, a few Americans, a Canadian, and several Europeans. Each of us, in our own way, welcomed the Sabbath. The evening meal solidified our friendship as we lingered in celebrating the beginning of that special Shabbat.

As we talked, it became more and more meaningful that, in eternity, we will celebrate God's mercies and foresight for creating the Sabbath. God built the world, and us, with a firm foundation. The majority of translations and paraphrases of Genesis 1:1 use this phrase: "In the beginning God." God's creation ended on the sixth day, and He closed the week but then began with the creation of the Sabbath—a sacred time we will keep throughout eternity.

With brothers and sisters, whether from India, Israel, or anywhere else on this planet, our Sabbath *beginnings here on earth will lead to a foretaste of the joys of the Sabbath throughout eternity.*

Jim Jeffery is dean emeritus of the School of Education at Andrews University. He writes from Cascumpec, Prince Edward Island, Canada.

The Sabbath and I

R. Clifford Jones

My parents married shortly after my father arrived in Trinidad from Barbados, and they had three sons before I was born. They were humble people of modest means that rented a first-floor apartment from a Seventh-day Adventist family who lived above them.

It did not take long for my mother, who loved Scripture, to begin studying the Bible with the landlords. The Bible lessons were intense and interesting, and she looked forward to them. At first, going to church on Saturday, something that my mom quickly began to do, was a bit strange. My father flatly refused to join her, although he regularly took her to and from church.

Of the nine children God blessed my parents with (seven sons, two daughters), I was the first to be raised in the church. When my mother was baptized, she told the rest of the family that I would become a minister, which I did, because of the impact her Bible studies had on me.

The Sabbath was all I knew as a child. I grew up keeping the Sabbath and looked forward to the day with the same anticipation and excitement that I felt when I looked forward to Christmas and my birthday. Sabbath meant going to church, singing songs with my friends (many of whom I had not seen all week), and listening to stories of Bible characters that thrilled our souls. Sabbath also meant the opportunity to witness, as Sabbath afternoons were spent going door to door with literature. Some of my neighborhood friends could not understand how and why my family went to church on Saturday, robbing me of a prime day to play and frolic. Yet, I did not experience the Sabbath as a loss but as a plus.

It goes without saying that I have studied the Sabbath extensively. As a pastor and evangelist, I have preached countless sermons about the Sabbath and can convince any sincere seeker for truth that the Sabbath has not been done away with. Yet, for me, what makes the Sabbath compelling and awe inspiring is its link to Jesus Christ. The Sabbath is not a stand-alone phenomenon. It is a dynamic force because it causes me to focus on Christ, the Lord of the Sabbath. Without Christ, the Sabbath would be little, if anything at all. In Christ, the Sabbath comes alive and is vibrant. It provides an opportunity for me to reconnect with Christ, repose in His rest and salvation, and fellowship with God's people. In short, the Sabbath is about relationship. It connects me to Christ and His marvelous creation in ways that lead to my transformation and contribute to my growth.

R. Clifford Jones is the dean of the School of Theology at Oakwood University in Huntsville, Alabama, United States.

Resting in a Relationship

Helgi Jónsson

I was raised in a Sabbath-keeping home, but I must admit that when I was a kid, Sabbath was not always a fun day. I was raised in Reykjavík, Iceland, where I still live and, because of Iceland's placement on the planet, we have quite a difference in Sabbath hours. In December, it can start as early as 3:30 in the afternoon; and in late June, sundown is as late as just after midnight.

As a youngster, I felt that Sabbath was a day when I could not do stuff. But, as I grew older, it became a day of value. When I studied medicine at the University of Iceland, the Sabbath became a day of true rest from books and projects. Back in the early 1990s, the university did not have lectures on Saturdays, but examinations could still take place on that day. I believe it was my first or second year when we had an exam on brain dissection. At each station, we were expected to solve different problems. The whole class walked from one station to the next until all of us had dealt with the problems. This type of examination was also complicated for the professor, who had to set up the specimens and administer the test.

The test was challenging, but to my disappointment, this important test was scheduled on a Sabbath. To make things worse, the professor was well known as a strict man who did not tolerate nonsense or silly questions. What was I supposed to do? *He would most certainly turn me down anyway*, I thought to myself. Some of my Sabbath-keeping friends would not have given it much thought and just taken the exam on the Sabbath. God would not turn His back on them for that, I reasoned. But the Sabbath had always been a part of my life, for better or worse. I had never attended school on a Sabbath, not as a kid nor as a teenager in high school. But this was different. At the university, I was dependent on the individual professor's goodwill, and no school regulations would help me.

I prayed and said to God, "OK, if You want me to take this test, You have to help me out! Give me the courage to ask, and make my professor kind and willing to help me out—please."

One day I mustered the courage to ask him. The prompt and kind answer surprised me.

"Yes, no problem. I will do that for you. Come to me by the end of Friday, the day before the exam, and we will do it then. You just have to promise me one thing. Don't tell any of your classmates the questions!"

That Friday night, the week's work was finished. That Sabbath, I rested well and contemplated on a new experience of God and His guidance. I knew Him a little more, trusted Him a little more, and was comforted in the thought that He is with me.

God and I—that is the Sabbath.

———

Helgi Jónsson is a psychiatrist in Reykjavík, Iceland.

Some Things We Miss Are Priceless

Nigel Lewis

The phrase "Step back and see things better" is familiar. Hold a picture too close, and our vision becomes blurred and the details are lost. Many beautiful pictures in our lives are blurred because we hold them too close. One such picture is the Sabbath—a day designed by the Creator and given to us as a restorative experience. Yet, many, when they hear the word "Sabbath," think of regulations, restrictions, and a loss of freedom.

I will share an experience, with the permission of my son Ray, that made me see the beauty of the Sabbath. Our son graduated with his master of science in engineering and began his first job in our hometown. He was a high-performing, results-oriented person with an excellent work ethic. On the religious side, he questioned everything from God's existence to whether religion was the cause of or the solution to world problems. Initially, none of these intellectual adventures were worrisome to me, but then he began to be somewhat carefree about the Sabbath.

One Sabbath, he wanted to spend the day walking with friends through Central Park in New York. Another Sabbath, he was not interested in going to church—he just wanted to stay home. These variations from the norm in our household were noticeable but not earth-shattering. But then, one Sabbath, he announced that he was going to work in order to finish a project and get a head start on another. I cannot tell you how this shook our family. When your adult child challenges years of established practices that you believed they would always adhere to, it is devastating. As I dressed for church, my wife and I wondered how to dissuade him from going to work that day. I stepped back for a moment and asked myself the question, *What does Ray highly value about Sabbath keeping to which I could appeal?* And the answer came almost immediately—family time. Yes, Ray loved being with his family.

So I picked my moment and said to him gently, "Son, I can't tell you what to do with your life. You are a grown man now. But before you give up precious things that you will need later on, think carefully about this. Every family has its way of spending quality time together. As a family, we do this on Sabbath. If you give it up, you could spend the rest of your life regretting that you gave away something so precious."

It worked! He continued dressing, but instead of going to work, he went to church with his mother and me.

Now Ray is married and has his own family, and you cannot get between Ray and the quality time he spends with family on Sabbath. Thank God I stepped back and saw the bigger picture, even the picture from his perspective. What a difference a step back can make in how we view the Sabbath.

At the time of this writing, Nigel Lewis was the associate pastor at the Atlanta Belvedere Seventh-day Adventist Church in Atlanta, Georgia, United States.

Sabbath and Our Family

Brian and Esther Liu

During the COVID-19 pandemic, the Sabbath has taken on a new and fresh meaning for our family.

When COVID-19 first reared its ugly head, we did not know what to expect. But I (Esther), a physician on the front lines and chair of my department, knew that I would be called to help lead the fight. And sure enough, I was.

Not wanting to put our family at risk, the kids and I (Brian) went to Florida to stay with my parents. While we were hoping it would only be a short time, it ended up being three months.

During this time, I (Esther) missed both kids' birthdays. It was not easy for them to be away from their mother, but as challenging as this was for us, we also realized we had so much to be thankful for. For us, it was an inconvenience. For others, it was life and death.

This pandemic has taught us several things. First, we are so blessed to have each other as family. Second, it has taught us that there is a lot of suffering in the world. Many people—our neighbors, friends, students, and patients—are suffering. It is in this context that we have come to view the Sabbath differently.

Yes, we miss seeing our friends and reconnecting at church, but the Sabbath is also a time for us to reconnect as a family. And the way we reconnect is by serving others. We do not do nearly enough, but we now spend our Sabbaths doing service projects—passing out food boxes to those that need it more than us, putting together baskets for the homeless, helping at-risk students find a safe place. The Bible tells us in Matthew:

"For I was hungry, and you fed me. . . . I was a stranger, and you invited me into your home. I was naked, and you gave me clothing." . . .

And the King will say, "I tell you the truth, when you did it to one of the least of these . . . you were doing it to me" (25:35, 36, 40, NLT).

We have much to be thankful for, and doing our small part in helping others is what Sabbath means to us.

Brian is a musician and teacher and Esther is a physician in Columbia, Maryland, United States.

My Sabbath Choice

Bruce Manners

For the first fifteen years of my life, I attended church on Saturday *and* Sunday. As I write this, it sounds a little crazy, but that was my reality.

I grew up in Port Wakefield, a small country town an hour's drive north of South Australia's capital, Adelaide. Before my time, my town was a significant port, shipping copper, wool, and grain to Adelaide and other parts of Australia. When I arrived on the scene, fishing and farming were the main industries.

As if to prove the point, my mother was a farmer's daughter, my father a fisherman. Their relationship was complicated because my mother was a Methodist and my father was a Seventh-day Adventist. For a while, my mother attended the small Adventist church, a half hour's drive from home, but then she stopped.

My father went fishing on Sundays and returned on Thursday afternoons to get his catch to the market in Adelaide on Fridays. He never attended my mother's church, except for weddings and funerals. And for his own funeral—conducted by his Adventist pastor.

Both of my parents were serious about their respective churches and, for a time, were elders in their churches. I have wondered if that could gain a mention in *Guinness World Records*.

Having to go to church twice on weekends was a bit of a chore, but the real annoyance was how it affected sports. I enjoyed sports. At school, I played cricket, football (Australian rules), and tennis, but I could not play on Sabbaths when *real* sport with adults was played. Tuesday's table tennis did not have the same excitement, but I played it because I could.

At the age of fifteen, I committed fully to Christ. As I considered my two in-house examples of Christianity, I chose to become a Seventh-day Adventist because I recognized that the seventh-day Sabbath is a valid, biblical teaching. More than this, it was what Jesus did, and I wanted to follow in His ways.

That step was easy. Explaining it to my mother? Not so easy.

Several decades later, this remains a standout decision. Not every Sabbath has been a highlight, but each has been important in my walk with God. Better yet, I now see more clearly how the Sabbath is a gift in which I can truly "delight" (Isaiah 58:13).

Two years ago, I was invited back to my mother's church for its 150th anniversary. With the invitation came the opportunity to speak for a few minutes.

On that day, the small church was packed, and I was surprised at how many people I recognized. My main message was one of thanks. I thanked the members for being a safe congregation that had helped my Christian journey. My challenge was for each of us to be the people Jesus wants us to be.

Following Jesus and His example is what shaped my life and led me to choose the Sabbath.

———————

Bruce Manners is a retired pastor in Melbourne, Australia.

The Magnificent Seventh

Lionel Martell

I was born in a Harlem, New York, hospital in 1956 to a very special Caribbean lady who loved and feared God. She was a single parent who lived and survived in some of the roughest, toughest areas of New York City.

I grew up in some difficult areas of New York. My mother raised my six siblings and me in a strict religious atmosphere closely connected to the church. Although I was only seven, I remember going to church every Sunday, then having to stay upstairs and read Scripture after church. I dreaded the feeling of house arrest.

One Sunday, I was in my room, supposedly studying the Scriptures but listening instead to the kids playing street games. I was so frustrated that I could not participate that I took my Bible and slammed it down on my bed. When I looked down at the bed, the Bible was open to Exodus 20:8, which says, "Remember the Sabbath day, to keep it holy."

Although only seven, I started thinking about what I had read. *If the Sabbath day is the holy day,* I thought, *and the seventh day is the Sabbath day, then the seventh day is the holy day. Sunday—the first day of the week—could not be the Sabbath.* I told my mom we were worshiping on the wrong day. I developed this argument so I could go outside to play, not because I was convinced of the sacredness of the Sabbath. My mom ignored me.

Years later, my eldest sister shared a passage of Scripture with me. It was Matthew 24:20, where Jesus says, "Pray that your flight will not take place in winter or on the Sabbath" (NIV). After that, my sister and I started keeping the Sabbath. We then found the Ephesus Seventh-day Adventist Church in New York, and we were both baptized. Later, I became a Seventh-day Adventist pastor, and I had the privilege of baptizing my mother just before she died on November 7, 2015.

The Sabbath has been important in our family. I praise God for His matchless love and His soul-saving power.

———————————

Lionel Martell is a pastor at the Spring Valley Seventh-day Adventist Church in Spring Valley, New York, United States.

A Squirrel Called Peter

Edwin McBride Jr.

My parents, especially my mother, were intentional about how we spent our time on the Sabbath. She really wanted us to enjoy the sacred hours. As I recall, Sabbaths were filled with love, laughter, learning, and rewards.

Of the many beautiful Sabbath experiences, one that particularly stands out to me was when my parents, siblings, and I received a powerful lesson from a squirrel. This particular Sabbath is vivid in my mind. I still remember that we sang "Blessed Assurance" as the closing hymn at church. When we returned home, my mother gave my siblings and me a sermon quiz during the Sabbath meal. Although everyone received dessert, the winners of the examination received more. Sad to say, I did not win that day.

However, what continued to make this Sabbath unique and memorable was a nature walk in a park we had not visited in a while. We must have walked for a mile or two, picking up sticks and skipping rocks in the lake, before we sat down to close the Sabbath. My parents spread out a blanket for us to sit on and brought out a bag of mixed nuts.

As we sang songs and shelled the nuts, we noticed a squirrel coming closer and closer. I am not sure which of my siblings first threw a nut in the squirrel's direction, but before long, we were giving them away to the squirrel. My parents quickly seized this opportunity to teach a lesson about the bravery of the squirrel. On that Sabbath, as the squirrel came closer and closer to us to collect the nuts, Peter's bravery to walk on water to meet Jesus was brought to life with more meaning. To drive the point home, we affectionately and illustratively named the squirrel Peter. That Sabbath, we learned that trust in God would help us be just as brave during impossible moments as Peter the disciple *and* Peter the squirrel.

My mother has since passed away, but because she made the Sabbath enjoyable, we had many experiences that made learning about the Bible adventurous and amazing. These experiences have helped me make my children's Sabbath experiences and my own a time to remember.

Edwin McBride Jr. is a youth pastor at the Kansas Avenue Seventh-day Adventist Church in Riverside, California, United States.

The Sabbath and Others

Joi McClellan

Growing up as a Sabbath keeper, I was never the kid that loathed Friday sundown. Sabbath was indeed a high time of the week, thanks to family, dessert, and too many guests to count. It has always been my kind of day.

I thought I had appreciated Sabbath to its fullest in my younger years, but going away to Southern Adventist University, I realized I had barely scratched the surface. Who knew the relief of reaching sunset at the end of a hectic week? Convinced that God had students in mind when He made the day, I was determined to make the most out of the opportunity to rest, catch up with friends, and pause studying. I relished a day intended just for me!

So that is how I kept Sabbath for my first three years of college: run myself to near exhaustion, fall headlong into Sabbath, skip Sabbath School, make a point of attending later services in order to catch up on much-needed sleep, hang out with friends, go hiking—then after sunset, hit the week again. And every so often, I did some sort of benevolent outreach project.

One Sabbath afternoon, I found myself with no specific plans or people around. Helping me solve my plight, my roommate suggested joining a group that was going on an outreach event. This was by no means what I envisioned for my precious Sabbath, and I bristled at the disturbance it caused my resisting conscience. I would go on outreach sometimes, but as a norm? No.

Jesus understood my busy student life, right? But the more I tried, the harder it was to recall examples of Jesus chilling by the Sea of Galilee every weekend. I did not appreciate the confrontation—especially when the implications could affect the next 3,120 Sabbaths I might see in my lifetime.

As I think of this pivotal moment in my Sabbath keeping, my mind wanders to Isaiah 58, where God confronts His people about their disregard for others while pursuing "righteousness" and "obedience." He drives the point home by bringing up the Sabbath issue, presenting a better way to spend this special day: "If you turn away your foot from the Sabbath, from doing your pleasure on My holy day . . . then you shall delight yourself in the LORD" (Isaiah 58:13, 14).

The promise is certain. I will find delight in God and in His precious day by centering on Him, not on self. He has blessings of rest for me that can be found only in giving myself and time to Him. I am not saying it is evil to physically rest or take the day easy; it is just that I have discovered the Sabbath is not all about me.

So what did I do? My conscience got the better of me, and I joined the outreach group. That day was a turning point in my approach to Sabbath, and by God's grace, these twenty-four hours are no longer all about me.

Joi McClellan is a dental student at the University of Michigan School of Dentistry in Ann Arbor, Michigan, United States.

Sabbath Keeping: My Consistent Examples

Brian S. McDonald

For as long as I can remember, the Sabbath has been a part of who I am and has formed my biblical worldview. As I was growing up in the New York suburb of Mount Vernon in the 1980s, Sabbath began in our home in the hours preceding sunset on Friday. My siblings and I completed our chores so the house was tidy and our clothes were ready for church the next day. My responsibility was vacuuming and polishing my shoes in addition to those of my dad and younger brother. My father was consistent in ensuring the family attended Sabbath School and worship services every Sabbath. As a result, we learned over the years through practice and example the sanctity of the day. During this time, I also remember our Sabbath walks and Sabbath lunches and potlucks—all pleasant childhood memories.

To be certain, Sabbath observance also had its challenges. It was not easy for everyone to finish chores and other activities on time. My siblings and I were students in public school for primary and middle school, and my parents did not permit us to participate in some of the extracurricular activities on Saturday.

The Sabbath habits formed in childhood influenced my outlook on Sabbath observance as a young adult. I always informed my employers of my unavailability to work on Friday evenings and Saturdays. Although sometimes apprehensive as to how this limitation would be received, I saw it as an opportunity to share my faith, as there were some who never had a knowledge of the Sabbath in the context of Christianity and only associated it with Jewish tradition.

Before deciding to undertake the rigors of law school part-time while being employed full-time, I had to have a plan for how I would accomplish the feat. For many who work full-time while attending law school, a full weekend of study on both Saturday and Sunday is critical to their success. I prayed and believed that God would bless my efforts in completing law school if I remained faithful to Him in keeping the Sabbath. I especially enjoyed the blessing of the Sabbath after working long days and nights throughout the week. The Sabbath was a welcome reprieve for rest and fellowship with family and friends.

As I reflect on the impact of the Sabbath in my life and on my worldview, it is clear that the admonition of Proverbs 22:6 to "train up a child in the way he should go, and when he is old he will not depart from it" rings true in my life. The example my parents set for me in keeping the Sabbath has remained with me to the present. I have strived to model the things my parents taught me to my daughters, and I pray that they will be faithful in keeping the Sabbath and find the blessings in keeping it, as I did.

Brian S. McDonald is a banking attorney in New York City, New York, United States.

Sabbath—A Family Legacy

Paulette McLean Johnson

My paternal grandparents gave me two precious gifts—my family and the Sabbath. My parents were separated and did not attend church when I was a child, but my grandparents made sure I attended church every Sabbath. Sabbath was a day of worship, eating our packed lunch at a friend's home, returning to church for Bible study, and enjoying youth meetings and other activities.

Sabbath Community

Later, my grandparents moved to a developing town with a church nearby, and at age nine, I went to live with them. I was introduced to early morning worship, Friday preparation for Sabbath, sundown worship, and appropriate home behavior during the Sabbath hours.

On Fridays, Grandmother shopped and cooked. My cousins and I tidied the house, cleaned the yard, prepared our clothes and shoes, and took our showers. My grandmother prepared breakfast and dinner and placed items in thermoses on the dining room table, covered almost like the Communion table. There was no cooking or warming up of food on Sabbath. Sabbath dinner usually included the best sweet potato pudding that was ever made.

It was a delight meeting and greeting neighbors and other Sabbath keepers as we walked to and from church. I had friends who lived on the same street, and together, we walked just ahead of our parents and grandparents, dressed up in our finest Sabbath clothes. At eleven years old, I decided to be baptized because I wanted to go to heaven.

Two years later, I immigrated to Canada to live with my mother. She did not go to church but did not prevent me from attending. However, she wanted me to do chores on the Sabbath. This created some conflict, and I started spending the whole day away from home. These actions did not help the situation, and the youth pastor had to make a visit. He offered me some practical suggestions for doing chores before or after Sabbath and communicating with my mom. He also encouraged my mom to support my involvement in church.

As I grew older, I started thinking about how I would honor God in my studies and choice of work. Fortunately, I was never asked to compromise Sabbath in any of my jobs. Sabbath observance was easy until I was exposed to different ways of observing the Sabbath by friends from different cultural backgrounds. I got married, and we had kids. We asked ourselves, "What is the meaning of Sabbath? How can we make Sabbath a happy day for the children? Will there ever be times for quiet study and reflection again?" Opening and closing the Sabbath with worship remained, but new practices emerged—haystacks, popcorn, and hot chocolate while enjoying Bible videos and many other Sabbath activities.

Sabbath is still a happy and special day to worship and give thanks to God. During this past year, the Sabbath has truly been a refuge from social and political unrest, the global pandemic, and losses. Whether worshiping alone, online, or in a socially distanced congregation, I have been truly grateful for this oasis in time. Today, my parents are Seventh-day Adventists. What a surprise that will be for my grandparents when we all meet on the new earth.

Paulette McLean Johnson is the dean of libraries at Andrews University in Berrien Springs, Michigan, United States.

89

For Time and Eternity

Cyril Millett

I believe that God sent Mrs. Myers into my life for time and eternity.

To begin with, I grew up on the island of Bermuda, and the only colleges were overseas. In 1976, I found myself studying at the University of Windsor in Windsor, Ontario, Canada. The rigors of university study were not easy on me. The pressure of academics and feeling homesick wore my relationship with God thin.

At the start of my third year, with summer work in Bermuda behind me, I headed back to Windsor with my sister, Theresa. She was in a preuniversity program. I anticipated that she would quickly settle, and I would be all about my schoolbooks. What I did not anticipate was that, with the schoolbooks, another book—the Bible—would absorb a lot of my time!

One of the friends that Theresa made during the opening weeks at university was another girl in the dorm who talked with her about the Sabbath. As Theresa and I chatted, sometimes I was baffled by what Christianity commonly teaches about Sunday worship. Soon I was asking Theresa's friend questions, and she arranged to introduce me to Mrs. Florine Myers. I was told that Mrs. Myers could address most, if not all, of my inquiries.

Mrs. Myers was so patient with me. I wanted to rush to the topic of the Sabbath, and she wanted to make sure that first I had a well-established understanding of salvation through Christ alone. For her, the Sabbath was a poignant and prominent part of her day-to-day relationship with Jesus. For months, she and one of her daughters studied with me. She made sure that my confidence in a loving Savior was solid.

With Jesus in my life again, learning about the Sabbath was exciting. What was not exciting was staying in my dormitory room to shut out the world as I tried to experience Sabbath rest! Thankfully, Mrs. Myers was not a Seventh-day Adventist who just studied with you and left you to figure out how to practice your newfound faith. Having young-adult children, she appreciated a young person's need for a socially fulfilling Sabbath. Mrs. Myers kept inviting me to church and lunch in her home after service—and I could not refuse her invitations! Besides, her children were around my age and our conversations on Sabbath afternoons were rich.

Today, because of dementia, Mrs. Myers does not remember that she was used by God to introduce my sister and me to the joys of the Sabbath. Even so, one day, in the twinkling of an eye, she will behold our Best Friend—Jesus! What an experience of rejoicing and sweet fellowship those Sabbaths in eternity will be with Him.

Cyril Millett is a pastor and superintendent of education in the Bermuda Conference of Seventh-day Adventists in Hamilton, Bermuda.

Margaret and the Sabbath

Maxroy Mitchell

My first job after law school was at a large New York City law firm. I was deeply concerned about reserving twenty-four hours for religious observance because of the lore about endless hours and nonexistent work-life balance for many lawyers. To be sure, almost none of that was exaggerated.

Back then, some senior lawyers had not quite adopted the word-processing tools that are abundant now. Instead, these lawyers relied heavily on professional administrative assistants to record their time, take dictation, type documents from handwritten notes, and generally manage administrative tasks. Partners and senior lawyers were the priority. I was not a senior lawyer.

Junior lawyers shared the services of an administrative assistant with a partner and a midlevel associate who had been at the firm for a few years. First-year lawyers were at the bottom of the priority list. Our team's administrative assistant was a very special woman whom I will call Margaret. An immigrant from Barbados, she was a diligent, pleasant person—and a faithful Sabbath observer.

Margaret had paved the way for my Sabbath observance by her conduct and example in our law office. Her smile and character meant that I did not have to explain or apologize for my Sabbath observance. I could say, "I am a Seventh-day Adventist . . . like Margaret."

Margaret had a network of friends and allies in the firm on whom she could depend for getting work done. And just as importantly, Margaret often worked late, doing favors and helping her fellow admins hit their deadlines. Her colleagues knew that they could depend on her as much as she depended on them. She was somewhat senior in years herself at that point, but she was not a stranger to new technology. She was adept at using the firm's tech resources. Her age and bearing also reminded me of the deaconesses at my home church. The experience at firms can be isolating and competitive, but some of that isolation was mitigated because I had a "deaconess" sitting outside my office.

Margaret made sure my time was entered, even though I was a lowly first-year attorney. And like clockwork, at around noon on Friday, she would begin looking over her glasses at me with what I came to recognize was effectively an early Sabbath bell. She was a valuable part of my successful Sabbath observance as a young lawyer, because her faithfulness and diligence were imputed to me.

For me, the Sabbath has been a symbol of community. The Sabbath is many things, but for me, it has been a welcome point of contact, a junction at which we can link arms with others—like my friend Margaret.

Maxroy Mitchell writes from New York City, New York, United States.

The Gift

Sabbath and Growing Up Latina in America

Elizabeth Muñoz Beard

I am a third-generation Seventh-day Adventist and the first generation born in the United States. My maternal and paternal grandparents all became Adventists in their youth and raised their children in the church. In the 1950s, they immigrated to the United States from Peru with very little money and few English skills. They came seeking better opportunities for their children and, more importantly, a good Adventist education.

I grew up with devotion time every morning at breakfast, along with Wednesday night prayer meetings, Friday night vespers, Sabbath church worship, Sabbath vespers, and game nights Saturday nights at the church. The Sabbath was sacred. We prepared everything on Friday—we bathed, cooked, and cleaned—so that on Sabbath, we were prepared to rest from the busy week.

The best tradition of all was and still is our Sabbath lunch. Rice, beans, enchiladas, *tallarines verdes*, or vegetarian *lomo saltado*. The smells, the sounds of laughter, and chatter around the table are nostalgic and something to look forward to each Sabbath.

We did not start to feel the generational and cultural gap between the older generations who grew up in Peru and us, the younger American-born generation, until we hit our teen years. We no longer wanted to go to our family's more conservative Hispanic church for vespers or church. We wanted to go to a more contemporary church with our friends from school. The music was more upbeat and current than the old hymns (although today, I am more of a hymns girl, to be honest). My sister and I did not want to wear matching dresses with tights. We wanted to wear the new fashions without tights (gasp). Furthermore, we wanted to wear makeup and jewelry (more gasps). My parents chose their battles wisely with each change. I attribute my spiritual growth and commitment to my church to how they handled their independent, Americanized children's way of thinking.

Now, we might not have cousins, aunts, uncles, parents, and grandparents all gathering together, but even with just two of us in our home, we still hold cherished traditions close to our hearts.

Elizabeth Muñoz Beard is the principal of La Sierra Academy in Riverside, California, United States.

My First Sabbath

Pardon Kandanga Mwansa

After seriously battling in my heart about the points that my schoolmate, a Seventh-day Adventist, had made about the Sabbath being Saturday and not Sunday, I finally made up my mind that I would go to church on Saturday. I dressed up, prepared my hair, and accompanied my friend to the Mansa Main Seventh-day Adventist Church in Mansa, Zambia.

What my friend never told me was how to go to church on Sabbath. I was used to my Catholic way, which was usually a brief church attendance. He did not tell me that I would be asked to stand in front of many people, that members would greet me and sing a song to welcome me, that I would be assigned a class to attend Sabbath School lesson study, that I would be expected to have a hymn book and a Bible, and that I would be the center of attention by all these Adventists who would view me as a soul saved from hell.

If he had alerted me to all of these expectations—even just one or two things—I would have "prepared" the best I could. Instead, I was shocked! Everyone at church was overdressed (at least, more so than I), looked more knowledgeable than I, and wanted to greet me.

With my Soweto T-shirt and my Rastafarian hair, I was the center of attention. I loved it. It felt that everyone was telling me that I was saved now. Even though I was shy when asked to stand up, I loved the introduction and welcoming song.

I left thinking, *This is the place. They even have school at church where everyone says what they think about a Bible verse!*

And the best was at the end—the meal! I was invited to eat as a first-time visitor, and the meal was delicious. I noticed that they did not serve meat, but what they served tasted very good. At the end of the meal, they invited me to a second Sabbath meeting they called the Bible study.

"What?" I asked my friend. "Do you stay at church the whole day?"

My friend's response made me see the seriousness of these people. "Yes, this afternoon there is a Bible study. After the Bible study, we will take a break for about thirty minutes, and then we will go for vespers."

"What is vespers?" I asked.

He told me it was a sermon for ending the Sabbath. When the sermon ended and we prayed, then we would have "closed the Sabbath."

Because the topics were all helpful and the music, fellowship, and sermon were good, time went fast. From that day on, I was hooked on the Sabbath!

Pardon Kandanga Mwansa is the vice-chancellor at Rusangu University in Monze, Zambia.

The Gift

One Friday Evening

Andy Nash

I will never forget my first Friday evening in Jerusalem—and the surprising clarity it brought to my Seventh-day Adventist faith.

As my family and I strolled through the Old City, we found ourselves joined, at an eager pace, by Jewish families, hand in hand and sharply dressed. We turned onto David Street, where, for the past few days, shopkeepers had been yelling at us to buy something. But no longer. The marketplace was silent; everything was shutting down in anticipation of Shabbat.

Drawing near the temple mount, I expected the serenity and solitude of Orthodox men rocking back and forth in prayer at the Western Wall. But as the plaza came into full view, another emotion filled the evening air: joy!

Circles of Jewish teenage girls danced hand in hand, singing. Not far away stomped a spirited line of Jewish boys, their hands on each other's shoulders, their yarmulkes hanging on for dear life. Closer to the wall, hundreds of Jews of all ages gathered socially in close conversation: the women and men in their respective quarters. Laughter and tears, hugs and clasps. The whole place burst with emotion. I was stunned by the pulsating energy of the place.

Every so often, a Jewish man or woman broke from the socializing to approach the wall and pray—then returned to the community, walking backward. Some Jewish worshipers did not turn away from the wall all evening. Why would they want to turn away? This wall once protected the temple of the Lord!

Watching these children of Israel, I found myself marveling. What an interesting people to whom God chose to reveal Himself! What an interesting way they dress and worship and act. Then I remembered. God did not choose a people who dress and worship and act this way. These people dress and worship and act this way *because God chose them.*

Suddenly I had the strangest sensation wash over me—*familiarity.* I somehow felt right at home. How could this be? I was at a place I had never been before, with thousands of people I had never seen before. No one had really made any effort to welcome my family and me. We were not even *Jewish.* We were *Christian.* How could we feel right at home?

I looked around the plaza at other Christians standing there. They also seemed happy to be part of the evening. Still, by the looks on their faces, they seemed out of place. Their expressions seemed to say, "What an interesting experience this is. It's a little like church Sunday morning—except that it's not church, it's not Sunday, and it's not morning."

That was true. It was Friday evening under the stars—as it was for the first humans. And that is why I felt at home—not because of the people or place, but because of something that transcends both people and place.

94

Because of *Shabbat*—the sign of the Jews—I had never felt happier to be a member of my own Judeo-Christian faith community.

<hr>

Andy Nash is an Adventist author and the owner of Tabgha Tours to Israel in Chattanooga, Tennessee, United States.

Sabbath: A Day of Remarkable Memories

Willie and Elaine Oliver

We both grew up in Seventh-day Adventist homes, so we have no idea what it is like not to experience the Sabbath each week. What we do know—to be sure—is that Sabbath has always been a day of wonderful experiences we have relished since childhood, indelibly etched in our minds to this day.

My (Elaine's) childhood home was one with multiple generations living under the same roof. I was raised by my Jamaican grandmother—Gwendolyn Marnock Powell—who was the constant authority figure in my life until I got married and left home. She was a devoted Seventh-day Adventist, and all of the members of our family called her Ma.

Those early years from my childhood—first in Brooklyn, New York, then in Clinton, Massachusetts—have left enduring remembrances of Fridays as the preparation day for celebrating Sabbath in our home.

Getting ready for Sabbath meant cleaning the house, ironing clothes, and cooking meals that produced wonderful smells, which filled our home with memorable aromas that still bring joy to my heart. These happenings that I joined in after getting home from school culminated with welcoming the Sabbath at sunset to delightful piano music being played by one of my aunts and the joyful singing of "O Day of Rest and Gladness."

Recollections of Sabbaths during my (Willie's) childhood are incredibly similar to Elaine's, with the exception that in my home, they were framed by a nuclear family that included my parents, my siblings, and me.

My dad was a Seventh-day Adventist pastor, and Sabbaths were jam-packed with church activities from Fridays at sunset to sundown on Sabbaths. I thoroughly enjoyed every bit of it. When my parents were missionaries in Honduras (I was in grade school during this time), Sabbath included attending two congregations every week—one Spanish-speaking and the other English-speaking—both in the same building. Of course, this meant wall-to-wall church services from Friday evenings (Spanish youth meetings) to Sabbath afternoons (English youth meetings) and double everything in between.

What fills us to this day with warm memories of childhood Sabbaths are the extraordinary feelings of anticipation for a day that was special because our families said it was and made sure it was so. They engaged us in unforgettable worship and missionary experiences that are still the foundation of our spiritual lives today. And in our minds are still magnificent memories of delectable and delightful dishes that made their appearance on our childhood dining room tables every single Sabbath. These encounters made us long for each week to hurry by so we could welcome the Sabbath again and get to live in that exceptional space yet again.

We can only imagine what Sabbath in heaven will be like, with Jesus leading the celebration around God's majestic throne. Thus, our collective aspirations assert, even so, come Lord Jesus!

———————————

Willie and Elaine Oliver are the directors of family ministries at the General Conference of Seventh-day Adventists in Silver Spring, Maryland, United States.

What the Sabbath Means to Me

Dionisio Olivo

The Sabbath has always been a delight in my life. As a young boy, I memorized Isaiah 58:13, and it has long been my favorite Bible text:

"If you turn away your foot from the Sabbath,
From doing your pleasure on My holy day,
And call the Sabbath a delight,
The holy day of the LORD honorable,
And shall honor Him, not doing your own ways,
Nor finding your own pleasure,
Nor speaking your own words."

I was six years old when my mother became a Seventh-day Adventist. She had to make a courageous decision based on strong faith, because my father threatened to leave us if she joined the church. Unfortunately, thereafter, my father was only minimally involved in our family life.

I did not really comprehend what was going on, but I sensed that my life was somehow changing. We started attending church worship services, which was a new experience for me. Life was hard, but fortunately, the church members supported my mother and me. There were about three or four families who, every Sabbath after service, took us to their homes to eat. I started looking forward to the Sabbath, as it was a special day and the families who invited us became our close friends.

Life was improving for my siblings and me. The time came when others were invited to our home for Sabbath meals. That was possible because Mother was able to purchase a sewing machine and earn some income. We enjoyed that fellowship.

My siblings and I enthusiastically looked forward to the Sabbath. The Sabbath was truly the best day of the week. On Sabbath, we worshiped and enjoyed the fellowship of other church members.

Sabbath became a day of unity—unity in our family, unity with church members, and unity with our Lord.

Dionisio Olivo is vice president for Hispanic affairs at the Atlantic Union Conference of Seventh-day Adventists in South Lancaster, Massachusetts, United States.

God's Answer to Our Prayer

Lester Parkinson

My mother, a devoted Christian, suddenly passed away during my preteen years. My memory of her was cemented in my mind through storytelling by my maternal grandmother, Henrietta Lowe. I trace the Christian values I hold today to these two women. Those values shaped my worldview, and I am a disciple of Jesus because of their influence.

After Mom's untimely passing, Dad relocated us to a new home. This house was in a middle-class neighborhood and sharply contrasted to Granny Lowe's one-room apartment. Shortly afterward, we were introduced to his new wife, whom we hoped would be our "new mom." However, we soon discovered that this new home was very unlike our spiritual upbringing and lifestyle—we were now occupants of a secular home. We all silently yearned for our regular routine of Friday sunset and Sabbath observance, with Sabbath School and youth meetings in the afternoon.

Suddenly, by a stroke of divine favor, our father decided that we must resume church attendance. We were all elated to be obedient and faithful Sabbath keepers again.

Our new church experience was exciting, especially with our newfound friendships. However, we soon discovered that our church attendance was not accompanied by Sabbath observance; hence, we were confused and disappointed.

But God in His mercy intervened. Suddenly, all that changed one bright and beautiful Sabbath morning when we discovered that a Sabbath keeper resided in our neighborhood: Edna Dublin, a kind, warmhearted disciple of Jesus. When she invited us to dine in her lovely home, it was a dream come true. We did not hesitate. Our lives were back on the right path. She not only insisted that we regularly join her and her family to dine on Sabbaths, but we also were allowed to remain and spend the rest of each Sabbath afternoon until the sunset. Her long-lasting Christian influence and example solidified our faith and our walk with Jesus.

We long for the return of Jesus, when we shall all be reunited as one big family in Jesus. And what a joy it will be to see our own Edna Dublin. She was an angel sent from God, an answer to the prayers of a faithful mother and grandmother.

Lester Parkinson is senior pastor of the Sandton Seventh-day Adventist Church in Sunninghill, South Africa.

Sabbath Friends

Carl Ricketts Jr.

Sitting in church one Sabbath morning, I was supposed to focus on the worship service, but truthfully, my mind was elsewhere. What caused me to walk away from this Sabbath day with a smile? I met someone for the very first time who eventually made that Sabbath most memorable. Let me tell you about the encounter.

I had traveled to Daytona Beach, Florida, to attend a worship experience for church youth. I was new to the area and somewhat shy. Eventually, I connected with a group of teenagers from a sister church, and they made me feel welcome. My attention was immediately drawn to a young lady who was most distinct in her group. She was the shortest person in the group. I also quickly discovered that her personality was very appealing. We exchanged greetings, and as we did, I remember watching to see if she would look at me or look away. She looked directly at me, and I determined then that I wanted to get to know her.

Candice and I became best friends. We both participated in music ministry and the Bible Bowl contest. We became a strong and fearsome Bible Bowl team. We were known as the dynamic duo. Our friendship stood the test of time as we sang in gospel groups and attended college together. When I went away to graduate school, we stayed in touch and reconnected more than a decade after our first meeting.

Candice and I eventually got married, and we and our three remarkable children are now serving the Lord. Whenever the Sabbath comes each week, I cheerily reflect on the journey of our friendship and the joy we are afforded to share as a family. However, I cannot help but think of God's providence in allowing us to meet that Sabbath in 1993. What started out as a casual youth event turned out to be not only memorable but also the initial spark of the flames of love that burn brightly in gratitude each week. Oh, how I love the Sabbath!

Carl Ricketts Jr. is the director of chaplain services at Loma Linda University Health in Loma Linda, California, United States.

Married on the Sabbath

Jason Ridley

As a fourth-generation Seventh-day Adventist, I am learning more and more about how to appreciate the beauty and blessing of the Sabbath day. Unfortunately, when I was younger, a lot of my most memorable Sabbath experiences had to do with what I was told I could not do. For example, I was not allowed to ride my bike on Saturday or watch Saturday morning cartoons, as my neighborhood friends did. Probably the most memorable for me was what happened in high school when I was part of the football team, my favorite sport. I knew I did not have a future with the sport because I would never play on Sabbath, and many of the games were on the Sabbath. Therefore, I quit the team.

Even though my youth was filled with Sabbath challenges, a memorable and joyful experience for me happened on a Sabbath. On Sabbath, August 24, 2019, I married the love of my life, Aislinn Rebecca Freeman. The day was extra special, because not only was I marrying the one person that I wanted to spend the rest of my life with but we were also able to share that exceptional Sabbath experience with so many of our friends and family.

My wife and I were reminded of Creation week. God instituted both the Sabbath and marriage. I thank God for the Sabbath, for Aislinn, and for bringing us together.

Jason Ridley is the director of youth ministries for the Allegheny West Conference of Seventh-day Adventists in Columbus, Ohio, United States.

The Sabbath: Fulfilling a Deep Heart Longing

Beth Thomas

The Sabbath has always been the highlight of my week.[1] When I was a child, my mother created a special atmosphere on Friday evening, at the very start of the Sabbath. As the brilliant sun set, Mom would light our Sabbath candles, and Dad would choose calm, quiet music to set the tone for worship.

As I snuggled down into my spot on the couch with a cozy blanket, Mom would begin reading: mission stories, Bible stories, angel stories, or stories of God's intervention. After story time, we sang together—sometimes accompanied by Mom's guitar, sometimes by piano, other times a capella. I felt God's presence in a special way during those Sabbath worship moments.

When I was growing up, Sabbath was different from other days. It was more than just going to church. We did special things on the seventh day that we did not do throughout the rest of the week. We went to friends' homes for lunch; we took walks together in nature; we visited and encouraged the elderly who were lonely. Sabbath, to me, has always been about fellowship with God and others—that is where I find the most fulfillment. Even today, "good" Sabbaths are marked not only by an inspiring church service and sermon but by fellowship with others.

We moved a few years ago and, after settling a bit, began looking for a new church. The greeters at the first church we visited welcomed us warmly. The sermon was sincere and the music engaging, but what really made us feel at home was the invitation we received to go on an afternoon excursion with several other families. We visited with our new friends until long after dark and, when we finally left, we each looked at each other and said, "We have found our new church family."

I believe God intended the Sabbath to fulfill a deep heart longing we each have for community and for fellowship. He created us because He longed for a relationship with someone made in His own image who could reciprocate love in an intelligent way. He set the Sabbath apart at the end of a busy week to enjoy the work of His hands, including you and me. And, during that twenty-four-hour period, God invites us to put everything else aside and focus on reconnecting with Him and each other.

I am not sure what your plans are this Sabbath, but I invite you to join me in spending quality time with the Creator, gaining refreshment and renewal.

Beth Thomas is a freelance writer, pastor's wife, and mother of two in Michigan, United States.

1. A version of this story was first published in *The Journal*, a publication of the General Conference Ministerial Association.

The Sabbath in My Family

Astrid Thomassian

I was too young to remember when my mother became a Seventh-day Adventist, but my earliest recollection is her gathering my three siblings and me on Friday before sunset to welcome the Sabbath. My father was not persuaded to become a Seventh-day Adventist, and he did not affirm Mama's commitment to teach us children Adventist beliefs. Mama, however, was undaunted in her mission.

Friday was preparation day. On that day, the house was thoroughly cleaned, and fresh plants and flowers from Mama's garden decorated our living room. We had to ensure that every item of clothing we were going to wear on Sabbath was selected and ready. The smell of freshly baked bread together with the main course of Sabbath lunch wafted through our home—no cooking was done on Sabbath. Welcoming Sabbath was a delight and exuded warmth and tranquility.

Friday evening, the customary hymns we sang during weekday evening worships were traded for hymns referencing the Sabbath. "Don't Forget the Sabbath," "Lord of the Sabbath," and "The Dawn of God's Dear Sabbath" were among our favorites. We would recite the fourth commandment before Mama would animatedly share a Bible story about the value of trusting God.

Papa tolerated our home worships, but he was not at all open to our attending church on Sabbath. Unfortunately, the church was located in another town that he felt was unsafe. Nevertheless, on Sabbaths, when Papa left for work, Mama would take us to church. In order to get home before Papa returned from work, we left after Sabbath School. One day, the bus was delayed. Time was zipping by, and Mama was getting anxious. She prayed earnestly. As she peered intently for a bus, a black limousine pulled up. A gentleman introduced himself as the supervisor of bus transportation. He explained that bus drivers were preparing to strike, and he was evaluating the possible impact. He had observed Mama with her children waiting for a while. He wondered whether she would accept a ride in his limousine. She repeatedly thanked God that He made a way for us to arrive home before Papa.

Another Sabbath afternoon, as Papa lounged on the porch, my sister excitedly shared with him a bookmark she received for perfect Sabbath School attendance. Mama's heart sank as she overheard the exchange. Again, she prayed that God would guide her through the argument she knew was coming. When Papa confronted her, with a prayer in her heart, she stoically confessed that she was taking us to the Adventist church because she felt that was what God required of them as parents. Surprisingly, he conceded. Another answered prayer!

Sabbath in my family means more than rest, missionary outreach, and observance of God's creation. For me, in addition to those things, it embodies answered prayer, freedom to worship, and, above all, God's redemptive power on the hearts of individuals receptive to His biddings.

Astrid Thomassian is a retired educator and writes from Winter Garden, Florida, United States.

Sabbath: A Special Day for Connection

Asnel Valcin

I learned to keep the Sabbath from my adopted family in Léogâne, Haiti, a town 150 miles from my birthplace of Petite Rivière de l'Artibonite. It is unlikely that I would be raised observing the Sabbath if I remained with my biological family. My grandfather was a well-known voodoo priest and sought to influence my parents to inherit his spirits.

When I was five years old, my mother made the difficult decision to send my brother and me to live with the Henry family in Léogâne for religious, security, and social reasons. It was there I learned about the blessings of the Sabbath.

In the new family, I appreciated the secure environment where creativity was encouraged. However, the best gift I received was experiencing the Sabbath. We were given money to buy the treats we desired to make Sabbath special. Best of all, there were no punishments on Sabbath. Small acts of bad manners were met with grace and understanding. Even more precious, Sabbath was a time when Father Henry joined with the whole family and taught us songs and how to memorize scriptures. The Sabbath was a special day of connection for the whole family.

I have kept these memories alive through the years, and they influence how I minister today. As a chaplain in a New York hospital, I do my best to make my ministry about connecting with people in crisis. I do not regularly work on the Sabbath. However, one of the first times I visited an institution on the Sabbath changed my understanding of Mark 2:27, in which Jesus says, "The Sabbath was made for man, and not man for the Sabbath." I was called because no other chaplain was available.

I had no idea that God was about to show His love to one of His beloved children. I asked the nurse if there was anyone who could benefit from my visit. She said, "There is this miserable lady; let us see how you deal with her, Chaplain." As I approached, I asked for guidance from God.

At first, the patient was defensive and guarded. I noticed her speech was laced with Adventist lingo, and I recognized the Sabbath School quarterly next to the bed. She felt abandoned by both God and family. I told her I was a Seventh-day Adventist. To say that she was surprised would understate the emotions she expressed. At the end of her tears, she acknowledged that indeed God had never abandoned or forsaken her. The Sabbath bond with this person brought me back to my childhood days when Dad Henry bonded with us in worship. I was overjoyed—indeed, God leads us on the Sabbath to connect with one another as we connect with Him on His holy day.

Asnel Valcin is the director of pastoral care and education for Saint John's Episcopal Hospital in Far Rockaway, Queens, New York, United States.

Love My Neighbors—*All* of Them?

Dawn Jacobson-Venn

Sabbath took on a whole new meaning when our family moved overseas. My husband and I, with our eight-year-old son and six-year-old daughter, served as missionaries in

Bangkok, Thailand. It was the first time we had lived in a big city, so there were lots of adjustments and challenges. But through that experience, God drew us closer to Him, to each another, and to the Thai people.

In Mark 12:31, Jesus instructs, "Love your neighbor as yourself." That seemed doable when we lived in a small community. But how were we to reach those who lived in this massive, bustling city of more than ten million people? That was a lot of neighbors!

We reflected on the example of Jesus and stepped out in faith. We put our trust in God to equip us to serve and love His precious people living in Bangkok, one neighbor at a time. God quickly began opening doors, and Sabbath became the week's busiest day, filled with outreach activities at twenty-three church planting sites across the city. We rotated around the city to these different neighborhoods each week, resulting in some exciting and memorable Sabbath adventures.

The Lord inspired us to look for needs then gave us creative ideas and the energy and team to carry them out. We delivered truckloads of rice, a staple food in Thailand, to slum communities. Our team organized health expos around the city, offering free medical care and health education using the NEWSTART (Nutrition, Exercise, Water, Sunlight, Temperance, Air, Rest, Trust) program. We also went to prisons with volunteer health professionals and church members, providing medical, dental, and vision care. Through these practical acts of kindness, we built relationships. People were interested to know about God and requested programs for their children. Throughout the week, our team offered after-school classes in English as a second language, art, and music at our church plants.

During the six years we lived in Bangkok, God led us to go where the people were, giving them glimpses of His love and masterful handiwork. We had opportunities such as telling Bible stories in a beauty parlor, teaching temperance under a tree in an empty lot, hosting a living Nativity in a public school, and planning "nature discovery" activities at Bangkok's aquarium and beautiful parks. These were all ways we could show the Thai Buddhist people God's unconditional love in tangible, practical ways.

God has a way of nudging us out of our comfort zone so that we can receive the greatest blessings He has to offer. Serving others on those Sabbath adventures was a blessing to our family and a tangible way to show our children what it means to love our neighbors. And what better day to do that than Sabbath!

Dawn Jacobson-Venn is an administrative assistant for family ministries at the General Conference of Seventh-day Adventists in Silver Spring, Maryland, United States.

All Is Well—the Family and the Sabbath Are Here

Daniel A. Weber

During the height of the COVID-19 pandemic, I paused to reflect on the sudden hardships faced by people around the world as they struggled to live with the impact of an unknown and dangerous disease. My thoughts went back to my father's family during World War II and the struggles they faced. My troubles were nothing compared to what my family went through during the terrible days of World War II. Yet, I never once heard my grandparents complain about the past and everything they went through before they immigrated to the United States. Their trust in God gave them hope.

As a child, my fondest memory of the Sabbath was a song my family would sing as the sun set. The song held great meaning to my family, as it had always been sung no matter where in the world they were. The words, in German, went like this:

> Alles wohl, alles wohl!
> Wie der Herr mich führt, ist's gut,
> Er hält mich in treuer Hut.
> Alles wohl, alles wohl, alles wohl![1]

In English, the words are:

> All is well, all is well
> The way the Lord leads me is good
> He faithfully keeps me
> All is well, all is well, all is well

Although I did not understand all the German words, it was not Sabbath if we did not sing them. They helped me be part of the family, and I learned to cherish the Sabbath.

It is comforting that despite everything Satan throws at us, God has us in His hands and gives us the Sabbath as a day to rest, recover, and give thanks. The Sabbath draws us closer to Him and helps us bond with our family and loved ones. All is well when God is in control.

Daniel A. Weber is an assistant professor of film and photography at Andrews University in Berrien Springs, Michigan, United States.

---

1. Ernst Heinrich Gebhardt, "Alles Wohl!" (1880).

The Meaning of the Sabbath in My Life

Ted N. C. Wilson

The Sabbath is a special gift from God to all of us. It not only points us back to God as the Creator but also to God as our Redeemer and to God the Son, Jesus Christ, as our coming King. It gives us a needed break from the six-day cycle to restore our spiritual, physical, emotional, social, and mental capacity. It would take a long time to list all the blessings of the Sabbath.

God provides us with many assuring promises of His presence and creative power, such as Isaiah 43:5–7, which says, "Fear not: for I am with thee: I will bring thy seed from the east, and gather thee from the west; I will say to the north, Give up; and to the south, Keep not back: bring my sons from far, and my daughters from the ends of the earth; even every one that is called by my name: for I have created him for my glory, I have formed him; yea, I have made him" (KJV).

In order to help me remember that He is the Lord who made the earth and all living creatures, including me, He gave us the seventh-day Sabbath—a day to *remember* Him and His creative power. The very day I set aside to worship Him every week is the same seventh day that He created as a Sabbath at the end of the literal week of Creation.

The fourth commandment found in Exodus 20:8–11 is explicit regarding God's creative power and action, and it beautifully reminds me to "remember the Sabbath day, to keep it holy" (Exodus 20:8). In addition, the book *Patriarchs and Prophets* reminds me that "God saw that a Sabbath was essential for man, even in Paradise. He needed to lay aside his own interests and pursuits for one day of the seven, that he might more fully contemplate the works of God and meditate upon His power and goodness. He needed a Sabbath to remind him more vividly of God and to awaken gratitude because all that he enjoyed and possessed came from the beneficent hand of the Creator."[1]

That is why I, as a Seventh-day Adventist, worship God on the seventh-day Sabbath and am delighted to do so, honoring my Creator, who created this earth in six literal, consecutive, twenty-four-hour days of recent origin. The Sabbath is a sign (Ezekiel 20:12), or seal, by God for me to know that I am part of His remnant people and Advent movement at the end of time just before Christ's soon return. I fully believe we are living at the end of time, and Jesus is coming soon.

The Sabbath is an integral part of the three angels' messages of Revelation 14:6–12. It tells me where I have come from, why I am here, and where I will be going. It is plain to me that it is at the core of the great controversy theme, since it identifies God as the Omnipotent Ruler of the universe and my personal life.

I rejoice when the Sabbath arrives each week. There is an unexplainable feeling of sanctity and sacredness that arrives on Friday evening when the Sabbath begins. It is because God the Father, God the Son, and God the Holy Spirit blessed the Sabbath day and hallowed it (Genesis 2:3).

There is something special to our family about the Sabbath. As our children were growing up, the Sabbath was a time of worshiping, singing, studying God's Word, and offering Christian service. That spiritual setting continues in our children's homes with their families. My wife, Nancy, and I are grateful for the Sabbath hours. Even though, as a pastor, I find that the Sabbath can be full of spiritual activities, it is nevertheless a marvelous connection with the Lord every week. I love the Sabbath and am grateful we will have it throughout the ages to come (Isaiah 66:23) as we look forever to our Creator, Redeemer, coming King, and Best Friend, Jesus Christ. Because of His sacrifice on the cross and His current mediation as our High Priest in the Most Holy Place in the heavenly sanctuary, we will have the opportunity to worship Him on the Sabbath throughout eternity. Praise be to God!

Ted N. C. Wilson is the president of the General Conference of Seventh-day Adventists in Silver Spring, Maryland, United States.

1. Ellen G. White, *Patriarchs and Prophets* (Nampa, ID: Pacific Press®, 2005), 48.

Sabbath Witness

My Early Sabbath Test

Trevor Baker

For three months, I rode the New York City subways and walked the city streets looking for a job. I was nineteen years old and recently baptized into the Seventh-day Adventist Church. My job search became successful when I obtained a job with one of the largest banks in New York.

Within eight months, I was asked to be the head of the department that was responsible for reconciling each teller's transactions at the close of each day. That meant some days I had to stay late.

In the fall of the year, the sun sets earlier, and clocks are turned one hour back for daylight saving time. That presented a problem, for the Sabbath then started Friday afternoon before I could leave the bank. I presented my dilemma to my supervisor and asked to be transferred to another department, but the manager explained that there were no vacancies anywhere. He suggested that perhaps I could ask my pastor to grant me permission to work just for a few hours on the Sabbath. I told him the pastor did not have authority over the Sabbath—it was God who gave us the Sabbath. The manager could not grant my request, and I resigned from my position.

I met with managers at the bank's head office to explain the Sabbath situation. Although they were sympathetic, they said they could not grant my request. I learned that another person—a Jewish employee—also lost her position because she did not work on the Sabbath. My career at the bank was over.

Soon I faced another challenge. I was living with my parents, who were not Sabbath keepers, and they did not agree with my decision to leave a promising position. They reminded me often that, in their opinion, I had made a foolish decision.

I walked the streets of New York City looking for other jobs. Why did God not help me find another job? After all, I was faithful to Him and expected that He would bless me with another job. Yet, wherever I was interviewed, I was asked why I had left the bank. Once I explained, they told me I would have the same problem in that company.

While I was looking for a job, I had to admit I was avoiding a call from God. I had considered various professions, but down deep, I sensed that God was calling me to be a pastor. After three months of walking the streets of New York, I got a job at the New York Public Library, where my two supervisors were Jewish. They understood my request to have the Sabbath off and work alternate Sundays. I worked there for a while, but the next year I started preparing for ministry. I heeded God's voice, and He has led me all the way. Just recently, I completed fifty-three years of ministry.

God used the Sabbath as a way of reminding me what He wanted me to do, and for that, I am thankful.

Trevor Baker is the former president of the Northeastern Conference of Seventh-day Adventists in Jamaica, New York, United States.

A Fourteen-Year-Old Boy and the Sabbath

Henry Beras

I have been a Seventh-day Adventist from an early age, and the observance of the Sabbath has been an essential part of my Christian experience. Receiving the Sabbath on time and preparing to spend time with the Lord on His holy day has always been an exciting part of my weekly routine.

But the Sabbath took on a different meaning when I started working at only fourteen years of age. I helped with various chores in a top-rated store in my town. The owner was not a Christian, and sometimes he was uncomfortable when I left work to be at my house in time to receive the Sabbath. The Sabbath hours were special, and I wanted to spend every minute with God. Whenever I left work, I always said goodbye to the owner. He seemed annoyed when I told him "Happy Sabbath."

One day, auditors discovered that someone was stealing merchandise and committing fraud. The owner testified in my favor, saying that if I was faithful to God, he was sure that I was also honest with him despite the pressure he had put on me. The person involved with the theft was discovered and consequently fired.

The owner told me that he was willing to employ more people like me, even if they did not work on Saturdays. I took him at his word and invited other young people from the church to work for him. There was even a time when all but two of the employees were Sabbath-keeping Adventists.

You can imagine that it would be difficult for the business to operate on the Sabbath with so many Adventists. Yet we were surprised when the owner decided to close on Saturdays. Soon after his decision, another businessman questioned him about his seemingly foolish decision to close on Saturdays, but the business owner quickly replied, "God blesses me twice during the weekdays so that I can close on Saturdays."

Eventually, an employee learned about Jesus via the Adventist employees and decided to be baptized. The town's main warehouse closed on Saturdays, winning many individuals for Christ after this experience. All of this started because the Lord helped me, a fourteen-year-old boy, be faithful.

Henry Beras is president of the Greater New York Conference of Seventh-day Adventists in Manhasset, New York, United States.

Put Your Foot Down

Jeffrey O. Brown

I love writing. But as an editor, I put my pen down on the Sabbath. You see, I learned the hard way that Sabbath is not about my pleasure; it is about His pleasure.

I grew up attending a Baptist church and was part of a youth organization called the Boys' Brigade. I became sergeant of the brigade and captain of our company's football (soccer) team, the district football team, and the city football team. My Seventh-day Adventist grandmother (we called her Gran) often took my siblings and me to her church. I went to the Baptist Christmas party on Saturday and the Adventist Christmas party on Sunday. Life was good.

One day, Gran said to me, "Jeff, you have to make a choice." While I was successful on the football field, I was also starting to realize the importance of the Sabbath. It was about putting aside my personal pleasures and calling the Sabbath a delight (Isaiah 58:13). I knew a major game was coming up, and I would have to have "the talk" with Skip, our Boys' Brigade leader. I dreaded it. But the incredible happened. After listening to my struggles, Skip relieved all my pressure. "Jeff," he said, "always follow your convictions."

I did not play that Saturday. Instead, I went to church. I thought about the text, "Delight yourself also in the LORD, and He shall give you the desires of your heart" (Psalm 37:4).

My heart was resting as I thought about my Lord—but my mind was racing as I thought about my team. How were they playing? I found out soon enough. The faces were long. The looks were accusing. The silence was deafening. They had lost the cup final.

Skip approached me. "Jeff, how could you let your team down like that?" he asked. This was the same person who, seven days before, had said, "Jeff, always follow your convictions." Now he was singing a different tune. "Jeff, next week's game will decide the championship. Your team needs you. What will you do?"

Next week meant the next Sabbath. With Skip looking at me pleadingly and with the team looking at me imploringly, what would I do? What should I do? What did I do? Did I play? Yes, I did. Did we win? No, we did not. We lost the game, and I lost respect—some from my team members and some from myself.

Sometime later, professional scouts came to my house. They asked if I was interested in signing up to play for Aston Villa, an English professional football club. I was seventeen years old. I asked if games would be played on the Sabbath. They said yes. I said no. They said I would be missing out on a great career. But by then, I understood what the Psalmist meant: "I delight to do Your will, O my God, and Your law is within my heart" (Psalm 40:8).

So on Sabbath, I put my pen down now—because I put my foot down then.

Jeffrey O. Brown is the associate editor for *Ministry*, an international journal for pastors, in Silver Spring, Maryland, United States.

Sabbath and Graduate School

John Brunt

Our lives were the busiest they had ever been. My wife, Ione, was working on a graduate degree in nursing, and I was doing the same in New Testament studies. We had moved from our home in Washington State to Atlanta, Georgia, to study. We coveted family time together with our first- and third-grade children.

Sabbath was our oasis, and we decided we needed to plan and make the most of it. We came up with the idea of making a list of interesting activities to enjoy together after we had worshiped at church in the morning. The list was long. It included hikes to the top of Stone Mountain or walks through the nature paths of Fernbank Science Center with the ponds full of ducks and frogs. There were also opportunities to join the singers visiting seniors in care facilities, attend a concert of religious music, to invite friends for dinner and conversation. Drives to places like Lake Lanier contrasted with just spending a quiet afternoon together on the back porch looking out over a forest. More than forty activities made up the list.

At the beginning of every week, we took turns choosing the activity for the next Sabbath. In the first week of the month, our son, Larry, chose. For the second week, Laura, our daughter, chose, and so forth. That gave us the opportunity to anticipate our Sabbath oasis all through the busy week.

Toward the end of our time in Atlanta, I faced comprehensive exams. One of those exams lasted a week and involved using the resources of the library to write a paper on a New Testament passage. I walked into the professor's office at 9:00 on Monday morning. He handed me an envelope containing the passage. I had to translate the passage from Greek with an annotated translation explaining my word choices. Then I was to present the history of how the passage had been interpreted from the time of the early church to the present, give a verse-by-verse exegesis of the passage, and finally discuss its theological and ethical significance. The next Monday morning, I walked into the professor's office with a seventy-page paper.

My fellow students knew about my Sabbath observance, but after I turned the paper in, one of them said, "I'll bet you worked on your Sabbath this week!" I was happy to say that though it was one of the most grueling and sleep-deprived weeks of my life, from sundown Friday until sundown Sabbath, I put the project aside and enjoyed my weekly oasis in time with God and my family.

John Brunt is a theologian, author, and pastor of the Edmonds Seventh-day Adventist Church in Edmonds, Washington, United States.

Standing Tall

Tracey-Ann Carter

I was a candidate to become the chair of my department at the university where I was a professor. During the process, I made it clear I would not be available from Friday sunset until Saturday sunset, as these hours were my Sabbath, and this was my time to fellowship and commune with God.

After I was appointed, I settled into my new role of leading the faculty in my department while continuing to mentor students and teach. On Fridays, I prepared for the Sabbath as usual. My Sabbath days were full of family time, reflection, and the awareness of God's blessings in my life. The Sabbath represented a time to recharge and reflect. I was increasingly becoming more grateful for the Sabbath as my new role was becoming more demanding.

Then came March 2020, and everything changed because of COVID-19. The pandemic caused our university to transition all in-person classes to an online learning environment. The job responsibilities became 24-7; emails took the place of in-person conversations.

Students and professors were faced with unprecedented challenges due to the rapid transition to remote learning.

My responsibilities increased exponentially. I was asked to assist in training all the faculty on the different web-conferencing software programs available. Never before did sunset Friday arrive so quickly, and I found myself in a dilemma. Should I continue my roles and responsibilities after sunset during the crisis?

There were times I was faced with the dilemma of wanting to continue working because of the current situation. However, I reminded myself that from Friday sunset to Saturday sunset, I would be in a state of worship. During the pandemic, I realized that my Sabbath is more than a religious routine; it is more than just the seventh day of the week. It is a time when I need to turn off all notifications on my phone. My Sabbath is a day to mentally break free from the racing thoughts and deadlines of the world.

My Sabbath is not just about communicating with Christ but also about seeking Him for answers and listening to His Word. I am recharged each Sabbath because I know that the Lord will deliver me from all my fears and uncertainties.

It is the Sabbath that keeps me strong and allows me to be still in a time of deep uncertainty. It is the Sabbath that transforms me into what God has called me to be. I have a newfound appreciation for the Sabbath.

———————

Tracey-Ann Carter is an assistant professor of human services at Allen University in Columbia, South Carolina, United States.

Keeping Sabbath in the Most Populous Muslim Country

Donny Chrissutianto

Indonesia is the most populous Muslim country in the world. In 2021, out of a population of about 270 million, approximately 240 million are Muslim. However, Indonesia is not *officially* a Muslim country. The law protects individuals who wish to follow other faiths, although in practice it is hard to do so.

My father was a Muslim before he had a dream that prompted him to become a Christian. He then married my mother, who was a second-generation Seventh-day Adventist. Since my father was a naval officer, my family usually lived in a port city. I spent my childhood years in Makassar and Surabaya, two strict Muslim cities.

My first three years of elementary school were in Makassar. I faced questions about my absence on the Sabbath day. In the beginning, my teachers accepted the reason for my nonattendance, but when it happened continually, they punished me every Monday by making me stand for an hour next to the flagpole.

When I was nine years old, we moved to Surabaya, where I went to a government school. In this school, the rules were stricter. There was a regulation in this school: if the absences were more than 10 percent of the total days of school, the student was not allowed to continue attending. Only by God's grace did I complete elementary school and receive an award as one of the best academic achievers. I was the only Christian who received the award.

I went to the best government junior school in my region, wherein the attendance rules were again strict. It was a miracle that the teachers allowed me to miss the Sabbath exams and take them on another day. During this time, my friends asked me about my faith. As a result, some friends went with me to church on the Sabbath.

The experience of keeping the Sabbath in government school without expulsion ceased when I went to high school. The principal called me and threatened to kick me out without a recommendation to continue my study in other schools if I continued missing classes on the Sabbath. The other option that he gave me was to resign from that school. I chose to resign.

When I left the government school, I missed my opportunities to share Christ and the Sabbath truth with my classmates. I enjoyed the times we discussed spiritual themes together. Those experiences led me to study for the ministry, and today I am privileged to be a pastor and Bible teacher.

<hr />

Donny Chrissutianto is an assistant professor of church history and systematic theology at Adventist International Institute of Advanced Studies in Silang, Cavite, Philippines.

Sabbath—Pain Turned to Joy

Nigel David

I remember like it was yesterday, the day my father said, "I am not signing any contract for you to play professional soccer on Sabbath—absolutely not." I was very angry and hurt. Playing professional soccer was my aspiration. I had dreamed about playing soccer, and now that I was at the age when I could, my father prevented me from doing it. And he refused to change his mind.

I could not understand what Sabbath had to do with me. I argued from the perspective of ability, because I did not ask for the talent to play soccer. God had given it to me, and, in my mind, there was absolutely no justification why I should be penalized because of a day that I neither cared about nor wanted to be involved in.

For years after, I resented my father and saw Sabbath as a day that robbed me of the chance to be a great soccer player with the prospect of financial security for life. That was until a series of events nearly ended my life. It was then that I began searching for inner peace.

I was not keen on church; worship; or, to say the least, listening to sermons. But in the midst of my anger, I heard a preacher paraphrase Mark 2:27: "Man was not made for the Sabbath, but the Sabbath was made for man." This simple statement stirred my curiosity, so I began to explore the Bible. It was this quest that led me to see God's desire for communion with His people on the Sabbath. I was convicted that such communion with God meant I would need to put aside my agenda so that I could spend intimate time with Him.

The conviction of my intellectual pursuit was also physically and supernaturally affirmed when, one Sabbath, at my home church, I personally experienced the presence of God. I sensed a mysterious shift in the molecular structure of the room where we were gathered for worship. I was completely overwhelmed by this unusual but beautiful occurrence. It was then, in that same moment, that I heard a distinct voice that I now know was God saying to me, "I want you to serve Me; I am going to use you." On that

Sabbath day, I accepted the call to pastoral ministry.

The day my dad objected to my dream of playing professional soccer changed my life's desires, but the day I experienced God changed my whole life. The Sabbath became and remains a joyful blessing.

Nigel David is a chaplain at Kaiser Permanente Medical Center in Vallejo, California, United States.

What I Remember Every Sabbath

Sandra Finley Doran

The Sabbath has always been very special to me. To help you understand, I need to tell you about my father. My dad, Jim Finley, lived for eighty-nine years and was never able to figure out where he came from. He remembered, as a child, being passed from one relative to another, feeling like a burden wherever he went.

One of his earliest memories was riding on a train as a young child, all by himself, traveling from Georgia to New York City. He spent his childhood trying to survive poverty during the Great Depression of the 1930s, attending seventeen schools in eleven years.

At the age of seventeen, he joined the United States Navy and found himself serving on the ship that photographed the testing of the atomic bomb in Bikini Atoll. Relishing the opportunity to learn, he went on to become a machinist, First Mate.

My parents met during World War II, when Dad was stationed in New London, Connecticut. They were married on a snowy day in January and spent many of those first years apart as Dad was shipped out and transferred. His term of service finally ended on his twenty-third birthday.

Soon life settled into a comfortable routine. We lived in a small house across the street from the large Catholic church that my mom, brother, sister, and I faithfully attended every Sunday.

When I was three years old, my dad took a job working nights at Bostitch, a tool manufacturer. There he met a Seventh-day Adventist man who worked the day shift. Each night this man, Al, reviewed the orders with my dad. Somehow the two arrived at the topic of religion.

Al sensed that my father had a searching heart and recommended that he take Bible studies through the mail. My dad studied the Bible for three years. When he learned about the Sabbath lasting from sundown Friday night to sundown Saturday night, he knew he could never work another Friday night again.

It was not an easy decision. He had three children, and my mom was expecting the fourth. But Dad made a commitment.

With God's blessing, Dad rented two machines and started his own business. The early years were hard. We were poor. My sister and I took turns wearing a winter hat one cold February. But Dad was committed to keeping the Sabbath. He ran his little machine shop and kept his faith.

God was good. The business grew. Dad eventually bought his own building. My grandpa, who had started as the only employee, found himself working beside two dozen others. And Finley Screw Machine Products put all four kids through Adventist colleges.

So, you see, by keeping the Sabbath, I honor the faith of my dad. I remember his difficult childhood, how far he came, and how God had a plan for his life. By keeping the Sabbath, I thank God for blessing my family and putting this reminder of His love in my life every seventh day.

Sandra Finley Doran is an educator and writer in Land O' Lakes, Florida, United States.

The Impact and Blessings of the Sabbath: As Told by a Busy Nurse

Portia Dowden

As a little girl, I always had a strong desire to help others, and that propelled me to become a nurse. This decision led to challenges, struggles, and blessings involving Sabbath keeping.

One challenge that stands out vividly occurred at the beginning of my nursing journey. A requirement for entrance into the nursing program included an exam that was scheduled on Saturday. Without hesitation, I refused to sit for that exam on the Sabbath. This stance was met with disparaging remarks from the school's director. "Why would you ruin an important chance like this just because you fear missing one Sabbath attendance at church?" she wanted to know.

I was brokenhearted by that remark and thought that nursing was no longer an option for me. However, I was determined to trust God and His process for my life.

But the words "God moves in a mysterious way His wonders to perform"[1] came to mind. A week later, I was notified that because I had high scores in a previous course, I was exempted from taking the entrance exam. The utter joy and delight of this experience inspired more confidence in God's promise that if I am faithful and obedient, He will go before me (Psalm 84:11).

Today, I work as a registered nurse in a very hectic environment. The experience is fulfilling and exciting, yet challenging and exhausting. I recall, prior to my clinical rotations, planning a routine that would allow me to observe the Sabbath hours while at work. But the realities I face working twelve-hour shifts at a frantic pace have often made it difficult to maintain a focused mindset, especially when duty calls for me to work on the Sabbath.

I have developed some practices to help me find fulfillment in doing ministry in my workplace on the Sabbath. I enjoy the subtlety of changing casual conversations into reflective discourses that celebrate the wonders of God's creation, including the marvel of the human body to recover from illness, injury, or childbirth.

Despite the bustle and buzz of the environment, I am still able to find quiet moments and places during breaks that give me the opportunity to worship privately. This private time with God, however, does not limit my penchant for singing softly or humming hymns while making my rounds.

The blessings of the Sabbath bring me a different kind of inner peace. Caring for the sick on the Sabbath is a true blessing. The joy, grace, and confidence amid the chaos that often arises help me minister gently, bringing hope to patients and their families during times of pain, uncertainty, fear, and death.

Many years have passed since that consequential juncture. But God keeps inspiring my conviction with amazingly beautiful Sabbath experiences.

Portia Dowden is a registered nurse in Southern California, Unites States.

---

1. William Cowper, "God Moves in a Mysterious Way" (1774).

What Monday Morning Taught Me About the Sabbath

Victor Dyman

Monday morning, the first words from my third-grade teacher were, "You, get out of my class! I am fed up with your 'day of rest' excuses!"

I had missed school for three Saturdays in a row. For two years, I attended my school every day, including Saturday. But toward the end of the second grade, I did not feel right being in school on Saturday.

I grew up in a Seventh-day Adventist family in Ukraine during the Soviet era, and we kept the Subbota (Sabbath) as a day of rest and worship. It was a special day. Mother cooked borsch only for Subbota. The delicacy of wild mushroom gravy was reserved only for Subbota, as it was served with buckwheat kasha (cereal). On Subbotas, we were doing many wonderful things—meeting other believers, getting the latest news from other congregations, worshiping in secret, attending children's meetings, going to the parks. Every Subbota had an aura of specialness!

After starting the first grade, the first Subbota was fast approaching. I asked, "Mom, where should I go tomorrow, to church or to school?"

"Son," she said, "it is time for you to make your own decision. But whatever you decide—you should be ready to stand for it."

Caught between what I really wanted to do on Sabbath and the unknown but scary consequences of breaking the state law, I went to school on that first Saturday. And on the second. And on many others. But going to school on Sabbath made me feel like a traitor, miserable and alone. The summer before my third grade, I decided not to attend school on the Sabbath. And that is what made my teacher angry on Monday morning. She sent me to the principal. I froze in front of the door to the principal's office. How was I to tell him that I could not attend school on Saturdays anymore? And why now? Would my explanations matter to him, a Communist in Ukraine during the Soviet era?

Finally, I knocked on the door, and the principal told me to come in. He read the note from the teacher. We discussed it, were silent for a few minutes, and then he spoke.

"If it is your decision alone, then I will report to the authorities that I have punished you adequately, and they should not go after your parents," he said. "Every Monday, you will stand in the corner in front of the class for the entire day."

"That's it?" I asked.

"Yes, that's it."

I was jubilant and returned to my classroom. I asked my teacher which corner she wanted me to stand in.

"This one," she said and pointed to the right front corner. Most classmates were sympathetic. Some were picking on me with their jokes. But it did not bother me much.

I felt whole again. That Monday morning taught me a lot about the Sabbath. The Sabbath became an important part of my life, and it is still part of my life.

Victor Dyman is a pastor at the Poughkeepsie Seventh-day Adventist Church in Poughkeepsie, New York, United States.

My Testimony

Leonard Gashugi

I grew up in eastern Democratic Republic of the Congo, where my parents had settled after migrating from Rwanda. Although my family was not Seventh-day Adventist, other kids and I joined the few Adventists in the village to sing songs from their hymnal.

Then in 1972, I providentially met an individual who had been an Adventist missionary in the same region of Africa from which I came. I invited him to stay with me instead of a hotel during his visit.

After his visit, he returned to his home and subsequently invited me to come and spend Thanksgiving weekend with his family in Berrien Springs, Michigan. I did not enjoy the weekend. I did not appreciate the restrictions of not smoking, not drinking coffee, and not having a glass of beer. I could not wait to return to my familiar surroundings.

The following year, I was responsible for distributing auto products in the Caribbean and parts of South America. While there, I kept receiving Adventist literature, such as *Signs of the Times*, from my Adventist friend. I threw it all away.

I was living a secular life, and in time I began reaping the fruits of what I was sowing. It was time to reconsider where I was heading. As I contemplated the future, my eye caught sight of a book on my bookshelf that I had not read. It was the Bible. On the first page was the following handwritten message: "Leonard, may this always show you the Way, the Truth, and the Life." It was a birthday gift from a group of Lutheran youth. I decided to read the Bible in its entirety.

As I was walking on the beach in San Juan, Puerto Rico, one day, I met three guys who invited me to attend their church on Sunday, and during the service, I responded to the altar call. My life was transformed.

The following week, I went to a prayer meeting during which the minister preached a sermon on Genesis 12—Abram's call. I remember telling the Lord that I also wanted to go where He wanted me to go.

Soon after, I received a pamphlet from my friend that read, "Which day did God rest on and sanctify?" This time I paid attention and read all of the content and the references in the Bible. I accepted the new revelation in my heart.

I was soon transferred to New York. I decided that it was time for me to leave the company and ask the Lord if He had something else for me to do.

I reached out to my Adventist friend, telling him about my conversion, and he suggested that I consider coming to Andrews University in Berrien Springs, Michigan. I went there and took classes in the seminary, including one called History of Sabbath and Sunday.

Even before taking the class, I began attending the Spanish Seventh-day Adventist church in town. It was a wonder to me to be singing some of the same songs that I used to sing back in the Congo, but now with new conviction. I was baptized on November 6, 1976.

Leonard Gashugi is a professor at Loma Linda University in Loma Linda, California, United States.

The Gift

Sabbath and Eschatology

Lawrence T. Geraty

During the first year of my doctorate program at Harvard University, during the 1966–1967 school year, I made friends with a fellow graduate student named Elizabeth Platt. She was a minister in the United Presbyterian Church, as was her father, Charles A. Platt.

Elizabeth and I often talked about our respective beliefs, including why I kept the Sabbath and the role it might play in last-day events. She was incredulous that anyone in this day and age would be persecuted for keeping the Sabbath. She said, "Nowadays, anyone can do anything they like! No one is going to care what day you keep!" As proof that that situation might change, I countered with the fact that there was an organization called the Lord's Day Alliance whose purpose was to push for Sunday legislation. She said she had never heard of it, so it could not be all that active. Elizabeth spent the following Christmas vacation with her parents in New Jersey, where she told her dad about our conversation. He said, "Elizabeth, I'm president of the Lord's Day Alliance!" So she came back from her trip to say, "Larry, you need to meet my dad and talk to him about the concerns of the Seventh-day Adventist Church."

So, while visiting my parents in Takoma Park, Maryland, where my dad was associated with the General Conference of Seventh-day Adventists, I went to the Public Affairs and Religious Liberty Department and got all of the literature I could about Sunday legislation. I then made an appointment with Dr. Platt, gave him the literature, and talked about Adventist expectations of future Sunday legislation. Dr. Platt said, "No one in the Lord's Day Alliance would want to deprive Adventists of their right to worship on Saturday! I'll tell you what, in the future, whenever we press for Sunday legislation, we'll make sure to include an exemption clause for Adventists, Jews, and other Sabbath keepers."

Since Dr. Platt's term of office in the Lord's Day Alliance was coming to an end, I introduced his successor, James Wesberry, to Samuele Bacchiocchi, who had done his dissertation on the Sabbath at the Pontifical Biblical Institute at the Vatican and was then teaching in the religion department at Andrews University. And that is how James Wesberry came to invite Bacchiocchi to address the Lord's Day Alliance in various venues around the United States.

One never knows, of course, what the future holds. But I have, at times, wondered whether I might have played a role in delaying Sunday legislation, thus possibly temporarily shielding Adventists from their long-expected persecution for keeping the seventh-day Sabbath according to the commandment.

Lawrence T. Geraty is an archaeologist and president emeritus at La Sierra University in Riverside, California, United States.

A Miracle Even Communists Couldn't Deny

Pavel Goia

I grew up in Communist Romania. As a young adult, I had a profitable glass-cutting shop. Individuals and businesspeople from the region came to me for their glass needs.

The leader of the country, to get rid of the nation's deficit, announced that we had to increase our production by 25 percent. Those who did not meet the quota were threatened with termination from their work or imprisonment.

The supervisor in my area told me that I was a problem, because I did not work every day of the week. Despite his demands, I told him I would not work on the Sabbath. The Sabbath, I told him, was God's Sabbath.

"I'm not playing games," he said. "I will make you work. You must listen to me. If not, I have the power to put you in prison and teach you that there is no God that will protect you from the Communist government!"

He ended his harangue by calling me a traitor.

I went home shaking. The threats were real. I poured out my heart to God, and God gave me peace with the decision to honor Him by keeping the Sabbath.

When I went to work on Monday, I found four damaged boxes of glass in front of my shop. The supervisor told me the glass boxes were damaged because they were sitting in the rain on Saturday and Sunday, since my shop was not open. I knew that was a lie because I had seen the damaged boxes of glass at the warehouse before they were brought to the shop. They had been there, outside in the elements, for years.

What to do? I hired a crane to remove them. As the crane started to lift a box, the bottom of the box fell away. Over one ton of glass slipped out of the box, but then it just stopped and hovered in midair! I could not believe my eyes. And neither could the people walking by. Some of them knelt, raised their hands, and praised God—an extraordinary scene in a Communist country.

The leader of the cooperative, an enterprise of many shops, witnessed the miracle and was shocked. His last words to me were, "Just ask your God to not curse my family. We don't want you around. We are afraid of you. Please leave."

That day I went home and told my father, "God protected me."

My father shook his head and said, "He did not do it for you. God did it because He loves those people and wants them to know that there is a God and to give them a chance for salvation. That's what happens when you put God above everything else."

Keeping the Sabbath, even at the threat of prison or death, helped me experience the importance of trusting God.

———

Pavel Goia is associate ministerial secretary and editor for *Ministry*, an international journal for pastors published by the General Conference of Seventh-day Adventists in Silver Spring, Maryland, United States.

Sabbath Trial

Clifford Goldstein

Although Jewish, I was raised a secular Jew and never kept the Sabbath a day in my life. Then one day, I was born again and met Seventh-day Adventists in a health-food store. They told me all about the Sabbath, as I was clueless and never really knew what it was and what it meant.

At this time, I was all but broke and needed a job. Outside the health-food store, I met a guy, Barry, who had a custom tile business, and he offered me a job right then and there. I agreed to take it.

Meanwhile, I had a little medical issue, so I asked Steve, one of the Adventists in the store, about it. He told me he would look into it for me.

The next day, I drove to Barry's to start my new career as a custom tile installer. Things went well until Barry said that he would need me to come with him on Saturday to a wholesale supplier to look over tiles.

Although still not fully convinced about the Sabbath, I could easily see the validity of the seventh-day Sabbath. Yet, I agreed to go, knowing that I should not have done it. We shook hands.

As I drove away, I was crushed, as if a giant thumb were squashing me like a bug into the car's console and seat. Finally, I remember saying to myself, *Cliff, it is 1979; people just do not do this.* I turned around, went back to the store, and told Barry I could not do it.

"Look, I am not able to work on Saturday." He shrugged, and that was the end of my career in custom tiles.

Anyway, I went back to the store, and Steve, behind the counter dealing with customers, seemed excited. He said to me, "Cliff, don't go. I need to talk to you right away!" Once the customers left, he handed me a bottle of vitamin supplements. And then he told me that fifteen minutes earlier (at the time I got fired over the Sabbath), a man whom he had never seen had come into the store, walked to the vitamin shelf as if he knew exactly what he wanted and where it was, grabbed this bottle, and came over and said to Steve something like, "This is a great cure for—" and he mentioned my exact ailment. Steve, dealing with customers, told the guy to wait, that he wanted to talk to him. The man, however, turned around, put the bottle back on the shelf, and walked out. When Steve ran after him, he was gone.

An angel? I do not know. But a reward for faithfulness regarding the Sabbath, something that, at the time, I did not fully understand? Definitely!

Clifford Goldstein is the editor for the *Adult Sabbath School Bible Study Guide*, published by the General Conference of Seventh-day Adventists in Silver Spring, Maryland, United States.

My Transformative Sabbath Experience

Michael Harvey

The Sabbath experience that changed my life for the better took place on August 10, 1985. That unforgettable afternoon was when I responded to the love of God expressed in the gospel and was baptized.

In Westmoreland, Jamaica, I was wandering through life as a careless and hopeless young adult without a sense of purpose. After my father migrated to the United States, I felt neglected and abandoned. I got caught up in disruptive behaviors that included fights, gambling, and nonattendance at school.

My prowess at playing dominoes resulted in me traveling throughout the island to play in several tournaments. While playing one evening, I remembered receiving an invitation from a former primary school classmate to attend a nearby youth evangelistic series. Despite my love for the game, I stopped playing and alerted my friends that I would return after attending the meeting. I did not return.

The sermon topic was Noah and the ark. The preacher spoke of the importance of heeding God's call. Although I initially resisted responding, I tearfully walked to the altar, and my life was changed forever.

At first, I was nervous about attending church on the Sabbath, as I grew up going on Sundays. Thankfully, the experience was very positive. When a baptismal call was made, I decided to be baptized that afternoon. I developed a hunger for the Word of God. I became the first Seventh-day Adventist in my family and decided to be a pastor. Since then, I have baptized my mother, father, and two of my brothers.

When I wake each Sabbath morning, the day's unique nature is explicit—this day is different from all other days. Sabbath releases me from all mundane activities of life. It reminds me of the essence of salvation. The Sabbath is my weekly oasis. It is a day of healing from anxiety and my emotional and mental scars.

Not only does each Sabbath remind me of my loyalty to God but it also reminds me of God's loyalty to me and His attention to my well-being. I could not read at the age of twenty-one, but God answered my simple prayer of desperation offered in faith: "Lord, please help me read, and I will serve You for the rest of my life." I not only learned to read, but God also enabled me to complete a PhD. Therefore, each Sabbath experience is unmistakably the most appropriate way to remember, not just the day of rest and worship but the celebration of my salvation.

However, my Sabbath experience is not only one that looks backward to my rebirth but it also nourishes a forward-looking frame of mind. Each Sabbath, I celebrate, with anticipation, the final rest day when Jesus returns.

The Sabbath experience matters. I see and live the Sabbath as a gift of grace. I see and live the Sabbath with eager expectancy of the Sabbath on the earth made new.

Michael Harvey is a pastor for the Maranatha District of Seventh-day Adventist Churches in Mandeville, Jamaica.

The Nonnegotiable Conviction

Guillermo Henry

In 1980, I enlisted in the United States Army. A sergeant took me under his wing and assisted me with the transition from civilian life to military life.

Soon after my arrival, I was assigned to a mission that required me to work on Saturdays. For me, this was nonnegotiable. I explained to my immediate supervisor that, due to my religious belief, I was requesting an exemption from working on Saturdays. I offered to work on Sundays as a substitute for the time. He, however, ordered me to comply with the directive to join the mission on Saturdays.

I appealed to a sergeant, who informed me of my rights, including exemption from Sabbath work. He promised to accompany me to every appeal meeting, even though he did not have to. The captain in charge of the hearing denied my request.

I immediately appealed to a higher command and was referred to the battalion commander. My supportive sergeant accompanied me to the appeal. He told me that he deemed it his responsibility to ensure that my religious rights were protected.

A few minutes later, standing before the battalion commander, with the sergeant at my side, I was asked about my refusal to follow the order to work on Saturdays. I explained that working on the Sabbath was a nonnegotiable religious conviction, and I offered to join the mission scheduled for the next day, Sunday. After a lengthy discussion, the battalion commander told me that the presence of the sergeant made a positive impact in my favor and that he would take my request under advisement.

On our way back, the sergeant reassured me that all would be well and authorized me not to report for the mission the next day, Sabbath. Even though I knew that there could be significant punishment for my refusal to follow a direct order from my superiors, I decided to trust God. I was convinced that the consistent support and prayers of my wife, Berta, along with some church members, would bring a positive resolution.

Indeed, for the remainder of my time in the military, God answered our prayers. I never heard anything more about having to participate in the mission on Saturdays. In fact, subsequently, God performed another extraordinary miracle—I was promoted to acting sergeant.

Finally, the time came for me to renew my contract to either stay in the military or leave. After much prayer and conversation with Berta, I decided to leave. When I informed the military of my decision to leave, I was asked to stay and offered a new contract with a large bonus, but I declined the offers.

I thank God for making it possible to enjoy Sabbath blessings during my military service.

Guillermo Henry is retired and lives in Riverside, California, United States

Hidden Strength

Donna Jackson

One summer Sabbath afternoon, my son, Danny, entered the world after a threatening placenta previa birth struggle. My husband, Dan, left the side of my hospital bed only to deliver a short sermon on Noah and the ark. (The members later told him that he renamed Noah Jonah throughout the entire message!)

Fast-forward about fourteen years to another summer Sabbath afternoon. Danny and I were invited by friends to visit a park in Naramata, British Columbia—a park we would have never seen. He was enthusiastic as the family had two teens. After we arrived, the teens jumped out of the van and jaunted off in one direction while the host couple led me in another direction, where we perched on large rocks, enjoying the lovely sights and a pleasant conversation.

Suddenly the wife blurted out, "I hope the kids are safe! I just remembered the waterfall has jagged rocks and a very steep drop-off into Okanagan Lake! They would never survive if they fell in."

Stunned, I jumped to my feet and demanded, "Which direction is it?" They quickly rose, and the husband began running, with his wife and I following close behind. Eventually, the waterfall came into view, and I bolted past them.

In the distance, I caught sight of my son trying to cross a rapidly moving waterfall by jumping from one boulder to the next. I looked downhill to where the waterfall became more treacherous and then dropped off into a steep fall. I looked back at Danny just as he fell and was horrified to see him struggle, unsuccessfully, to stand up against the current. Frozen with terror, I expected that, at any second, he would be swept past me to his death. Suddenly, I sensed an inaudible command: "*Move!*" I ran up to the edge of the waterfall and, putting one foot in the water, thrust out my right arm and screamed amid the roar of the falls, "Grab my arm!" Danny thrashed about in the water but could not reach me, so I screamed the command again. Somehow we connected, and I pulled him up and thrust him against a rock wall beside the waterfall. With a little embarrassment and probably annoyance, he eventually said, "OK, Mom, you can let me go." Now it was my turn to be embarrassed, but relief and gratitude quickly took over.

Before writing this story, I wanted to check the accuracy of my memories of the waterfall experience with my son. He shared the following: "While trying to cross the falls by jumping from one big boulder to the next, I fell in and struggled to stand up against the waist-deep current but couldn't because it was moving so rapidly. Then I saw you running toward me and, in one motion with one of your arms, you grabbed my arm and swung me up out of the water and onto the side against a rock wall. If I'd been swept down into the falls, I wouldn't have survived."

I believe that on those two Sabbath days—Danny's birth and the waterfall rescue—both my son and I found an inner strength fueled by our heavenly Father's vastly superior strength to meet the ordeals that we encountered. What God did for us on those Sabbaths is part of our sacred family heritage.

Donna Jackson writes from British Columbia, Canada. She is a former associate ministerial secretary for the North American Division of Seventh-day Adventists.

I Will Not Be Able to Attend on Saturday

Karen R. Johnson

I left my home country, Jamaica, to pursue a master's degree at one of the Big Ten campuses in the United States. During that time, I was encouraged by two professors to transition to the doctoral program. My biggest hurdle was the lack of funding.

Soon one professor was appointed editor in chief of a leading journal in my field of study, and I was offered a three-year position to work as managing editor. A three-year employment contract with tuition, health-care coverage, and travel benefits, plus pay, was the blessing of an answered prayer.

One significant responsibility was to assist with planning editorial board meetings. As we met to discuss the first board meeting scheduled for Washington, DC, I realized that historically, meetings were held on Saturdays. My heart sank immediately, because working on Sabbath is contrary to my beliefs, and I needed to be present at board meetings. As I sat contemplating when I should address the situation, I silently prayed for God's direction, and I heard a gentle whisper saying, "Speak." I mustered up the courage and said, "I will not be able to attend the board meetings on Saturdays."

My professor questioned, "Why not?"

I responded, "It's my day of worship."

He asked, "Are you a Jew?"

I answered, "No, I'm a Seventh-day Adventist."

From the startled look on his face, I knew he had never heard of Seventh-day Adventists. "Tell me about your faith," he replied. Honestly, I was nervous and dumbfounded.

Where I grew up in Jamaica, it seemed like everyone knew about Seventh-day Adventists. I explained that we are a Bible-believing church, we believe in the second coming of Christ, and we worship on the seventh day of the week—Saturday. The Sabbath begins at sunset Friday and ends at sunset Saturday. On Sabbath, we take a break from work to focus on our Creator through worship, fellowship, and rest. He made a note to find out if the dates could be changed. I prayed they could.

Thank God, at our next meeting, he announced that the dates were rescheduled. To my surprise, he had done his research. He shared findings from a study on the longevity of Seventh-day Adventists in Loma Linda, California, that directly correlates to biblical beliefs and a healthy lifestyle, including rest.

Now, as a tenured professor in a public university, I often find myself repeating the same words: "I will not be able to attend on Saturday." I ask God to use my voice in shareable moments to introduce the blessings of the Sabbath to others, especially in today's high-pressure work environments where deadlines loom and efforts for work-life balance diminish. Every week, I look forward to the change of space and pace that Sabbath brings, where I continually grow in relationship with Jesus, family, and community, and reset for the week ahead.

Karen R. Johnson is an associate professor at the University of North Texas in Denton, Texas.

Sabbath Spelled Trouble

George R. Knight

Sabbath spelled trouble for me. I was not a Seventh-day Adventist (or a Christian of any sort) and had no desire to be one. But I had a Sabbath-keeping, non-Adventist wife who would not stop talking about the topic. Even if I wanted to keep Sabbath, my job, unfortunately, would be a major problem. It paid very well, but in the retail world, the most important business day was Saturday. The last thing I was going to do was quit over some Sabbath foolishness.

But the good lady could not keep still. So I told her I would keep every seventh day—every Wednesday, as I recall. That ploy worked for about forty-eight hours and then collapsed, since the Ten Commandments specifically state that Sabbath is *the* seventh day of God's Creation week.

To buy peace in my young marriage, I agreed to quit my job and not work on Saturday. Ten months of nagging had had its effect. So in June 1961, I took a construction job that paid roughly one-half of what I had been making. And on top of that, my zealous young wife wanted me to start paying tithe. Would there be no end to it? It was a tough road for an agnostic.

The second round of my Sabbath trouble showed up that August, during the annual two-week summer training of my army reserve division. To this day, I am not certain what had gotten into my mind. While there, I realized that having risked so much to keep Sabbath in my work, I had apparently begun to think it must mean something. And I had also concluded that I would no longer carry a weapon, since I could not see how a person could love one's enemy and kill him or her at the same time.

There I was in the late summer of 1961: a trained infantry combatant without church affiliation who had decided to no longer drill on Sabbath or carry a weapon. Those decisions set me up for major conflict.

The crisis hit the first Friday of training camp, when I let my superiors know that I intended to keep Sabbath. They firmly replied that I was in for serious trouble. Even the chaplain refused to back me, indicating that I could be up for a court-martial.

It was at that point that my company captain showed up. Taking me aside, he noted that even though he was not especially religious, he had a Jewish heritage. In short, he understood Sabbath. He told me that the next morning I was to study my Bible in his office while the others drilled.

That was a turning point in which I began to see Sabbath as a blessing rather than trouble. The next month, I attended a series of evangelistic meetings, was baptized, and joined the Seventh-day Adventist Church. Autumn 1962 found me at Pacific Union College studying for the ministry. The rest is history. And it all started with Sabbath spelling trouble.

George R. Knight is a minister, historian, and author living in Rogue River, Oregon, United States.

When Courage Bears Fruit

Richard P. Lehmann

This story takes place in Cameroon, Africa, at the Adventist school of Nanga-Eboko, where I was president in the 1970s. The school year was ending, and the final-year students were preparing intensely for the state exam that would allow them to enter a university or hold important positions. The exams were previously scheduled from Monday to Thursday, covering all the subjects taught during the school year. Each examination was two to three hours.

But then we received disturbing news—the exams were moved to Wednesday through

Saturday. What a shock! As president, I wrote a letter to the minister of education and explained the difficulty for young Adventists of having an exam on the Sabbath day.

The minister's reply was swift. He wrote that there were Adventists in his service who were working on Saturdays. He, therefore, did not see why there was a problem for young Adventists to take an exam on a Saturday. I sent him another letter telling him that there were young Adventists for whom this was a case of conscience.

The examination day came. We prayed with and encouraged our young people but left it up to them to choose what to do. A teacher accompanied them to the city of Yaoundé and stayed at their disposal for any need. The students knew that a failure in the exam would force them to repeat the school year.

Three-quarters of them did not go to the exam on the Sabbath. In the end, sixteen candidates out of the twenty-two were admitted because they had good grades. The average for the other schools was generally 50 percent failure. For us, it was only 22 percent—a very good level.

But there is more to the story. At the beginning of the next school year, the government representative in charge of youth and sports came to see me about organizing the interschool sports meetings. I told him that we were open to such meetings, but of course, not on the Sabbath day. He replied angrily that a circular from the Ministry of Education asked that nothing be organized on Saturdays because of the Adventists. At the end of the school year, we were happily surprised to find that no exams were scheduled on the Sabbath—from elementary school to university level. This had never happened before. The Holy Spirit used my second letter to open the minister's heart. The courage and faith of the young people finally convinced him. Their testimony was stronger than my letter. Thanks be to the Lord!

Franklin Roosevelt, in his first inaugural address, said, "The only thing we have to fear is fear itself."[1] When we rely on the Lord, we have nothing to fear.

Richard P. Lehmann is an emeritus professor at Campus Adventiste du Salève in Collonges, France.

1. Franklin D. Roosevelt, "Inaugural Address of the President" (speech), March 4, 1933, Washington, D.C., National Archives, accessed March 2, 2022, https://www.archives.gov/files/education/lessons/fdr-inaugural/images /address-1.gif.

Sabbath Is Way Better Than Playing Ice Hockey

Mike Lemon

Without question, hockey was my love, my life, my all! Whenever I got the chance, I would lace up my skates, put on my uniform, and hit the ice with my buddies. Weekends especially found me at some arena on the shivering prairies of Saskatchewan, Canada, blasting a puck at the net or bashing my opponents into the boards.

One day, my grandmother checked me out of the orphanage, drove me to her house for the weekend, and prepared for me home-cooked Romanian treats. Because I love to eat, my grandmother kept piling the pierogies and cabbage rolls on my plate, all the while talking about God.

"So, Michael, I have been praying that God would lead you to the truth."

"Uh-huh," I mumbled as I stabbed another plump pierogi and stuffed it into my mouth.

"Did you know the seventh day is the Sabbath?"

My forehead creased. "So?"

"Let me show you the calendar. See, the seventh day is God's holy day."

"But I play hockey that day!" I protested.

Tears welled up in my grandmother's eyes. "Michael, I know you love hockey, and God is happy you love to keep active having fun with your friends." She smiled. "But how much happier will you be if you experience the blessing of resting on God's holy day? Giving your time to God is the best investment you can make. When you trust God, you never lose!"

At that moment, my grandmother gave me a Bible study on the Sabbath. I knew absolutely nothing about the topic, but I saw she was right. The dedicated life she lived showed me she was bang on! As much as I loved the game, when I witnessed my grandmother's faith, the allure of playing ice hockey on the Sabbath lost its grip. I still played the game, but never again on Sabbath.

Because I lived in an orphanage forty-three miles from where my grandmother lived, I could go to church on Sabbaths only when she came to fetch me. However, a program called *It Is Written* came on TV, and I watched it during the weekends that I had to stay at the orphanage. I had no idea that one day I would become the speaker and director for It Is Written Canada.

Early in my life, there were two things I decided I would never do: I would never become a pastor, and I would never go to Africa, where I was certain people did not play ice hockey. However, as I kept reading the Bible every morning and observing the weekly Sabbath, God transformed my life, turned me into a pastor, sent me to Africa for fifteen years, and gave me a beautiful, godly wife. We have two lovely daughters who, as tiny tots, delighted each Friday evening in hauling their mattresses into Mommy and Daddy's bedroom to have a sleepover, welcome in the Sabbath, and crash on the floor while we all chattered into the night.

That is way better than playing ice hockey!

Mike Lemon is the speaker and director of It Is Written Canada.

Sabbath in a Communist Country

Igor Lorencin

I was born in a country that no longer exists. Yugoslavia was controlled by Tito, a ruler committed to Communist ideology. Sabbath was a regular workday, and kids were obligated to attend school every second Saturday. What was a Seventh-day Adventist boy—who regularly attended Sabbath worship services—going to do? For me, it was not a big question, since I knew that my place on Sabbath was at church. But how would the school authorities react?

My dad visited the school director and had a pleasant conversation with her. She had no problem with my skipping school on Sabbath, as long as I did not neglect my school performance. But that was her own opinion, which was not necessarily shared by the teaching staff. After I skipped school a couple of Sabbaths, my language teacher was angry. She called my name and made me stand in front of the whole class.

You can imagine what it meant for a small school boy to stand in front of the whole class because of his faith. My father and mother were not there to support and encourage me. I felt alone. In front of the whole class, the teacher harshly asked, "How can you stay at home and enjoy your time when others are working hard at school?"

She continued mocking. I started crying, tears rolling down my cheeks. I was publicly shamed in front of the whole class.

The teacher realized that something had gone wrong and let me sit down. After discussing the case with other teachers, she learned that I was a Seventh-day Adventist, and she apologized to me privately. But the burden of public shame in front of my comrades did not go away. A couple of weeks later, my chemistry teacher decided to test my knowledge of the material covered in class on the previous Sabbath. She called my name and gave me an oral exam in front of the whole class, asking me only questions related to the material covered during the previous Sabbath, when I was not in school.

I never wanted to avoid learning, and my custom was to regularly go to one of my school comrades on Sunday and inquire about the material covered on Sabbath. I learned that new material on Sunday and was prepared for future classes. Thus, I knew the answers to all the questions my chemistry teacher asked. She was surprised that I did not miss anything. She publicly rewarded me by giving me the best possible grade.

I thank God for intervening in a difficult situation.

Igor Lorencin is the assistant professor of New Testament studies at Friedensau Adventist University in Friedensau-Möckern, Germany.

The Sabbath Challenge in School

Miroslav Lorencin

I grew up in Medulin, a town on the southern tip of Istria, Croatia. Each day our family prayed and read the Bible. Each Sabbath we went to church in the city of Pula. This was during the time of Communism, when few people attended church; thus, our family stood out. While others went about their daily activities, the people in our town saw us go to church to worship God. Some considered our conduct an affront to Communism.

In those days, it was customary to go to school on Sabbath. During the first four years of school, I had the same teacher and did not have major problems for not attending school on the Sabbath. When I started fifth grade, the situation changed. My main teacher—known as a loyal Communist—taught German and mathematics classes on the Sabbath. After I was absent several Sabbaths, he warned me in front of the class, "Listen, you little Sabbatarian, if you don't come to school on Saturday, you will fail my classes and never complete the fifth grade."

Afterward, that teacher used every opportunity to humiliate me. On one occasion, one of the boys swatted the legs of some girls with nettles, causing blisters. The leader of the boys was the teacher's son, but the teacher protected his son and claimed that I was the culprit. After that, it was announced in each classroom that I was responsible for the terrible act and that the principal would punish me. Even though I had nothing to do with it, I was proclaimed the guilty one.

When the semester grades were issued, I was disappointed that I was given a failing grade in math and German. The teacher showed how he, a Communist, treated believers. "Religion," he said, "is the opiate of the people. God does not exist. Soon we will bury the few old ladies who still go to church, and we will make the churches into museums."

With tears in my eyes, I showed my parents the report card. "God will take care of you," they told me. We prayed about the situation. With fear in their hearts, my parents sent me off to school for the second semester. To our surprise, the teacher did not come to school. We heard that he was admitted to the hospital. In fact, he never returned to school—he died.

My school circumstances improved. I successfully completed elementary and secondary school. I have been ministering for more than fifty years in the Seventh-day Adventist Church. Over the years, I have witnessed many challenges to our faith, particularly regarding the Sabbath, but God has never abandoned us. The gospel is being proclaimed, and individuals are choosing to respond to God. And unfortunately, my teacher is not around to see these good things happening.

Miroslav Lorencin is a retired president and pastor for the Croatian Conference of Seventh-day Adventists in Zagreb, Croatia. His story was translated by Nikolaus Satelmajer.

A Missionary Every Sabbath

Shelly Lowe

"As the Father has sent me, I am sending you" (John 20:21, NIV). I have always thought of this verse as a commission to be an overseas missionary—maybe to the jungle, a desert area, a city with few church members, or some small island.[1] Many people I know have gone on mission trips and served overseas, but I have never felt impressed to go. My focus has been on ministry at my home church every Sabbath and doing what I like to call "caring ministry."

In the summer of 2021, though, I felt the call to be a missionary in my own country!

As churches started reopening after COVID-19 restrictions, the church I often attend during the summer again started in-person Sabbath School. It is a very small church, so the members are stretched with many responsibilities. On Sabbath, three to four children attend, plus a visitor occasionally, but when the church restarted in-person Sabbath School, no one was available to do anything for the children.

Seeing that nothing was being done for the children, I went to their Sabbath School room to see what was available for an impromptu program. Unfortunately, the supplies in the room were not organized. It broke my heart that there was nothing planned for these precious children to learn about Jesus.

The next day, I, along with my mom, aunt, and cousin, went to the church to organize things, see what was available to decorate the room, and look for program props. Over the next couple of weeks, we gathered props and music and put together a program. My own home church graciously allowed us to borrow some materials.

From the generosity of others, my family and I worked together to put pictures on the wall, hang decorations from the ceiling, and make the room inviting. On Sabbath, it was such a joy to see the children's faces light up as they came in and saw the changes in the room. The children noticed all of the new special touches, like the flowers that had been added and the clouds hanging from the ceiling.

The next Sabbath, the children walked into church with big smiles and great anticipation about their own program. They enthusiastically participated—learning Bible stories and doing crafts. After a couple of weeks, they were already answering questions about what they had learned. I received a blessing knowing they were so happy to learn about Jesus each Sabbath!

I may not feel called to go overseas as a missionary, but I am a missionary each Sabbath and share God's love right where I am. Whether it is making food for a sick neighbor, keeping in touch with an elderly church member, babysitting for the young family at the end of your pew, or helping in a children's division, each Sabbath can be a special day.

Jesus has a mission field for each one of us—it may be just a step away in your own church or community.

Shelly Lowe is the senior editorial assistant of the Ministerial Association of the General Conference of Seventh-day Adventists in Silver Spring, Maryland, United States.

1. A version of this chapter was first published in *The Journal*, a publication of the Ministerial Association of the General Conference of Seventh-day Adventists.

I Messed Up and God Fixed It

Carol Lynton-Dunbar

It was the busiest period of the year—the "winter season," as it is called in the hotel industry. It is the time when representatives from the Caribbean hotels meet for a marketplace convention in January to discuss performance and sales strategies for the year ahead and meet new business partners.

As I did every year, I registered those attending, including the owner and other individuals. While making travel arrangements, I was notified that a chartered plane was available at a reduced cost. The plane was scheduled to depart on Saturday. I had already booked our tickets but at a rate more than twice the cost of the chartered plane. We were scheduled to arrive on Sunday, which was ample time before our meetings started on Monday. In light of the savings offered by the chartered flight, I was not surprised when the owner called me to book the team on that flight. With a heavy heart, I did as I was instructed to do.

For days, I was troubled that I had not stood up for Christ with my boss and allowed God to work things out as He has promised He would. I earnestly prayed that God would help me sort out this situation and forgive me for my distrust in His power and love for me.

It was now time for me to prove the power of God. So, I canceled my booking on the chartered flight and rebooked my seat with the scheduled airline for Sunday. But now, the price was three times higher than the chartered fare. How was I going to explain this travel expense to my boss when there was a less expensive option? So I changed my mind and quickly called back to reserve a seat on the chartered flight, but . . . there were no seats available. *I'm in trouble!* I thought. *In trouble with my boss and my God!* I constantly prayed that God would forgive me for my distrust and weakness in my inability to stand up for Him. In one of my prayers, I said, "Lord, just cancel the chartered flight—please."

While in a meeting, I received a call from my boss informing me that the chartered flight was canceled and to quickly book a flight for everyone. Tears overwhelmed me as I saw how God had fixed my mess, and the seats I booked for my boss and coworkers were now more expensive than mine.

I shared my testimony at church that Sabbath. And, praise God, it helped someone who was struggling with the Sabbath issue decide to give their heart to God. God is truly amazing!

———————

Carol Lynton-Dunbar works in the hospitality industry in Montego Bay, Jamaica.

I Lost My Job for the Sabbath

Easton G. Marks

The end of my junior year at the University of the Southern Caribbean in Trinidad coincided with the issuance of my immigrant visa to the United States. The timing was perfect. I would travel to New York, find a summer job, and earn the tuition for my senior year. After waiting a month, the other needed documents arrived, and the job hunt started.

I interviewed for various jobs, but I was frustrated after each interview. Working on Saturday was a requirement. Then it happened. As the last interview closed, I thought that I had heard correctly—I would not be required to work on Sabbaths. I accepted the job, although that meant I could not retain my mustache and beard. Company employees were not allowed to have facial hair. I decided to keep my eyes on the prize—earning enough to return to school and graduate the next June.

Clean-shaven, I reported for duty on Monday. The hours became days, and soon it was Friday.

"I will need you to come in tomorrow to assist with inventory," the manager told me.

I was sure he had mistaken me for another employee. Realizing that I was stunned, he explained that it did not happen often, but there were a few Saturdays when it would be necessary to report for work. I reminded him that at the interview, he had assured me that I would not be required to work on Saturdays.

Clearly annoyed, he said, "If I am coming in, you have to also."

On my way home that Friday evening, I wondered why this was happening. I could not afford to be unemployed now. Seeing I was discouraged, my mother tried unsuccessfully to lift my spirits.

During the Sabbath worship service, I told my cousin what happened. He assured me that everything would be fine when I reported for work on Monday. As it turned out, he could not have been more wrong. My time card was not in the rack with the others. That was my cue. The manager confirmed that I was fired because of my failure to report for duty on Saturday.

I stepped onto the street in a daze, but God was about to intervene. It took one phone call to get an appointment for an interview that same day with another company. I was hired immediately. The only day's income I lost was for the day on which I was fired.

As a pastor, I hear from members who lose their jobs because of the Sabbath. Being able to commiserate, I remind them that God knows our needs and will lead them to another job. God cares for us.

Easton G. Marks is a pastor at the Flatbush Seventh-day Adventist Church in Brooklyn, New York, United States.

Ministering to the Community on the Sabbath

Philip B. McDonald

At Ignite-LA, a ministry in Los Angeles, California, our focus is community service. Through this ministry, church members are the helping hands for Jesus, doing God's work on the Lord's Day.

We bring in the Sabbath on Friday night with a spirited youth-oriented worship service as a way of rallying our group for a planned community-organized event on the Sabbath. Our members visit prisons, group homes, orphanages, and homeless shelters. We usually partner with already established ministries linked to one of the many professional sports teams in the city of Los Angeles. We network with like-minded individuals about future endeavors and events to serve our community.

Another feature of our Friday night service is interviewing other community service groups about their ministry for the Lord. These interviews often encourage others to start their own ministry.

Some Sabbaths, we link up with a national charity and distribute meals for the homeless at an off-site location. We also visit many homeless individuals (Los Angeles has one of the largest homeless populations in the country) and distribute meals, along with handwritten messages of encouragement, hope, and love.

This way of spending Sabbath strengthens my walk with Christ because the focus, in addition to food distribution, is on prayer, reading the Bible, and sharing the Word. Focusing on various individuals in our community gives us the opportunity to share the love of Christ. This type of ministry also gives us the opportunity to fellowship with fellow believers.

Philip B. McDonald is a radiologist and television medical analyst for the National Basketball Association in Los Angeles, California, United States.

Lawful to Do Good on the Sabbath

Timothy P. Nixon

"How much more valuable is a person than a sheep!
Therefore it is lawful to do good on the Sabbath."
—Matthew 12:12, NIV

I was the associate pastor of a two-thousand-member church in Brooklyn, New York. The senior pastor was Rupert Young, a seasoned minister, who was a genuine model of servant leadership. He was a soft-spoken person, unassuming, with great depth and wisdom. His mentorship is something that has stayed with me.

One Sabbath morning, as we were preparing in the pastor's study, Pastor Young received a call from one of our deacons about a distraught member who was being evicted from her apartment that morning and had nowhere to go. After a discussion, Pastor Young turned to me and said, "Let's go! We have to move this sister. It's lawful to do good on the Sabbath."

While driving to the member's home, he explained to me the details of what had happened. When we arrived at her apartment, there was a rental truck outside, and two of our deacons from the church were already moving our member's belongings from the apartment into the truck. Pastor Young and I immediately joined them. Once we finished, we were off to a new apartment.

I cannot tell you how the new apartment was found on such short notice, but God always provides for His people. We were able to unload the truck and get our member settled. The greatest satisfaction of all was to hear her heartfelt thanks and see the pure joy on her face when we were leaving. We had prayer with her, thanking God for His providence and intervention, and then we were on our way. No amount of money could have bought such fulfillment. Selfless service for Jesus Christ is always its own reward.

As we were driving back to the church, the sun having set by then, I said to Pastor Young, "This has been the greatest Sabbath experience I have ever had in my life." He laughed in the way that only he could. It was one moment that we shared together, and it will stay with us for eternity. *What a Sabbath!* I thought.

So when I think of the words of Jesus—"It is lawful to do good on the Sabbath" (Mark 12:12, NIV)—I think back to that glorious Sabbath day when, through the hand of Divine Providence, I was placed in the charge of a true servant leader who understood what that phrase spoken by Jesus Christ really meant and who was willing to implement it. Thank you, Pastor Rupert Young, and thank God for Jesus Christ, the Lord of the Sabbath.

Timothy P. Nixon is a pastor at the Ephesus Seventh-day Adventist Church in New York, United States.

Them That Honor Me, Will I Honor

Leslie Pollard

During my preteen days, I idolized the great football hero Gale Sayers. Sayers was the running back from Kansas who took the National Football League by storm from 1965 to 1971. I imitated his evasive moves by high-stepping through uneven fields, dodging trash cans in alleys, sidestepping doorjambs, and leapfrogging tacklers on the playgrounds of my New Orleans, Louisiana, neighborhood. When I got to high school, my dream was to play football. In tenth grade, I became a member of the team.

A few years earlier, the evangelist E. E. Cleveland came to New Orleans. I was fascinated by his preaching, particularly his Bible prophecy presentations from Daniel and Revelation. I was baptized, even though at the time of my baptism, I was the only Seventh-day Adventist in my family. A few years later, I faced my first spiritual crisis. I was fifteen years old when I became a junior varsity member of the football team. That was manageable because the games were played on Thursdays. Next, I desired to join the varsity team. Unfortunately, that team played on Sabbaths.

"I am not going to be able to continue playing football," I said to Coach Brooks after one of our practices. "The Sabbath begins at sunset Friday, and all of our high school games will be on Friday nights. So I'm quitting the team." He was astonished. His dream was for me to play the key role of quarterback. "Leslie, I understand your dedication to your religion. I am dedicated to mine too. I'm a Catholic. Couldn't your minister give you special permission to play just on Friday nights, and you can still go to church on Saturday?"

I replied, "No, Coach, that's not how it works."

The next day, the coach came to our house and asked to see my mother.

"Ma'am, I know you didn't expect me to show up at your house like this, but I want to talk to you about your son. We have plans for him. I want him to stay on the team. Can your minister give him permission to play on Friday nights?"

I will never forget mother's response. "Coach, this is Leslie's decision. No one has put any pressure on him. He is under conviction. And I can't help you change his mind."

I can still see the sadness on the coach's face. "I understand," he said.

That decision fifty years ago to honor God's Sabbath has enriched the rest of my life. Instead of winning a possible athletic scholarship to a university, I went to Oakwood University. Instead of pursuing athletic stardom, I pursued God's calling. I met a young Adventist woman who has been my wife for more than forty years, and I rejoice that various family members have also joined the church.

Thank God for the Sabbath. We are invited to honor God and watch His blessings move from generation to generation (Isaiah 58:13, 14).

Leslie Pollard is the president of Oakwood University in Huntsville, Alabama, United States.

The Sabbath and Public University Campus Life

Alanna Rodriguez

A secular academic campus may not seem like the ideal place to experience a Sabbath blessing, let alone observe the Sabbath. Yet I chose to attend a public campus for the purpose of being a witness to my faith and, of course, the blessings of the Sabbath. I was a communication major at Michigan Technological University in Houghton, Michigan. This quote encouraged me in my choice of institution: "There are those who, after becoming established, rooted and grounded in the truth, should enter these [secular] institutions of learning as students. They can keep the living principles of the truth, and observe the Sabbath, and yet they will have the opportunity to work for the Master by dropping seeds of truth in minds and hearts."[1] The Sabbath was one way to share my faith with my fellow students.

I started by having many conversations in my study groups with my Muslim, Hindu, and secular classmates as to why I could not meet them from sundown Friday to sundown Sabbath. I wanted to invite my classmates to my church, but I did not think the worship service would appeal to them. Our church had about twenty members, and most were older. The church wanted to minister to the university students, but their question was how to connect with us.

So we church members started to pray and ask God to guide us. Little by little, change took place. There were three of us university students that started participating in adult Sabbath School and helped with potluck cleanup and other little things. The church started seeing a cross-generational community being built!

Eventually, after much discussion, the students led a collegiate worship service. The university students were excited with this opportunity to invite our classmates to church. Everyone enjoyed singing together, and they were blessed by the sermonettes.

The service was a bit different, so I wondered what the church leaders would say. I still remember when one of the key leaders shook my hand after the worship service and, with tears in his eyes, said, "The church is in good hands." I knew that God had blessed all of us that day and that it was just the beginning. My friends from the university stayed for the meal.

Now the student involvement in the church service is more frequent, and God has given us more boldness to invite others to church. Some of them decided to be baptized. On more than one occasion, my Muslim and Hindu friends have also attended. God opens the doors, and the Holy Spirit continues influencing the students who come to our church.

Alanna Rodriguez is a university student, who is involved with public campus ministry for the Michigan Conference of Seventh-day Adventists in Lansing, Michigan, United States.

---

1. Ellen G. White, *Selected Messages*, vol. 3 (Washington, DC: Review and Herald®, 1980), 234.

The Sabbath on a Public Campus

Alanna Rodriguez

Gabrielle

The Adventist student ministry at the University of Michigan provides a "little heaven on earth" for Gabrielle Umana, a psychology major.[1] The student organization hosts weekly Bible studies, Friday night vespers on campus, and church on campus each week. As a result, Gabrielle has been able to grow in her relationship with God through the fellowship of worship, potluck provided through the local church, Bible study, and singing. In a campus where the dominant narrative caters to the secular mind, the godly conversations on Sabbath have given her that taste of heaven each week.

During her freshman year, Gabrielle lived in the dormitory, so she was always being invited to secular events on the Sabbath. She recalls that this was her favorite time to share about the Sabbath. When her dormmates and friends invited her to events, she politely declined due to Sabbath, and that usually gave her an opportunity to share about the Sabbath. "Students were always open to listening to what I had to say and never had a negative response. I could see that they understood what a blessing the Sabbath was."

However, not every student may have an Adventist organization to connect and have community with. Gabrielle suggests finding or creating an Adventist community on campus so that you can also enjoy fellowship on the Sabbath. If a student is not able to connect with an Adventist community, she suggests finding a quiet place where you can spend time with Jesus—a quiet room, nature, or even in your car listening to gospel music. Remember to enjoy that special time with God, especially on the Sabbath.

Rachel

The Adventist Christian Fellowship at Michigan State University provided a safe haven for senior Rachel Cowell, an animal science major. Due to the restrictions on campus, face-to-face meetings are limited. However, God has connected her with a genuine Christian freshman seeking community through the university's online portal for student organizations. Rachel invited this freshman to a small retreat, which opened the door for them to experience the Sabbath each week with the local students in their online gathering and face-to-face activities.

Rachel is thankful that she can put her studies aside each Sabbath and enjoy the fellowship of the local church, located just a block from her campus. Her advice to any Adventist student attending a secular campus is to connect with the local church, find community, and participate in the local church. "When you reach out to others, even one other person, it helps to give you support and encouragement."

Alanna Rodriguez is a university student, who is involved with public campus ministry for the Michigan Conference of Seventh-day Adventists in Lansing, Michigan, United States.

1. Information provided in this chapter was gleaned from separate personal interviews between the author, Alanna Rodriguez, and the interviewees, Gabrielle Umana and Rachel Cowell.

Court-Martialed Due to the Sabbath

Kirsten Anderson Roggenkamp

"Private First Class Numan Haffner, guilty as charged.
"Private First Class Harold Massey, guilty as charged.
"Private First Class Robert Nelson, guilty as charged.
"Private First Class Richard Spencer, guilty as charged.
"You are all sentenced to six months of hard labor, your pay will be reduced by thirty dollars a month, and your rank will be reduced to private." The military judge read the verdict.

On February 4, 1954, at Fort Richardson near Anchorage, Alaska, these young men were court-martialed for refusing to obey the officers' order to man a roadblock for a practice alert on Sabbath, January 23. They, along with several other servicemen, attended the Anchorage Seventh-day Adventist Church, as did our family. They had been guests in our home and sometimes stayed to play games with us Saturday nights. My brothers and I regarded them as big brothers.

On a wintry Sabbath afternoon, January 30, many from the Anchorage church attended a service in the chapel in the stockade at "Fort Rich." We wanted to encourage the young Adventists who were imprisoned because of the Sabbath. As we walked through the chapel door, Hal was playing the piano, and Bob, Hap, and Spence were singing "All the Way My Savior Leads Me." My twelve-year-old heart was touched. The service that afternoon was meant to encourage the imprisoned men, but it also encouraged the rest of us to be strong in following Jesus in every circumstance.

Originally, our four friends had been charged with mutiny. Spence worked at the fort's veterinary clinic. The other three, Hal, Bob, and Hap, worked at the fort's dental clinic. Dentist Captain Harry Slough, also an Anchorage church member, worked at the same dental clinic. Dr. Slough was put on house arrest and charged with being the ringleader of the mutiny, a charge that carried a penalty of twenty years in a penitentiary.

Two ministers, G. W. Chambers from the North Pacific Union Conference of Seventh-day Adventists and Roy L. Benton from the Pacific Union Conference of Seventh-day Adventists, had come to Anchorage to meet with the military officers in an effort to obtain the release of these young men. After the church administrators and the local pastor met with the general, the mutiny charges were dropped, and Captain Slough was released from house arrest. Still, these four young men were court-martialed and found guilty of disobeying an order because they honored God's Sabbath over the country they loved.

Eventually, the senators from their home states were notified of what had happened to their soldiers. These senators contacted the Pentagon, the headquarters of the United States military, and the four servicemen's sentences were suspended. Each was sent to a different base in Alaska. We missed having them worship with us but were delighted that they had been freed.

Seeing my friends imprisoned for their loyalty to the Sabbath and the Lord of the Sabbath made me determined to be faithful to Jesus. Oh Lord, give me the courage and conviction of Hal, Spence, Hap, Bob, and Harry.

Kirsten Anderson Roggenkamp is an educator and author living in Loma Linda, California, United States.

Introduced to the Sabbath While Living in a Muslim Home

Emmanuel Rugambwa

I was born into a family of practicing Catholics. When I lost my family during the Rwanda genocide in April 1994, I developed an attitude of skepticism toward God. I had always thought God was a God of love, but the vicious murders of my parents and siblings caused me to question those beliefs. I wondered why God allowed my loved ones to be killed, and I never found an answer.

In 2001, I moved to Dar es Salaam, Tanzania, and was hosted by a family of Muslims. While living with this family, I found a box that contained the book titled *The Great Controversy*. I assumed it was about military wars, in part because the head of the family was a retired colonel.

After I read one of the chapters, I wanted to locate the local Seventh-day Adventist church. I met an Adventist neighbor, the one who gave the book to my host family. She took me to an evangelistic meeting. The messages were riveting. The speakers called for those who were ready to keep the Sabbath and be baptized. I heard the Holy Spirit urging me to step forward. Without a change of clothing, I stepped forward and was baptized in the clothes I wore to the meeting. I was joyful. However, this marked the beginning of a difficult journey of Sabbath keeping.

Prior to my baptism and even for some time after, my Muslim family and I were on good terms. They did try to persuade me to become a Muslim. One day, my host asked me why I chose to be an Adventist. This led to more discussions, and other family members, especially their daughter, were affected.

Things became worse when the daughter started reading my Bible and *The Desire of*

Ages. Then one day, she requested to attend church with me. She staunchly professed her conversion to Christianity. Her words, though pleasing to my ears, also surprised and scared me. I deliberated on how the father would react when he learned about his daughter's conversion to Christianity.

When he found out about his daughter's conversion to Christianity, my relationship with him soured, and I was driven from the family. This also inflamed numerous misunderstandings between the daughter and her parents. She was exiled to Uganda to live with another relative. She was resolute and stayed determined in her acceptance of Jesus as her Savior and King. With this turn of events, my time with the family ended. Unfortunately, I have since lost contact with the daughter, but I pray that her faith in God is still strong.

I accepted the call to pastoral ministry after academic preparation in Uganda and have pastored various congregations. Praise be to God for leading me to Jesus Christ!

———————

Emmanuel Rugambwa is a pastor in Kigali, Rwanda.

Ruth's Story

Ruth I. (Nutter) Satelmajer

On Sunday, July 25, 1965, Nikolaus Satelmajer and I were married at the New York Center (a church outreach facility), located in the Times Square district of New York City. It was one of the hottest days of that summer and the air-conditioning system did not work. It was a memorable ceremony and we enjoyed the reception with family and friends.

Following the ceremony, we drove off in a Chevrolet for our honeymoon, heading for northern parts of New York State and the New England states. While driving, we saw a sign that read "Camp Cherokee, Seventh-day Adventist Youth Camp." We did not know that the church had a camp in this location. We took the road to the rustic waterfront camp and met some of the staff, who invited us to join them for the evening campfire.

Unfortunately, our plans were interrupted by a series of unanticipated events that evening. After checking into a nearby motel, we decided to go to a local lake. Nik jumped into the lake while I stood on the dock, holding the car keys, until they fell—*plunk*—into the dark lake water. Nik's valiant efforts to impress me with his water skills did not produce the keys.

We walked back to the restaurant next to the motel, and soon our problem of lost keys became a shared challenge in that rural community. The restaurant owner called an off-duty police officer, who brought his diving equipment. However, his numerous dives did not produce the lost keys. By now, our dilemma had become a cause for all those in the restaurant. They were determined to get the keys to our car. The next rescuer was a manager of a car dealership, who came from his home, picked up Nik, and drove some thirty minutes to create a new set of keys. Finally, we had access to our car. We were delighted, and so were the owner and restaurant patrons.

The first crisis in our marriage ended up being a joyful event because of what others did for us. But there were other good things in store that week. We visited many beautiful areas of northern New York. We even went to the North Pole—that is, North Pole, *New York!*

Our first week as newlyweds ended on a high note. We spent the Sabbath at Camp Cherokee, the youth camp we noticed earlier that week. Years later, our children, and other children who lived with us, attended or worked at that camp. Our family visited that camp many times, and we made many great memories there.

But our fondest memory of that week was the first Sabbath we spent together as a couple in a beautiful part of the state with others who also cherished the Sabbath. We have been married for more than fifty-five years, and God has blessed us with nearly three thousand Sabbaths together. However, that first Sabbath of our marriage will always be special.

Ruth I. (Nutter) Satelmajer is a retired educator and pastor's spouse and lives in Silver Spring, Maryland, United States.

Celebrating Sabbath With Dirty Pigs

Artur Stele

During my compulsory military service near the Arctic Circle in the former Soviet Union, I was always looking for a hiding place to spend the Sabbath. In the summer, it was much easier because I could hide in the bushes and the forest just behind the military unit. The main challenge was to not get lost in the forest and to find something to eat. Although it was a punishable act to leave the territory of the military unit, most of the time, I managed to escape without being noticed.

But winters presented a much bigger challenge. The winters in the area are very cold. The coldest temperature was –37.6 degrees Celsius, which is equivalent to –35.7 degrees Fahrenheit. However, when the wind chill was taken into account, the temperature felt much lower. Regularly in winters, the constant winds are 11.27 kilometers per hour, and that brings the temperature down to –46.9 degrees Celsius.

At the start of each week, I kept an eye out for a new, safe, warm hiding place. It was vital to constantly change these hiding places; otherwise, I would be found, ridiculed, mocked, and pushed to work on the Sabbath.

As time passed, I discovered more reliable places to spend the Sabbath. The Lord sent people who helped me. I spent many Sabbath days in a warm office, for which a key was miraculously given to me. In the same room was a desk where I could hide a very small New Testament. In this office, I could also hide some food for the Sabbath day. Sabbath with food was much more joyful!

One Sabbath, though, I could not go to the office, so I found another hiding place—with smelly pigs. God pointed me to a soldier in charge of a pig farm just outside of our military complex, who caringly allowed me to hide in his "pig kingdom." The smell was terrible and the grunting of the creatures was absolutely foreign to me, but it was warm enough and nobody found me! Sabbath with dirty, stinky pigs. I felt and smelled like the prodigal son. It might sound paradoxical, but it was better inside with the unclean pigs than outside with people.

For me, Sabbath keeping was a weekly challenge, but the Lord provided a warm, safe place to spend the Sabbath and the food that I needed.

Artur Stele is general vice president for the General Conference of Seventh-day Adventists in Silver Spring, Maryland, United States.

Sabbath: A Prickly Problem or Positive Potential?

Dick Stenbakken

The voice on the phone was stressed.

"Chaplain, I have a problem. I need your help," said the navy chief.

It was not unusual to hear that request. I was intrigued and asked how I might be of assistance.

"Well," he continued, "I am making up a duty roster for guys to stand watch, and there is an Adventist guy who tells me he wants to be off duty on Friday nights and Saturday because he worships on Saturday. The problem is that it is hard to distribute weekend duty. If I let one guy off regularly, it looks like favoritism. At the same time, I want to accommodate his religious needs. That is why I called. I'm in a bind."

I was a Seventh-day Adventist army chaplain near the naval base of Pearl Harbor in Oahu, Hawaii, so the chief called me. After talking for a few minutes and listening to the needs for both the command and the Sabbath keeper, I asked, "Chief, how difficult is it for you to get guys for Sunday duty?"

"Oh, Chaplain, it is one of my biggest headaches! The guys like to party Saturday nights, and they are hungover and call in sick on Sundays. It's really tough."

I suggested that he consider asking the Adventist sailor if he would be willing to pull permanent Sunday watch duty in place of Friday nights and Saturday rotations.

"Do you think he'd be willing to pull duty every Sunday?" the chief questioned. My response was, "Give it a chance and see what he says."

The chief was skeptical but said he would follow through and then be in touch with me.

About half an hour later, the chief called back. This time his voice was lighter and happier than before.

"Chaplain! You have just solved one of my biggest headaches! I talked with the young sailor, and he says he would be delighted to pull watch every Sunday and be off duty for Sabbath. It's a win-win situation."

I noticed how the chief, having talked with the Adventist sailor, was now calling Saturday "Sabbath."

Sabbath looked like a problem, but when seen from a slightly different perspective, it became a blessing not only to the Sabbath-keeping sailor but to the chief as well. After all, the Sabbath was blessed by our Creator; that makes it a positive reality rather than a problem. The exchange with the navy chief helped enhance my understanding of the Sabbath as an ongoing reminder of God's blessings and His ability to make prickly problems into positive potentials.

Thanks, Lord, for the Sabbath!

Dick Stenbakken, a chaplain having reached the rank of colonel in the US Army, is now retired and living in Loveland, Colorado, United States.

The Diploma Exam Scheduled on Sabbath

Marija Trajkovska

My dream was coming true. I was finishing my English language and literature studies. After graduation, I could look for a job.

I was studying at the University of Niš in Serbia. Most of my lecturers were visiting professors from the Faculty of Philology from Belgrade, some 160 miles from Niš. Their lectures and exams were Friday and Saturday mornings. I did not attend the Sabbath classes, and after I appealed, they gave me permission to take the exams on a different day. And then the decisive moment came.

The final diploma exam was scheduled for Sabbath. I was studying, praying, and hoping that the schedule was somehow going to change. But it didn't, and I missed the June exam.

The next chance was in September. I studied and prayed again, but the exam was again scheduled for Sabbath, so I missed the September exam.

I was hoping for the October opportunity. But it was again scheduled on Sabbath, and I missed it.

The next opportunity was in January of the coming year. When the schedule was published, again, the final exam was on Sabbath. I was disappointed.

The last chance would be in February. My professors knew I could not come due to my religious convictions. I spent hours explaining my reasons to them and pleading for them to give me another date. The department chair said to me, "The diploma exams have been scheduled for thirty years on Saturdays. We do not see any reason to change it now. The diploma exam will stay on Saturday, be it your Sabbath or not." I was devastated but determined not to take the exam on Sabbath.

That Wednesday evening, on my way home from prayer meeting, a lady from church inquired about the cause of the deep concern she saw on my face and promised to fast and pray for the exam date to change. She encouraged me to stay calm and confident and to go on Friday afternoon to check the exam schedule again.

I earnestly prayed but was reluctant to go check the schedule on Friday afternoon. I was afraid of finding everything unchanged. But to my surprise and joy, on that Friday afternoon, I found a note on the exam board, written in large red letters:

DUE TO THE SUDDEN ILLNESS OF THE MAIN EXAMINERS, THE ENGLISH LITERATURE DIPLOMA EXAM IS POSTPONED AND TRANSFERRED FROM SATURDAY TO MONDAY

I began laughing and crying, jumping and hopping on my way to church to begin the Sabbath and share the news with my church family.

I passed the exam six months later than originally scheduled, but I received a higher grade than my colleagues who took it earlier. Six months later, I got a job as an English teacher in the Yugoslavian Union Theological Seminary and Adventist High School in Maruševec, Croatia. Our God proved to be the God who hears prayers and changes schedules, even at the last moment!

———————

Marija Trajkovska is director of women's ministries and the Shepherdess ministry for the South-East European Union Conference of Seventh-day Adventists in Belgrade, Serbia.

What Do You Do When Sabbath Is the Busiest Day? You Close the Store.

Roger and Joyce Windover

After we moved to the Adirondacks, a picturesque region of the northeastern part of New York State, I thought I would take some time off and work our newly acquired little farm. But, after a few months, I felt I needed some variety in my life. One day, coming back from town, I told my wife I would like to stop at the local hardware and feed store. We were casually acquainted with the owners. I asked the manager, who was also the son of the owners, if I could be of help at different times at the store. He thought for a moment and told me, "Let me get back to you." Several days later, he called and said he would like to meet with me. That evening, the owners, their son, and I met. To my surprise, they asked me if I would be interested in buying their business. My wife and I were not sure if we should buy the business, and we asked the Lord to guide us.

We made the decision to purchase the store and completed the franchise application. A week before closing, the franchise company called and said everything looked good except that I'd made a mistake on the days of store operation. They thought I had mistakenly marked that we would be closed on Saturday and open on Sunday. I explained that I was a Seventh-day Adventist and did not do any business on Saturday. They were very concerned because, in their other stores, Saturday was the busiest day of the week. With reservations, they approved the application.

About a year later, the franchise representative told me of a visit he made to observe our store. He was asked to come by on a Sunday and sit in our parking lot to observe how many customers were actually shopping on Sunday. He sat there for about one hour and then drove three hours back home. The next day, he told the franchise company that the store was busy and the parking lot was full.

Indeed, for a few months, previous customers had to get used to doing their shopping on a different day. Also, two nearby competitors were open on Saturday, so we were concerned about losing our customers to them.

But God worked it all out. Within a year, we had to expand. We doubled the size of our building and added other lines of business. Within six years, we purchased land and built a new store eight times larger than the previous one. The store was not only a witness to the community but it also employed several Adventists who then did not have to contend with the problem of being asked to work on the Sabbath. These days, it is harder to go from door to door witnessing, but there are also opportunities when the community comes to our doors! Have faith in God and, as Joshua writes, "serve the LORD" (Joshua 24:15).

Roger and Joyce Windover are retired business owners in Meyersville, Texas, United States.

Sabbath Joy and Jubilation

Sabbath Food Traditions

Sheryl L. Beck

I cannot say that I'm a foodie, as such, but I especially enjoy learning about regional and traditional foods. When my husband and I travel, instead of going shopping for shoes or clothing, I drag him to the nearest food market or grocery store. I love going up and down the aisles to see what's different from what I have in my home food stores.

When I'm talking to a friend or family member about a get-together, my first question isn't about who's coming; rather, it's always, "What food are you going to serve?" Learning about food traditions is a delight for me. If you visited my house, you would see hundreds of different cookbooks on a variety of cuisines.

When I became involved in this wonderful book on the Sabbath, my mind naturally considered what kind of meals individuals prepare for the Sabbath. Do people have special Friday evening meals to welcome the Sabbath? Do they make a special breakfast for Sabbath morning? What meal is enjoyed after church? I knew just the group to ask. I am a member of a Facebook group called Best Adventist Recipe Swap, and I knew this group would help me out. After all, members of this group regularly share food ideas for various functions.

I asked this question of the Facebook group: "What's your favorite traditional Sabbath food?" The group didn't disappoint me—I received 581 replies! What a joy it was to my food-loving heart to read through every one of them. Some individuals even included stories with their responses. Some responses came from family traditions, others were from boarding-school traditions, and some were based on favorite ethnic traditions. I'm unable to display all 581 responses, but here are the top forty items. See which ones are part of your Sabbath tradition:

- Haystacks
- Cottage cheese/Special K loaf
- Salad
- Mashed potatoes
- Popcorn
- Green beans
- Fruit salad
- Homemade gluten steaks
- Lasagna
- Mashed potatoes and gravy
- Potato salad
- Corn
- Homemade bread

- Potluck dinners
- Baked potatoes
- Broccoli
- Peas
- Cinnamon rolls
- Garlic bread
- Homemade soup
- Spaghetti
- Baked beans
- Corn bread
- Dinner rolls
- Green bean casserole
- Pizza
- Veggie meatballs

- Au gratin potatoes
- Chocolate cake
- Coleslaw
- Cottage cheese patties
- Fruit soup
- Macaroni and cheese
- Oatmeal patties
- Rice
- Scalloped potatoes
- Worthington Stripples
- Sweet rolls
- Taco salad
- Tacos

Enjoy the Sabbath and savor your favorite Sabbath foods and the sweet memories connected to them!

Sheryl L. Beck is the editorial specialist for *Ministry*, an international journal for pastors published by the General Conference of Seventh-day Adventists in Silver Spring, Maryland, United States.

Tub Full of Dishes

Jeanette Bryson

"Hurry up and eat! No, don't take another plate out of the cupboard."

My younger sister and two brothers were not very happy about just bread and fruit for breakfast, but I didn't want dishes to wash. We were going to church!

When a great aunt offered to take us to Sabbath School, I thought it would be my first time in a church, but I soon learned that I had been born into a Seventh-day Adventist home. However, I had not been to Sabbath School since I was very young—younger than five years old.

That morning, the youth class leader welcomed me and asked if I would like to share the mission story the following Sabbath. I said I would if we had a ride. Transportation was provided from that day onward, and the ritual of reducing the number of dishes to wash along with going to Sabbath School and church Saturday mornings soon replaced sleeping late and eating a big breakfast.

Sabbath afternoon soon became a challenge. As I learned more about the Sabbath, I didn't want to work from sundown Friday until after sundown on Saturday. But coming from a big family, as soon as we reached home, we changed out of church clothes and were assigned afternoon chores. I helped my mother prepare lunch, and then there were the dishes to wash. The house and yard chores took up the afternoons.

Then the first of many special Sabbath afternoons started when a woman approached me after church one Sabbath and invited my siblings and me to her home for a Sabbath meal. We drove by our house to ask for permission—only my sister and I were allowed to go with the nice lady.

When we reached Mother Boseant's home, there were already other members of the youth class in the living room. The table was set with bowls of delicious food. I was not enjoying the experience. The stacks of dishes in the kitchen and more being used for dessert wearied my brain with thoughts of washing all those dishes and cleaning the kitchen. Then something amazing happened; everyone helped carry all of the dishes to two washtubs in the laundry room, the door was shut, and we prepared to distribute literature. Instead of doing dishes, we were going door to door telling people about Jesus!

Just before sundown, we met at the church to sing, share stories of our afternoon visits, and pray. That night we returned to that same house for popcorn and fruit.

I enjoyed that Sabbath so much!

We enjoyed many Sabbath afternoons in this way, and sometimes, my sister and I stayed for a sleepover. I did learn that those who stayed for the sleepover washed and cleaned the next morning, but the Sabbath hours were dedicated to worshiping, sharing, singing, and praying!

Jeanette Bryson is an educator in Beirut, Lebanon.

Sabbath—the Challenge and the Joy

Claudio and Pamela Consuegra

Not yet a Seventh-day Adventist, I (Claudio) attended a youth retreat during which I made my decision to be baptized. When I returned home Sunday evening, I received a message to call my boss at a prominent hotel in Washington, DC. He told me that the banquet business was picking up, and he wanted me to return to work on Tuesday. I had been laid off three months earlier, so I was happy to have a job again. But then I realized that if I started back to work on Tuesday, my last day of the workweek would be a Saturday. I requested the Sabbath hours off, offering to work any other day, at any time I was needed. My boss granted my request and made sure I worked every Sunday, holiday, and even some evenings, but I had the Sabbath off. Soon after, I was baptized into the Seventh-day Adventist Church.

Three months later, the manager of the food storeroom of the hotel, whom I had never met, offered me a job with a pay increase and a better schedule that made it possible for me to start college in the evenings, and I never had to work weekends. I was overjoyed at how God had blessed me on my first Sabbath test.

Fast-forward almost three decades later. Our youngest daughter, Hadassah, was in her first quarter of medical school. She called us on the first Sabbath afternoon and told us that a lot of her fellow students were gathering Saturday afternoons to study. She said, "Now, don't freak out. I'm not telling you that I will be joining them. I am telling you because medical school is extremely difficult, and I need you to pray that I can make it, even though I won't be getting the benefit of group study." We reminded her that the mind needs rest too, that God would be with her and bless her, and we assured her that she would do well despite not studying during the Sabbath hours. When the quarter ended, she called to tell us excitedly that, out of 170 students in her class, she scored seventh from the top. She never had to worry about the Sabbath, and

God blessed her during medical school, residency, and fellowship, and He continues to bless her now in her career as a colorectal surgeon.

When our daughters were small, we would light our Sabbath candle to welcome the Sabbath, bring out their special Sabbath toys, and enjoy our favorite Sabbath meals. We wanted them to love this special day and the loving God who made it for us. We also reminded them of His promise: "I have been young, and now am old; yet I have not seen the righteous forsaken, nor his descendants begging bread" (Psalm 37:25). The Sabbath has indeed been a blessing to us.

Claudio and Pamela Consuegra are the family ministries directors for the North American Division of Seventh-day Adventists in Columbia, Maryland, United States.

What Sabbath Means to Me

Ed Couser

Every week God has set aside a whole day—a special time—for you and me. We can celebrate our relationship with Him on Sabbath by experiencing His blessings, healing, and fellowship. I want to share with you a personal experience of each.

His blessings: I was not raised in a Christian home, but through a series of experiences, on October 11, 1976, I knelt on my bedroom floor and invited Jesus Christ into my heart. The next day, I drove to a local Christian bookstore and purchased my first Bible. I wanted to better understand what it meant to be a follower of Jesus. After months of study, I learned that Jesus was a Sabbath keeper. Why? Because He created it. In my heart, I made a commitment to keep the seventh-day Sabbath. A few days later—late Friday afternoon—my commanding officer (I was on active duty in the US Air Force) came into our office, walked over to my desk, and said, "Airman Couser, I need you to work tomorrow."

My heart was pounding, and my knees were knocking. This was the first time I had to stand up for Jesus and His Sabbath. I prayed silently. My response was, "Sir, with all due respect, I am not available to work tomorrow." There was silence. It seemed like minutes, but it was only seconds.

"Why?" the officer asked.

I said, "Sir, I am a Sabbath keeper, and the biblical Sabbath is Friday night sundown to Saturday night sundown."

Silence.

"Would you come in on Sunday instead?" the officer asked.

I said, "Yes."

I watched the sun set in the west that night with joy and thanksgiving in my heart. I praised God that I did not have to work on His Sabbath day.

His healing: Jesus healed on the Sabbath. One day, a member of our church called me. She requested an anointing service for herself. I called the church elders and scheduled the anointing that Sabbath afternoon. We read Scripture, prayed, anointed her, and sang together. Two weeks later, the member called, asking me to visit her again. During this visit, she asked me if I had "felt the wind" at her anointing. I told her, "No." We then talked about how, in the Bible, the wind is a symbol of the Holy Spirit. A few days after her anointing, she had additional medical tests—the results were most encouraging. We rejoiced and praised God for His special healing.

His fellowship: On Sabbath, fellowship with others is important. However, we need to remember that the centerpiece of our fellowship is with God. One of my favorite ways to fellowship with God on Sabbath is walking in nature. Watching the clouds roll across the blue sky, seeing the trees bowing gracefully in the blowing wind, and listening to the birds chirp their merry songs is a joy. As I experience the beauty of nature, I speak with Him and let Him know how thankful I am for His love.

God created the Sabbath to be a delight (Isaiah 58:13). The Sabbath is a weekly reminder that I am loved by my Creator and Redeemer.

Ed Couser is a pastor in Candler, North Carolina, United States.

A Place of Delight

Lidija Djordjević Runić

Growing up, before I understood all of the theological ramifications for keeping the Sabbath, I experienced the manifold joys of it. Every Friday, I came home from school to a home full of wonderful aromas. I would play a guessing game in my mind or with my brother, trying to decipher what scrumptious foods we would be eating that Sabbath. Would we have special guests? Would my dad (who was a pastor) be home? Would we go somewhere special to welcome the day?

We were relatively poor, but each Sabbath was a banquet. Sabbath was all about being together with God and each other—a day of delight!

As I grew, my appreciation for Sabbath grew as well. Childhood memories were replaced with those of my teenage years in the Maruševec boarding school in Croatia. Again, everything revolved around the Sabbath—our classes, chores, and fun activities. I remember our dorms being sparkling clean every Friday afternoon. I remember countless Sabbath afternoon walks, even in the rain. I remember one extra hard week and a long-awaited Friday night. As I looked at the stars, I was overwhelmed with gratitude toward God, who loved us so much that He ordered us to rest! I also remember grumbling early one Sabbath morning on my way to the cafeteria, where I was to help in the kitchen. But then I heard the squeaky sound of dry snow underneath my boots, a random bird chirping, and the Holy Spirit whispering in my ear—all things for which I could be grateful. What delight! Sabbath stood as a reminder that life is to be enjoyed.

The years have passed by. I have earned different diplomas, changed vocations, and moved to another part of the world. I have undergone a lot of changes, but Sabbath has remained as an anchor of the weekly rhythm of my life.

I am a pastor now. I have my own family and churches with whom I enjoy Sabbaths. My life is very dynamic, but each week when Sabbath comes, everything stops. Whenever we welcome the Sabbath, we gather around our living room piano or the one in the church to welcome the Sabbath. It is like the clouds part and the heavens open. We join heaven! We enter it, and it enters us. It is like a shift from what is seen to what is unseen, from what it is now to a glimpse of what is to come. A reminder of a place we have never visited before but call our home—heaven, a place of delight.

Lidija Djordjević Runić is a pastor and lecturer at Belgrade Theological Seminary in Belgrade, Serbia.

One Sabbath in Amsterdam

Richard Edison

After two days in congested and busy Amsterdam, we needed a break!

My father was a delegate to the world session of the General Conference of Seventh-day Adventists in 1975. After two weeks of enjoying Austria's stunning mountains, majestic vistas, and beautiful palaces and gardens, we were now touring Europe.

We had started in Switzerland, with its pristine cities and mountains. We had hiked steep hillside trails and admired quaint cottages and beautiful mountain valleys. Later we had boarded a train and headed to Amsterdam, with visions of idyllic Dutch villages, placid canals, wooden shoes, and fields of tulips filling our heads. Were we in for a surprise!

To say Amsterdam was not what we had expected would be an understatement. Although the city was fascinating, with its lovely canals, unique architecture, and friendly people, it was crowded and busy. For three people used to the quiet and peace of rural America, Amsterdam was a shock.

On Friday, with Sabbath fast approaching, my parents scoured tourist brochures for a place to get away for some much-needed Sabbath rest. Finally, they learned of a park hidden in the center of the city, with two small chapels and charming gardens. It sounded like just what we were looking for.

Sabbath morning, we found our way to this beautiful sanctuary. Surrounded by closely packed old homes, this peaceful spot was a calming oasis from Amsterdam's bustle and noise. As we walked the garden paths, enjoying the colorful flowers and the songs of birds in the trees, we felt God's peace, "which surpasses all understanding" (Philippians 4:7), sweep over us. This was what Sabbath was supposed to be like.

God, however, had another treat in store for us. Along a quiet garden path, we met a couple from Australia and started talking with them. At one point, the husband asked what had brought us to Europe. Dad replied, "I was a delegate to our church's General Conference session."

The gentleman looked taken aback for a moment, then inquired, "For what church?"

Dad replied, "The Seventh-day Adventist Church."

"We're Seventh-day Adventists!" the couple exclaimed in unison.

Soon we were all laughing and talking, discovering shared acquaintances and similar experiences, and just bonding in the unique way that is so common when Adventists meet unexpectedly. We spent the rest of the day together, enjoying each other's company, two families from opposite sides of the globe but joined by shared beliefs and the joy of belonging to the same loving heavenly Father.

In the years since, I have often looked back on that Sabbath day in Amsterdam as an example of what Sabbath should really be—a sanctuary from the bustle of the world. It should be a time for friends and family. A taste of what heaven will be like, a place where we are all brothers and sisters—no matter where we are from.

Richard Edison is a physician assistant and writer in Cashmere, Washington, United States.

A Physician's Sabbath Delight

Wayne Greaves

The leaves on the trees in my backyard were a kaleidoscope of brown, yellow, and orange. It was 7:30 on a sunny fall Saturday morning, and I was driving to the hospital to meet with my medical team. As the attending physician, I'm responsible for supervising and training the young physicians on my team. It was the weekend, so I expected the medical rounds to be brief, and I assumed I would be able to reach church in time for the Sabbath School lesson study—my favorite part of Sabbath services. Usually, our class of seven sat in a circle, and the teacher passed out a one-page handout with questions we'd discuss. He's a trained theologian but speaks so we can understand, and he makes each of us feel special.

At the hospital, there were only eight patients we needed to visit. The team members hoped to quickly review the patients with me so they, too, could leave early and enjoy the rest of the day. All went well, and I said goodbye to the team.

I was just a few steps away from the hospital exit when I received an urgent call asking me to see a young man who had been admitted to the hospital twenty-four hours earlier. My spirit sank—I wanted to attend Sabbath School. Was this really urgent? I reluctantly agreed, hoping it would be a quick visit. I reviewed the patient's chart and realized he was one of our young physicians and had been diagnosed with HIV.

At the patient's bedside, I realized this would not be a short visit. He was only twenty-eight years old, appeared gaunt, had a fever, and was extremely anxious—his eyes kept darting around the room. Each time I thought I had answered all of his questions and prepared to leave, he grabbed my hand and asked another question. He acknowledged his lifestyle had led to his condition. He was remorseful, sad, and angry all at the same time. He was afraid—he didn't want to die.

"Is there anything you can do, professor?" he asked. "Please, do something—you must be able to do *something* to save me."

He was clearly distraught and overwhelmed by his diagnosis. He was single, an adopted child, with few friends. He felt alone and begged me not to leave. Tears streamed down his cheeks as he told me again that he didn't want to die. I spent more than an hour offering comfort and solace. Finally, we reached an agreement. I promised to explore every treatment available and see him the following day. I never made it to Sabbath School that day, but I did make a difference in that young man's life.

I am reminded of Luke 14:5. Jesus asked the Pharisees and teachers of the Law, "If one of you has a child or an ox that falls into a well on the Sabbath day, will you not immediately pull it out?" (NIV). Some things need attention, even on the Sabbath, but we can still delight in the Sabbath.

———————

Wayne Greaves is a physician in Edison, New Jersey, United States.

Sabbath—Past and Future

Monica B. Jackson

For me, the Sabbath evokes feelings of happiness, stress relief, and peace.

I am a sociable person who likes to have fun. When I lived in a rural area in Jamaica, there were few social activities in which to participate or events to celebrate. I waited in great anticipation for Christmas and Easter to come, wishing they would last longer. Once these special days passed, I experienced a feeling of sadness.

In my adult years, my mother, who had become a Seventh-day Adventist, introduced me to Sabbath keeping. I accepted the Seventh-day Sabbath, was baptized, and began attending church on Saturdays. I heard the good news of eternal life, a gift from God.

I was overjoyed at church on Sabbaths. Worshiping God and fellowshiping with fellow believers was a delightful experience. At that time, I was very unhappy with the workplace environment of the company that employed me. Each day, I looked forward to the end of the workweek and the beginning of the Sabbath. On Fridays, I was especially happy because I knew that the Sabbath was fast approaching and that during the Sabbath hours, I would not have to think about the unpleasantness in my workplace environment. The Sabbath brought joy to my life.

When the Sabbath ended, I felt unhappy because the Sabbath was over, and I was faced with the reality of the coming workweek and the challenges it would bring. But one Sabbath evening, in the midst of feeling unhappy, a thought came to mind that transformed my thinking: I realized that it was at the end of each Sabbath that I started looking forward to the next Sabbath. On the new earth, I reminded myself, we will be celebrating the Sabbath each week, but that celebration will continue forever. Nothing—not even thoughts of a job I do not like—will rob me of my Sabbath joy.

Even before Jesus Christ returns, each Sabbath reminds me that one day God will make all things new. The hurtful things we experience on this earth will no longer exist. Therefore, the Sabbath tells me that I can look forward to a time of peace and joy. And so, just as a choir rehearses in anticipation of its grand finale, I, a Sabbath keeper, continue to praise God for the Sabbath. I look forward with great anticipation to eternity and the Sabbaths I will enjoy!

Monica B. Jackson is a retired social worker living in the Bronx, New York, United States.

I Was Born on Good Friday

Mark Johnson

I was born on a Good Friday. Mom and I didn't make it to church on my first Sabbath. The second Sabbath was my introduction to what became my favorite day of the week.

Dad, Mom, and I were part of a small church in Ashland, Wisconsin, a little town far away from any large city. It's located on Lake Superior, one of the world's largest freshwater lakes. We worshiped with wonderful, friendly people. We shared our pastor with several other congregations in far northern Wisconsin, so we saw the pastor only about once a month. Church members led out in Sabbath School and the worship service. Everyone was involved—from 6- to 80-year-olds. Visiting guests participated as well.

As a child living on a farm, I felt like every Sabbath was a reunion, as I was able to catch up with friends whom I hadn't seen all week long. The Sabbath School class was for all children—toddlers through teens. In many ways, it was like a large family taking care of each other. As a child, I couldn't imagine it differently.

After church and lunch came exploring the woods and fields around us on the shores of Lake Superior. Accompanied by the family dogs, Lassie and Laddie, we waded streams and discovered hawks' nests. We imagined what it would be like to live in the wilderness like the pioneers in the hills and valleys of the Chequamegon-Nicolet National Forest, located in our area.

Supper was a weekly popcorn feed, the biggest batch of popcorn I'd ever seen. Family and friends had a standing invitation to join us for Sabbath supper. It was a fun time. Everyone around the table told stories of the past week and things seen in nature.

As the sun sank in the western sky, we moved to the living room. We sang a couple of songs of faith, and Dad led the evening worship, telling one of the great stories of the Bible. Daniel; Moses; Elijah; John the Baptist; and, most of all, Jesus came alive. In my imagination, I could picture myself standing next to the heroes of the stories.

Sabbaths were full of fun, laughter, and fresh air. The gift of this special day of rest and worship was eagerly anticipated and energetically enjoyed as a memorial of God's creative and re-creative power.

Mark Johnson is the president of the Seventh-day Adventist Church in Canada in Oshawa, Ontario, Canada.

My Sabbath Story

Abraham J. Jules

I spent my formative years in Trinidad and Tobago as a fourth-generation Seventh-day Adventist. My maternal great-grandmother, who came from India, couldn't read or write, but she learned about the Sabbath and was baptized. My paternal grandparents were Seventh-day Adventists. The Adventist church and the Sabbath were a significant part of my life. Whatever went on in the church, we knew about it because we lived next to it.

During my teenage years, my sister, brother, and I moved to live with our parents in New York. There, I attended church, enjoyed the Sabbath, and relished being a Seventh-day Adventist. I had many friends, and we spent time together, participating in various activities.

On one occasion, something happened that forever changed my life. One Sabbath, the church I attended arranged a trip to Peekskill, New York. Many youth packed several buses for the trip. A few of my friends traveled with me in my father's car and followed the buses. The worship service, in a building near a lake, was wonderful. It was turning out to be a great Sabbath—as all Sabbaths were for me—until tragedy struck.

After lunch, I went to the lake with a few of my friends. I saw a small aluminum canoe in the water and decided to jump in and take some of my friends for rides. After several short excursions, I got tired and went back to the building that was our gathering place.

Within moments, a friend ran from the building, screaming, "They're drowning!" Immediately, my father, along with others, ran to the lake and dove into the water, attempting to save the drowning youths. Tragically, three of my friends drowned that day—two of them were with me in my father's car that morning. I was devastated. On that day, for the first time, I experienced death up close. I stood on the shore and watched others pulling bodies out of the water. Friends, who were alive just a few minutes earlier, were now dead.

That tragedy changed me. That Sabbath turned out to be a horrible day. When we returned to New York, many people blamed me for the tragedy. I became very discouraged. I lost the joy of the Sabbath and stopped attending church for a while. However, every week when Sabbath came, there was an emptiness in my heart because I was not in church.

One Sabbath, while playing handball, I was impressed to walk in the direction of a little church called Brooklyn Mission, now called Brooklyn Faith Seventh-day Adventist Church. I heard the singing and preaching. I stood outside and listened. Eventually, I walked into the church. When the pastor made the appeal at the end of his sermon, I responded. A couple of weeks later, I was rebaptized. Since then, I've never missed being in church on Sabbath.

After my rebaptism, a few months later, I enrolled at Oakwood College and prepared for the ministry. More than forty years later, I am still a minister. Today, the Sabbath is a delight. I praise God, thanking Him that He turned my sorrow into joy. God redeemed me and brought me back to Him on another Sabbath day.

Abraham J. Jules is the president of the Northeastern Conference of Seventh-day Adventists, located in Jamaica, New York.

Experiencing the Sabbath as a Contradiction

D. Robert Kennedy

The sun was just about to set, or maybe it had already set. You know what happens when your mind faces a contradiction. Your memory fails. This is how it was that Friday evening, the beginning of the Sabbath when we were standing around his bedside, holding hands and praying.

My dad was dying. A few days before, he'd had a stroke. We flew from all over the world to be at Dad's bedside. He died a few days later.

In the past, when we went home and the Sabbath was beginning, Dad gave the vesper call and would lead out. But this evening was different. It seemed a contradiction. As we stood around Dad's bed, confronting death, it seemed like the contradiction of all contradictions.

Death and the Sabbath—how can they be together? Maybe you have faced such a Sabbath at a loved one's bedside. And by way of reflection, you have wondered, *How can the joy be so mixed with bitterness?* Does the Sabbath tell us about God's intent for our lives without contradictions? While wondering, I looked back at the Sabbath when Jesus was in the tomb. On that Friday afternoon, He died, just before the Sabbath, and His friends buried Him (John 19:38–42).

Just imagine the feeling of contradiction for Joseph of Arimathea, Nicodemus, the women at the tomb, and the disciples. Their contradiction was in contrast to the religious leaders, whose consciences were seared. I cannot plow to the depths of all minds and emotions, but I am thinking of so many who come to the Sabbath with contradictions. Sometimes the joy of Sabbath is mixed with a bitterness of the soul.

But when we think past any Sabbath of contradiction to the reality of Jesus' resurrection and the promised Sabbaths of eternity (Isaiah 66:23; Hebrews 4:6–8), we can be clear that Sabbaths are not meant for contradictions. On the earth made new, we will experience Sabbaths of endless delight. Until then, we live with anticipation.

———

D. Robert Kennedy is a pastor at Emmanuel Worship Center, a Seventh-day Adventist church in Alexandria, Virginia, United States.

The Sabbath and Compassion

Eldeen King

My experience of Sabbath observance began on the picturesque island of Antigua in the West Indies, where my late parents, Alberta and Roland King, taught my siblings and me the sacred, solemn, and spiritual nature of the Sabbath. I learned that Sabbath observance had a specific time, from sunset Friday to sunset Saturday. There were also specific practices—church attendance and outreach activities. Even our behavior was different on the Sabbath, such as our not partaking in secular activities.

We were instructed that our thoughts and actions were to reflect the sacredness and solemnity of the day, a practice I still hold very dear. There was also considerable focus on the "dos and don'ts." The emphasis was on the letter of the law and less on the spirit of the law of Sabbath observance.

In my quest to balance my approach to Sabbath observance, I discovered that nothing we do makes the Sabbath holy. God has already done that. He declared it holy—a day set aside for acknowledging His creative and redemptive powers. Christ, in His life and ministry, displayed kindness and compassion on the Sabbath, showing us that Sabbath observance is not comprised of some legalistic set of rules, regulations, and restrictions. God calls us to show and display our love for Christ through our care, compassion, and service to others.

The Bible is clear; it is lawful to do good on the Sabbath (Matthew 12:12). It shows that Jesus practiced what He preached, for in it is documented seven miracles performed by Jesus on the Sabbath day:

1. Jesus healed Simon Peter's mother-in-law (Mark 1:29–31).
2. Jesus healed a man born blind (John 9:1–16).
3. Jesus healed a man with dropsy (Luke 14:1–6).
4. Jesus healed a crippled woman (Luke 13:10–17).
5. Jesus healed a man with a withered hand (Mark 3:1–6).
6. Jesus drove out an evil spirit (Mark 1:21–28).
7. Jesus healed a lame man by the pool of Bethesda (John 5:1–18).

In these acts of kindness and compassion, Jesus showed our responsibility to God and each other.

My understanding and experience of the Sabbath have been transformed. It is now inspiring and renewing. I now approach the Sabbath with great joy, with excitement about my personal intimacy with God, and with enthusiasm to meet the opportunity to uplift and encourage others. I invite them to grow deeper in their relationship with Christ and exercise care and compassion in the church and community.

Eldeen King is the executive secretary for the Northeastern Conference of Seventh-day Adventists in Jamaica, New York, United States.

A Day of Art and Joy in Cree Territory

Hadassah Koester

The Maskwacis Cree Seventh-day Adventist group has been meeting for many years on or near the First Nations Treaty 6 reserve set aside for the Plains Cree of central Alberta, Canada. We have always enjoyed sharing stories and songs on various Bible topics, and the topic of the Sabbath is no exception.

When kids arrive for Sabbath School, they are excited to take a sheet of paper and draw a picture of how they mentally picture the Bible story that they are listening to for the day. Beautiful depictions of what they imagined as they listened are created and then posted on the wall. It's always a big hit. Sabbath has consistently been a high day for the congregation, with lots of fun, stories, music, and laughter while we learn about God.

"What about the Sabbath makes it interesting to you?" I asked Hope Crier, who attends the Maskwacis Cree Sabbath gatherings. She was a student at Mamawi Atosketan Native School for most of her elementary and high school education, where she learned about the Sabbath.

"I think it's cool—especially with the singing and how the pastor makes the stories more interesting," responded Hope. "I think a day of rest really helps a lot. I notice how refreshed I am afterward. I definitely want my kids to grow up learning about these things like I did."

Another student offered her input. "I keep the Sabbath because when God made everything, He rested on the seventh day." She continued, "I like the church because I get to learn about God and other good stuff. I want to keep the Sabbath as I get older, and I would teach my future kids as well."

As Jesus said, "The Sabbath was made for man, and not man for the Sabbath" (Mark 2:27). The joy and happiness that the Sabbath brings, the life and color it adds to the week, and the beautiful relationships built from its weekly observance are the gifts that God has blessed us with as we worship in Maskwacis.

Hadassah Koester wrote this story with contributions from congregation members from the Maskwacis Cree Seventh-day Adventist group in Maskwacis, Alberta, Canada.

The Sabbath—Harold's Freedom Day

David R. Neal

His name was Harold Hudson.[1] It was 1975 in Oxford, England, "the city of dreaming spires." Combine Oxford's stunning architecture amid green meadows with its academic excellence, and it is a magnificent place to visit—it is also *the place* to study.

By Oxford standards, Harold was not privileged. He'd been invited by the United Kingdom government to immigrate to England from the Caribbean during the early 1960s to resolve a severe labor shortage, and Harold settled in Oxford with his young but growing family.

Harold's workplace on the outskirts of Oxford was as far removed from the dreaming spires as you could get. His world was industrial, controlled by the tyranny of the mass-production line at the automotive factory.

From Sunday to Thursday nights, Harold worked long, labor-intensive, tedious shifts from 9:00 in the evening until 6:00 the next morning. His "rivet-rivet" world in the assembly plant was controlled by the speed of the production line.

When the night shift came to an end, Harold's work was not over. As the father of eight children, he knew his sacred responsibility to provide and care for each. To do this, he took a second job, covering the early morning milk delivery to homes. If ever there was someone who embodied the phrase "He worked every hour God sent," it was Harold.

But, come Sabbath, this was his Freedom day! Free from the tyranny of the machine. Free from the conflict between management and labor unions. Free from the responsibility of getting fresh milk to the doorstep before breakfast. It was his time with God, his family, and his church family.

I watched him at church and could see he loved to serve. He was the head deacon—and he was serving his Lord, who meant everything to him. Sabbath gave Harold two very special gifts, both related to the other. First, God gave Harold the gift of space and time to serve Him. Second, the opportunity to serve gave Harold the gift of significance—"I am not just a cog in the means of production, who 'rivet-rivets' on demand, but I am created in God's image."

Sabbath afternoon meetings at church were youth-oriented, but in reality, they were intended for the whole family. In winter months, the meeting ended the same time as Sabbath ended, and we'd always close the meeting with the song "Day Is Dying in the West." It was Harold's favorite hymn—and he sang it with gusto, but always, always with his eyes closed. It was his prayer, thanking God for the Sabbath, for his Freedom day. He was ready with his Lord to face the new week.

David R. Neal is the communication and media director for the Trans-European Division of Seventh-day Adventists in Saint Albans, Herts, United Kingdom.

1. This article was first published in vol. 42, no. 2., of *Focus Magazine*, a publication of the Stanborough Press.

Sabbath Delivery

Carl Pean

Sabbath has always been a special time for me, right from the time I was born. My mother went into labor with me on a Sabbath, just as Sabbath School was starting. That story told to me has left an imprint on me. Sabbath was also always a time to worship God with the family and to fellowship with others. And most important, it was a time to bond with God.

There was a time when I walked away from the church. Yet I always felt that there was something missing that I could not find anywhere else except if I were in communion with God and in community with fellow believers. Again, I enjoy the Sabbath fellowship with God and church members.

As a physician, I'm not overjoyed when I have to deliver a baby on the Sabbath, until I quickly remind myself that someone delivered me on the Sabbath. It's a privilege to bring new life into the world.

As I get older, I appreciate more the Sabbath and what it means for me personally. The Sabbath provides physical rest, mental rest, and divine rest. It rejuvenates my soul and recharges my spiritual batteries.

There are times when I am blessed by worshiping God with others. Other times I am blessed when I am alone with God. That's the beauty of the Sabbath.

I write this piece during the COVID-19 pandemic. For our health, we have been told to shelter in place. I yearn for corporate worship, but social distancing has also challenged me to consider what I need to put into worship in order to get something out of it. I long to spend Sabbaths with other church members. Sabbath, though, is not only a day apart for us but also a day that God has set aside to be with us. It's a special day.

Carl Pean is a physician in Memphis, Tennessee, United States.

My Favorite Sabbath Routine

Grace Peno

Many of us would agree that Sabbath keeping can become habitual. Sometimes the habits become dreary and seem to be more of a requirement than a joy. Other habits, however, are traditions that we love, as they assist us in keeping our minds on Jesus—the essence of the Sabbath.

While in my last year of college, I developed my favorite Sabbath routine. It went something like this. Friday evening, a small group of us gathered to sing, share testimonies, and pray to welcome the Sabbath. Sabbath morning, I would rise early enough to dedicate an hour to Bible study and prayer. Next, I went into the orchard, where no one could hear me, and sang hymns and prayed among the birds and bugs for as long as possible. Sometimes this was twenty minutes, and at other times it was an hour. Then I would prepare for church. At first, it was church as usual, but then it morphed into just a small group due to the COVID-19 pandemic. A small group of theology students and staff—about ten of us—met for fellowship and group Bible study. Afterward, we had lunch and then would go for a walk together for an hour or two. Next, the same group met to discuss a spiritual book focused on end-time events. During this time, the Sabbath ended, and we sang and prayed together.

This routine was my favorite, because it combined all the essential elements of communion with God: Bible study—both personal and in a group—prayer and song, nature exploration and childlike wonder, and Christian fellowship. There was time for coming away with God alone in introspection and personal conversation with the Creator. There was time for encouraging and being encouraged by fellow Christians. There was a united spirit among the group, as the main desire was to know God through His Word and creation. There was space for joy and laughter and even pain and tears to be shared. It also filled the whole Sabbath instead of only a few hours. The entire Sabbath was dedicated to Jesus.

I have tried to implement these Sabbath components in different ways even though I am no longer in that setting or with the same people. I no longer have an orchard to sing in away from all listening ears, but I can sing on a walk, in church, or with my family. I no longer have a forest within walking distance in which I can dive into the wonder of the woods, but I can walk in my neighborhood and pray for the people I pass, or I can drive to a hiking spot.

My Sabbath routines continue to adapt as I move to new places, meet new people, and gain new insights. Furthermore, I now seek to add the aspect of service to my Sabbaths. Yet I know that I will always strive to preserve the elements of my favorite Sabbath routine—deep Bible study, prayer, song, nature exploration, and fellowship, because these things help me give myself over to the God who meets me every Sabbath.

Grace Peno is a ministerial student at the Seventh-day Adventist Theological Seminary at Andrews University in Berrien Springs, Michigan, United States.

My Favorite Sabbath Experience

Jonel Rainford

There are several Sabbaths that are memorable to me. Many of the worship services on those Sabbaths were inspiring and moving. I especially recall Sabbaths when the praise and worship were electrifying and the sermon touching. Yet the Sabbath that stands out in my mind wasn't spent just in a building but mostly outdoors, ministering to the needs of others.

It all started one Friday, in September 2018, with a Compassion Consecration service and rally. The Compassion ministry was always exciting and drew great anticipation because it enabled me to participate in serving needy individuals. So the rush home from the library on Friday and the quick turnaround of ironing clothes and getting dressed for the service were all part of the exciting buildup. Even with a stretched-out service that started at 7:30 P.M. and ended after 11:00 P.M., I was pumped for what would take place the next day. Walking home with friends in a rough Brooklyn, New York, neighborhood brought no fear because of our excitement. It was a blessing to know that as we kept the Sabbath, the Sabbath kept us.

Still pumped up from the previous night's experience, I woke up Sabbath morning and listened to some classic hymns. I ate a large breakfast in anticipation of a long day. We wore branded Compassion shirts that we received on a recent mission trip to the Dominican Republic. The words *Porque las acciones hablan más que las palabras*[1] were printed on the back, indicating that we were more about actions than words.

The indoor church service ended, and it was time to serve. The youth and some adults assigned to Compassion groups immediately set out on the streets of Brooklyn. As we left, the older members chanted, "The church has left the building!"

My team went to a nearby home for displaced families, where we distributed winter clothing. We had visited this shelter previously and, although it was fulfilling to see the appreciation on the faces of recipients, I was saddened to see some of the families were still there. Nevertheless, I maintained a happy face while we sang gospel songs.

On our walk back to the church, my friends thought it would be a great idea to transpose some hymns into hip-hop music. The creativity of rapping the four stanzas of "My Hope Is Built on Nothing Less" made the walk back feel shorter.

That afternoon, all of the participants of various compassion projects in the northeastern part of the United States and Bermuda paraded in. We marched for about an hour.

Talk about a great Sabbath! I wish all my Sabbaths were like this.

Jonel Rainford is a teenager and Gen Zer in Brooklyn, New York, United States.

---

1. Translated as, Because actions speak louder than words.

My Favorite Day

Amarissa Reid

The Sabbath is my favorite day because it allows me to spend more time with Jesus, so my relationship with Him can grow stronger. When I was nine years old, I was baptized by my dad. I got baptized at that age because I loved Jesus, but I was also inspired by my mom, who was also baptized at the same age. During the weekdays, I do a lot of schoolwork that makes me tired. The seventh day, Sabbath, is the one day that I can rest physically without doing any chores. Mentally, I can relax without stress from everyday life, and emotionally, I feel happy and refreshed as I spend time getting to know Jesus.

Additionally, Sabbath is a special day in that it gives me lots of time with my family. During the week, for the most part, we focus on our individual activities, such as study and work. However, most times on Sabbaths, my family and I go to the park and spend time together. When we go to the park, we talk about different topics, including issues taking place in the world right now, the blessings and meaning of the Sabbath, or just about our week. We engage in conversations that help us expand the way we think and act.

Hanging out with and talking to my close friends is one more compelling reason the Sabbath is dear to my heart. Because of school on weekdays, we don't have much time to talk to each other. However, when Sabbath arrives, I get more time to talk to my friends without thinking about doing school assignments and other related tasks. In addition to talking to my friends on the phone, sometimes my parents will take me to see these friends. In that way, I can spend time with my friends, chat for hours, and catch up with those I haven't seen in a long time.

The Sabbath is my favorite day because of the blessings it brings. It allows me to spend time with Jesus, my family, and my friends. I always look forward to the Sabbath.

Amarissa Reid is a twelve-year-old student at Crawford Adventist Academy in Pickering, Ontario, Canada.

The Best Sabbath Ever

Sandra Roberts

On the morning of my best Sabbath ever, we awoke to roosters crowing and a glimmer of dawn beginning to erase the dark night sky. We had slept on the cold, hard floor in a small school on the Mexican side of the Mexico–US border. Anticipation of what the day promised caused us to jump out of our sleeping bags and prepare for breakfast. Cold water in the bathroom sinks was all we had available to freshen up.

The smell of tortillas and beans filled the air, and the high school students hurried to the dining area, where the cooks had Mexican hot chocolate waiting. Sipping hot chocolate, we had worship, singing a few familiar songs and offering prayers. Chilaquiles and fresh tropical fruit completed the hearty breakfast, and then we loaded up in vehicles to drive to church.

We were greeted with hugs and calls of "Feliz Sábado" ("Happy Sabbath") from church members. Our group of forty more than doubled the attendance as the students led out in Sabbath School and worship. They poured their hearts into sharing with the welcoming hosts—singing, telling children's stories, giving testimonies, and preaching—all translated by a bilingual church member.

After church, we mingled at a wonderful potluck meal as we sat in a circle in the church courtyard. As we left, we invited everyone to come back to the church for vespers and an evening of fun, asking them to bring their neighbors.

The afternoon was spent at an orphanage about an hour out of town. The students brought craft projects and put on a short program for the children. Then they paired up and played, talked, and sang with them.

I had to pull them away from the precious children so we could head back to the church, where a large number of people had already gathered. The students presented a program to close the Sabbath, and the church members gave testimonies on what God had been doing in their lives in spite of their difficult circumstances.

Popcorn, tropical fruit, and sandwiches appeared as we set up for a family-oriented evening block party. Games were organized, songs were sung, and children kept arriving from the neighborhood as they heard the sounds of joy and laughter.

It was late by the time we cleaned up and drove back to the school. More Mexican hot chocolate awaited us, and the students, although exhausted, just wanted to talk about their day. For many, this was the first time they'd traveled across the border into Mexico. We would be getting up early to go back to the church to lay tile, install new equipment for the kitchen, and put in a sidewalk before heading home from our quarterly forty-eight-hour mission trip.

The students repeated over and over that it was the best Sabbath ever. It had stretched them. They had made new friends, eaten unfamiliar but delicious food, served, worshiped, and experienced in new ways what it was like to be part of the larger body of Christ. Best Sabbath ever!

Sandra Roberts is an executive secretary for the Pacific Union Conference of Seventh-day Adventists in Westlake Village, California, United States.

Thank God the Sabbath Is Coming

Nikolaus Satelmajer

When World War II ended in 1945, my parents and I were thrown into a Communist concentration camp. This was the fate of many ethnic Germans in European Communist countries. Some fifty members of my father's extended family, along with us, were herded to a field surrounded by barbed wire and guard posts. Housing was whatever the prisoners found—a shed or a crude shelter put together. My parents and I spent the winter in a barn. We endured misery in three different camps.

Sabbath observers faced a challenge every week. Frequently, the camp commander threatened to execute those who did not report for work on the Sabbath. Fortunately, the threat was not carried out.

I was the youngest (about one year old when we were taken to the concentration camp) in the extended family, and I survived only because my parents, aunts, uncles, and cousins did all they could to keep me alive. Once, I was taken to a section of the camp where parents took children to die—but death did not win. Even though the concentration camp is in the distant past and my memory of it is vague, occasionally, I have flashbacks of those horrible experiences.

To our surprise, we were released from the concentration camp on a Sabbath day and went to our damaged and vandalized homes. Life was hard. My father was forced to work on government projects without pay. Mother and I had to survive on our own. Fortunately for us, we had support from our extended family.

One day, two angry police officers came to our house looking for my father in order to take him to another work camp. Father was hiding in the forest behind our house. One of the officers demanded my mother tell him where my father was. The officer then stared at me—I was about six—demanding to know where my father was. Terrified, I held on to my mother.

Most days, we lived in an atmosphere of fear. Fridays, though, brought hope, comfort, and joy. On Friday, one of my parents would say, "Thank God, the Sabbath is coming." The other one would agree. Their words were unexpected but comforting.

No matter what happened during the week, the Sabbath came. And, as young as I was, I realized there was something special about the Sabbath. A horrible week did not destroy the Sabbath. I learned at a young age to look forward to God's Sabbath.

My parents, just as Isaiah wrote, called "the Sabbath a delight" (Isaiah 58:13, NIV). They did not allow anything or anyone to destroy that delight. Each Friday, many years later, I still tell myself that my parents were right—thank God the Sabbath is coming!

Nikolaus Satelmajer is the former associate ministerial secretary and editor for *Ministry* for the General Conference of Seventh-day Adventists in Silver Spring, Maryland, United States.

A Day of Delight

Kevin Sullivan

Several years ago, I had a memorable conversation with a colleague about my Sabbath observance. I explained that Sabbath is a day of rest introduced by God at Creation and that it's also included in the Ten Commandments.

"From sunset Friday until sunset Saturday," I said, "we refrain from our regular work, including housework and business appointments." As a busy professional who balanced home and work responsibilities, she seemed intrigued. After some additional questions, she said, "I wish someone would give *me* a day off."

While the Sabbath does indeed provide rest from work, the greater benefit comes from God's blessing—His presence—that makes the Sabbath a day of delight. Sabbath provides the perfect work-life balance. I work six days to earn a living, but as I rest on Sabbath, I'm free to enjoy the day with God and His creation.

I especially enjoy hiking in nature, because I get to witness the marvels of creation. On one recent Sabbath hike, for example, I saw a flock of Canada geese ascend from a nearby lake. An audible swish filled the air as the birds left the water. The geese then merged into their familiar V formation, and their honking echoed off the nearby hillside. I was moved by the simple grandeur of the scene and whispered, "Thank You, Lord."

I also recall a hike in the woods during a more tumultuous season of my life. I walked until I found words for my turmoil.

"How did this happen, Lord?" I tearfully asked. "What should I do?"

In the stillness, I sensed God's love and compassion envelop me. By the time I completed the hike, I knew what adjustments I needed to make. God used our Sabbath time together to provide me with a critical course correction in my life.

Sabbath, however, is not only for solitude; it also provides an opportunity for strengthening bonds with people. I get to connect with my wife, Evelyn, with our children and grandchildren, and with members of our church. Together we enjoy inspiring worship services, sacred music, and engaging discussions about God's Word. Our Sabbath meals, whether shared between only Evelyn and me or among a tableful of guests, are healthful, delicious, and unhurried. Sabbath time with our grandchildren allows us to mark their growth and invest in their development. I know my family and friends much better because of Sabbath.

When Sabbath ends, I often emerge rejuvenated because I have been with God, enjoyed His creation, and connected with His people. Keeping the Sabbath is intended to prepare us for heaven—it provides us with a weekly taste of heaven on earth. The Sabbath refreshes and empowers me to face the week ahead. What a delight!

Kevin Sullivan is an attorney in Sykesville, Maryland, United States.

I Have No One

Sigve K. Tonstad

One Sabbath during my first year of residency in internal medicine, I entered a patient's room at the Jerry L. Pettis Memorial Veterans' Hospital in Loma Linda, California. The patient was an elderly man. Like me, he spoke English with an accent. It turned out that he came from the Transylvania region of Romania and was a Jewish rabbi. He suffered from multiple myeloma, a bone marrow disease that, at that time, had a life expectancy of no more than three years after diagnosis.

There I was, an inexperienced Seventh-day Adventist medical resident tending to the needs of a Jewish rabbi. I felt we had common ground, he as an elder brother. My patient had been a rabbi in Sighet, Transylvania. The village name rang a bell. Could it be Sighet, the home of Elie Wiesel, the Holocaust survivor and author of one of the most widely read personal accounts of the horror? It was. The rabbi proceeded to tell me that Elie Wiesel—Elihu, he called him—had been in and out of his home as if he were a member of the family before the war years. Wiesel's account in the book *Night* had brought me to tears a few years earlier. I remembered why. It was not only his suffering or the loss of his sister and mother upon arrival at Auschwitz. It was even more the feeling of God's absence. Wiesel had a deeply religious upbringing. At Auschwitz, the God of his childhood was nowhere to be seen.

I had a long conversation with the rabbi that day. The encounter filled me with awe and a sense of privilege. Since then, I have always counted Sabbaths spent in the hospital as the most meaningful time. There may be more to do because we staff are fewer, but there is less commotion and less to distract from direct interaction with the patients. I arrive early in the morning, go over all the relevant data, and then I see every patient in person. Later in the day, I go back to see *him* or *her,* not just his or her *disease.*

Sabbath and hospital work have led me to ponder the Sabbath healings of Jesus in the Gospel of John for insights that earlier eluded me.[1] At the first healing at the pool of Bethesda in Jerusalem, Jesus wins the attention and trust of a man who has been ill for thirty-eight years (John 5:1–5). The text hints that the man has been abandoned by others. When Jesus intimates that there is hope, the man answers, "I have no man to put me into the pool when the water is stirred up" (John 5:7).

"I have no one"—this is the gist of the man's answer. "I have no one" means that he is abandoned by others, and it can also reflect a feeling of being abandoned by God. This feeling is written large in the era of genocide, with Auschwitz and the experience of Elie Wiesel as a searing example.

To the man who says, "I have no one," Jesus comes with a message of hope. By choosing the Sabbath to make God's presence felt in the man's life, Jesus revealed the primary meaning of the Sabbath. Contrary to the view that the Sabbath is primarily a divine *commandment*, as Jesus' critics saw it (John 5:10–16), Jesus made the Sabbath proof of the divine *commitment* (John 5:17; 9:4). "My Father is *working* until now, and I am *working*," He tells His critics (John 5:17, ESV; emphasis added). On a later Sabbath, as He is about to heal a man who was born blind, and He tells His disciples, "We must *work* the *works* of him who sent me while it is day; night is coming when no one can *work*" (John 9:4, ESV; emphasis added).

This "work" is the work of revelation, and the Sabbath is Jesus' chosen venue to bring the revelation home to the world (John 1:18; 5:17–20). In my work as a physician, I have entered the hospital on Sabbath mornings, thinking that I am a participant in that story and the meaning of the Sabbath. The thought has filled me with awe, gratitude, and a sense of purpose. Of all the days I have spent in the hospital, Sabbaths have been the sweetest.

My thoughts have frequently returned to my encounter with the rabbi at the hospital in Loma Linda and to Elie Wiesel and the millions of victims who, like the paralytic at Bethesda, felt existentially abandoned and undone. In John's Gospel, the Sabbath brings God's presence to bear on a man who says, "I have no one." By this criterion, the Sabbath—like nothing else—could be present truth and heaven's remedy for the biggest theological problem in our time, the problem of God's apparent absence.

Sigve K. Tonstad is a research professor of religion and assistant professor of medicine at Loma Linda University in Loma Linda, California, United States.

1. See Sigve K. Tonstad, *The Lost Meaning of the Sabbath Day* (Berrien Springs, MI: Andrews University Press, 2009).

The Sabbath—A Royal Dessert

Jonathan Walter

Oh, taste and see that the LORD is good!

—Psalm 34:8

Growing up in Austria, I was exposed to some of the world's most delicious, elaborate, and beautiful dishes. To a great degree, today's typical Austrian meals and desserts have their origin in the nineteenth-century royal cuisine of the Austro-Hungarian Empire. What fed and pleased the royal leaders of the empire then has now become the desired choice of food for the common citizens and has contributed to Austria's world fame.

In Austria, as in many cultures, desserts are typically enjoyed at the end of a multicourse meal to end on a sweet note and, in a way, to celebrate the diners' time together. As a child, I often wanted to jump ahead to the dessert instead of having to work my way through the different courses. I mean, who wants to deal with soup and salad when the promise of something creamy and chocolaty is so much more appealing? This was especially hard on Sabbaths, when my mother prepared one of her extra-special Sabbath desserts.

Today, I still enjoy desserts. However, my appreciation for the main courses has grown significantly. Austrian cuisine is, after all, the food of kings and queens.

As Christians, we are also invited to partake in the privileges of a royal lifestyle. The Bible defines all who believe in Jesus as royalty—sons and daughters, princes and princesses of the heavenly King. As His royal family, we are invited to reciprocate God's love, to adapt the King's lifestyle, and share it with the people around us.

Engaging in King Jesus' majestic way of life feeds us individually, as well as the people in our sphere of influence, with delicious spiritual meals of love and truth directly from heaven's royal recipe book. As we go through each day of the week and daily ingest or share each specially cooked dish of the Spirit, we are then prepared to joyfully partake in the King's favorite—the Sabbath dessert.

The Sabbath is a celebration of the multicourse meal of faithfulness that has been experienced throughout the week. It is a sweet and delicious time of happiness in which we *savor* a special time with our *Savior*, recounting His goodness to us and honoring Him with testimonies that spread His fame as the Master Chef of love to a world starving from empty calories of deception.

So what about you, my dear prince, my dear princess of God? What's on your meal plan this week? Will you enjoy Jesus' royal cuisine? Will you faithfully savor each course and invite others to join in its flavorful experience, so that when the Sabbath dessert comes around, there will be reasons to celebrate?

Jonathan Walter is the media and communication manager for the Ministerial Association at the General Conference of Seventh-day Adventists in Silver Spring, Maryland, United States.

The Joy of the Sabbath

Leon Wellington

I was born as a third-generation Sabbath observer to parents who spent their lives practicing the faith. Growing up in rural Jamaica more than seventy years ago, I felt that life was very routine—home, grocery shopping, school, and church. In those days, there was no television, electricity, or piped water, but in this rustic rural setting, I learned to love God and looked forward to daily worship and Friday evening vespers.

Friday evenings were special, because they marked the end of preparation day and the welcoming of the Sabbath at vespers with songs like this:

How sweet upon this sacred day,
The best of all the sev'n,
To cast our earthly thoughts away,
And think of God and heav'n.[1]

My joy peaked because the next day, there would be no school or work to perform. I would participate in church activities and spend time with my friends.

The reason I found joy in Sabbath rest was that, having divorced myself from all work- and school-related activities, I experienced a mental liberation that afforded me more time to develop my personal relationship with God. This relationship, forged at home, made my engagement in church-related activities a service that I rendered to God—they were not a duty to perform. This engagement in church life with friends who shared my values was a great source of support that nurtured my childhood faith in God and acted as a guardrail for my moral, social, and spiritual deportment.

I have often encountered non–Sabbath keepers who asked me, "What do you do for a whole day at church?" What they did not know was that for me, the Sabbath was never long enough. Often, I did not return from church until near midnight after closing the day with a youth social event. The joy I found in the Sabbath as a child has never diminished; instead, it has grown stronger. I was able to transmit this joy to my family and others through my ministry.

God invites us to establish a relationship with Him because He desires to be close to us. He demonstrated this desire by visiting with Adam and Eve "in the cool of the day" (Genesis 3:8) each day to instruct and fellowship with them. I can only imagine what that first Sabbath was like with Adam, Eve, and God. I look forward to the time when the redeemed from earth will spend our first Sabbath in heaven with family, friends, and God. I invite you to look forward to that wonderful Sabbath in heaven, but in the meantime, enjoy God's Sabbath now!

Leon Wellington is a former vice president of the Inter-American Division of Seventh-day Adventists in Miami, Florida, United States.

1. Eliza Lee Follen, "How Sweet, Upon This Sacred Day" (n.d.).

The Best Sabbath Experience Ever

BeVerly (Jeri) Zacharias

It was the end of October, and my husband and I should have been on our way to Oregon, but we were not. Loading the truck took longer than planned. It wasn't until the first Monday of November that we were on our way from Union Springs, New York, to Portland, Oregon.

The weather was clear and cold as we left our home of fourteen years. In Ohio and Indiana, the weather was beginning to get wet and icy, but the roads were passable. In western Nebraska, we hit our first big snow, which limited our visibility.

We had hoped to reach Portland on Friday, but the weather changed that plan. My spirits were about as dreary as the weather, for we would have to travel on Sabbath. We always made it a practice not to travel on Sabbath, except for emergencies or important trips we couldn't make other days. When we came to a mountain pass in Oregon, signs said not to proceed without tire chains. Drivers on both sides of the road were putting chains on their vehicles, but we didn't have any. After getting advice about road conditions from some truck drivers, we decided to try it without chains, following the path of the large trucks.

The snow was dry and packed, and that provided some traction for our truck. As we headed up the mountain, the sun came out, and it was a glorious sight. Large evergreens were laden with fluffy, glistening snow, and the sky was a special blue. It was as if the Lord were telling me that He was with us and it was time to enjoy His nature.

As I drove, I told the story of Daniel's life to my guardian angel. I remembered how Daniel and his friends traveled from Jerusalem to Babylon. Those young prisoners determined to be faithful to God in the new world they were about to enter. Telling the story audibly with the emotions Daniel might have felt, and as a narrator might speak, gave me the thrill I never dreamed a storyteller could experience! Had it not been Sabbath, it wouldn't have been the same. God knew I wasn't happy about traveling on Sabbath, so He gave me the scenery that made Sabbath exciting and beautiful. He helped me recall one of my favorite Bible stories to remind me of His love and presence, no matter where I was. Sabbath! What a glorious day it is and always will be when Jesus comes to take us home with Him.

BeVerly (Jeri) Zacharias is a teacher and musician who lives in Calhoun, Georgia, United States.

Sabbath Benefits

The Sabbath and Pain

Shawn Boonstra

There is something in the human heart that refuses to accept that the world, the way it is, was designed to be like this. We may have attempted to persuade ourselves over the past two centuries that we emerged quite by chance on a random planet at the edge of a minor galaxy. Some believe that we are but mere animals who currently—again, quite by chance—find ourselves at the front of the tooth-and-claw race between species. It may be what we see written in many textbooks, but our hearts don't quite believe it.

We are deeply dissatisfied with the way life plays out. Something reminds us of a better time and a better place. We stand at the edge of a grave, knowing *logically* that this is how it is for all of us: nobody gets off this planet alive. But tell yourself all you want that this is how it is and you will still find it deeply displeasing. Your heart screams, *It's not supposed to be like this!* We get angry at a God who, on any other day, we tell ourselves does not exist, sensing that *someone* is to blame for this mess.

Those profound emotions are not the malfunction of a brain that erroneously wired itself over millions of years; they are left over from what used to be. Or, as the wise man put it, God has "put eternity into man's heart" (Ecclesiastes 3:11, ESV).

There is something else left over from our distant past: the rhythm of life. We do not march through life in twos, fours, or tens, as you might expect—but in *sevens*. We find no astronomical reason for the seven-day week; it is the fingerprint of God on a world where rebels have deliberately tried to obscure His presence.

Every week the Sabbath comes. For me, it serves the same purpose as graveside angst. It reminds me that life on planet Earth was not designed to be this painful, and at one point in the now-distant past, it wasn't. It reminds me that I do not have to accept the present state of things, that the pain I experience is not God's design. And then it points forward to a day when that pain will be lifted, and God will personally wipe away my tears (Revelation 21:4). All week, I ride over the washboard road of life, arriving Friday afternoon battered, bruised, and irritated. Then the sun sets, and I am reminded that God has not failed to notice. "Come and sit with Me," He said, "and let Me show you that this life is only an interlude between Paradise lost and Paradise regained."

I sit there quietly, learning to trust. For twenty-four hours, He draws close and confirms my suspicions. "You are right," He says. "Life is *not* supposed to be like this. For the next twenty-four hours, I will give you a small taste of your future."

And before the final triumph, He begins, even now, to wipe away my tears.

Shawn Boonstra is the speaker and director for Voice of Prophecy.

My Introduction to the Sabbath

John Bowerman

I was baptized at Immanuel Lutheran Church in my hometown of Williamstown, Pennsylvania. From a very early age, I was with my family in Immanuel's back pew every Sunday morning. As I got older, I stayed after church for Sunday School and, later, for catechism classes. After three years of study, I was confirmed into the church (a rite known as the affirmation of baptism).

Our church was only a few blocks from our house, so, weather permitting, we walked there and back. When we got home, my dad would make breakfast for my mom and me. It was a family tradition. For my family, Saturday was a day to do the things that did not get finished during the week or, more often, drive the forty-five or sixty minutes to the nearest shopping mall, large grocery stores, and fast-food restaurants.

To the best of my knowledge, there were no Seventh-day Adventists in my town of two thousand people or any of the surrounding small towns. At least I had never met one. Everything changed for me in June 2017. At age forty-seven, I was blessed to meet Tissiana Kelley, who had been a Seventh-day Adventist for most of her life. She introduced me to the Sabbath, and it was life changing.

Not long after I met her, Tissiana invited me to attend a service with her at Harrisburg First Seventh-day Adventist Church. I agreed and enjoyed it. My discomfort began as she explained what honoring the Sabbath really meant. Given how I was raised, the concept of not shopping, eating out, or going to a movie from dusk on Friday to dusk on Saturday shocked me.

With great patience, Tissiana shared the importance of honoring the Sabbath and having that full twenty-four-hour period to commune with God, study Scripture, and truly rest both the mind and body. I resisted at first. I was selfish and did not want to give up what I had known and enjoyed my entire life. But I attended church each week and began studying the Bible and Seventh-day Adventist teachings in earnest, both with Tissiana and on my own.

Slowly, over a two-year period, my eyes opened to the beauty and blessings of honoring the Sabbath. Instead of thinking about the secular things I felt like I was losing, I began to get excited about everything I was gaining. Now I look forward to sunset on Friday in a way that I have never experienced before. The peace that Sabbath brings to my heart and soul is a gift I never anticipated and one that I will never underestimate. I thank God for opening my mind to hear and accept the wonderful message of the Sabbath.

John Bowerman is a quality assurance specialist in Laurel, Maryland, United States.

Gifts

Tissiana Bowerman

Receiving gifts has always been a struggle for me. On the one hand, I love receiving a gift from someone who truly cares. Even small tokens fill my heart with warmth. On the other hand, I am uncomfortable with the spotlight being on me. I worry that my reaction will not accurately express my appreciation, and there are times I find myself questioning the possibility of hidden motives. My feelings are very different when the role is reversed, and I have the opportunity to be the giver. The entire process is so much fun! I get to think about what the person enjoys, what they need, how to lighten their load, what would surprise them, and, most of all, how much they will enjoy what awaits them.

Sometimes I try to imagine how much fun God must have had during Creation week. I see Him laughing as He created the platypus and smiling to Himself as He painted the exotic flowers, birds, and fish. I see His furrowed brow as He thought of the lessons we could learn from watching the butterfly's life cycle or in understanding how a diamond is formed. I imagine His happy voice as He created puppies and kittens to be companions. I can feel the heaviness in His heart as He created Adam and Eve, knowing that the day would come when they and their offspring would no longer be in His physical presence. After six days, with millions of unique gifts created for generations of people, God gave the special gift, the one He saved for last, His Sabbath. Exodus 20:11 tells us that the Lord blessed the Sabbath day, that this gift was made holy.

Gifts can be deceptive. Sometimes we judge the packaging or react based on other people's opinions. There have been times in my life that I have overlooked the value of this Sabbath gift, times I have even felt like it was preventing me from doing something I wanted. Sabbath, one day of each week, approximately 14 percent of our existence, was given to us for the purpose of knowing the Giver. The poet Leo Christopher once wrote, "There's only one thing more precious than our time, and that's who we spend it on."[1] Our God, the Ruler of the universe, gave us twenty-four hours of sacred time each week. Time to breathe deeply; find renewal; enjoy His creations; and, most important, grow our relationship with Him. For me, Sabbath is an exquisite gift, one filled with meaning, purpose, and love. It was given by our Creator—evidence that our God truly cares.

Tissiana Bowerman is the principal of Spencerville Adventist Academy in Spencerville, Maryland, United States.

---

1. Leo Christopher (@Leo_Words), "There's only one thing more precious than our time and that's who we spend it on," Twitter, October 12, 2015, 12:37 A.M., https://twitter.com/leo_words/status/653444270142160896.

Our Second Date—and My First Sabbath

Gail Boyer

It was our second date, and the plan was to go to a *church*. To a *Seventh-day Adventist church*! I did not know anything about Adventists. I was a lifelong Lutheran. But I was curious about this new church, especially since I really liked this guy, Bruce. So we went.

Bruce and I arrived at Sligo Seventh-day Adventist Church in Maryland that Saturday morning. *What am I doing in church—Saturday is cleaning day!* I thought. We arrived between Sabbath School (that's what they called it) and worship. The foyer was packed with people from Africa, India, the Philippines—all sorts of places. As a Swedish Lutheran, I found this unique—I loved this international experience. People were smiling, shaking hands, talking in groups, and saying, "Happy Sabbath." (I had never heard that before!) Bruce introduced me to many people, and I felt welcomed—very genuinely, I must say.

We took a seat in theater-style seating. I noticed the front of the church looked different—very simple, with several chairs in a row and no altar. *At least they have an organ and a pulpit*, I thought. From the right side of the platform, men and women in street clothes walked in. One of them walked to the pulpit and made numerous announcements, and I thought, *This appears to be a busy church!* Another person led the congregation in a hymn. Now I felt right at home—we Lutherans love to sing hymns. Another person called the children to come forward for a story, and, right on cue, the little kids started taking money from the adults who were prepared. The storyteller was quite enchanting—the kids were attentive, and I was too. Then a person talked about giving tithe—I had never heard about that in the Lutheran Church. *I'll have to ask Bruce about that*, I told myself. We were then asked to kneel for the prayer. I had never done that in my church either.

I saw in the bulletin that the sermon was next, with a woman's name next to it. Now, it was getting intriguing—a woman preacher.[1] *Good message too*, I thought to myself as she gave a fairly lengthy sermon. Oh, good—another hymn, and one that I recognized. I saw the people sitting in a row in front of me get up at once and walk down the aisle—it looked like we were done! Wait, maybe not. Time for more visiting. Bruce talked to more people, made more introductions, told more people "Happy Sabbath," and then we headed out the door. "What is the delicious smell?" I asked. "The fellowship meal," I was told. Well, that's a story for another day.[2]

Gail Boyer is a speech-language pathologist, businesswoman, and church administrator in Frederick, Maryland, United States.

---

1. This occurred in 1983, and the Lutheran Church did not have women pastors at that time.

2. I married Bruce in 1984 and was baptized by Dr. William Loveless in 1985 at Sligo Seventh-day Adventist Church. We have three grown children and three grandchildren. I praise the Lord for this man of God who asked me to go to church with him—on our second date.

My First Sabbath at a Baptism

Euxhenia Bregasi

"While I was coming up out of the water, I expected the Holy Spirit to come in the form of a dove," said my friend, the youngest of us three girls who were baptized one Sabbath morning.

"And the melody of the violin that girl was playing beside the lake created a solemn atmosphere," said my sister, jumping in enthusiastically as we were heading toward our camping tent.

"Oh yes! The pastor said that there was a celebration in heaven because of our decision to give our lives to Jesus," I added.

By the time we finished our afternoon walk, the sun was hidden behind the mountains, and the holy Sabbath hours had passed. Slowly, the sounds of night embraced our Pathfinder campout, and the sound of calm waves lapping the lakeshore became more recognizable. It was in that lake just a few hours before that I immersed my old life to start a new life with Jesus.

Later, I took the short path leading to the lakeshore and glanced at our camping banner, which bore the slogan "A Big Dream." Those words took on a whole new meaning. For years, organizing a Pathfinder camping event had been the dream of the Seventh-day Adventist Church in Albania. This camping event was indeed a dream come true. As for me, the theme of our camping had a double significance. My biggest dream of getting baptized had been fulfilled that Sabbath, and I was looking forward to a future with Jesus.

Stepping into a future with Jesus would be the beginning of my journey with the Lord of the Sabbath. I had heard amazing experiences of people who enjoyed the blessing of observing the Sabbath since they were kids. I was even more determined to present this blessing to my secular family and friends in the most interesting way, despite the challenges that it could bring. In my heart, there was a burning responsibility to share this blessing.

Five years have passed since the Sabbath that I was baptized, and, in my heart, there is still the same excitement and love for the Lord. To me, Sabbath is one of the most significant gifts God gave to His children. It is a foretaste of the heavenly world that points us to the love of our Creator and Redeemer. Our loving God is waiting to welcome all those who have experienced the blessing of the Sabbath on this earth and are looking forward to enjoying the Sabbath in eternity.

Euxhenia Bregasi is an Albanian ministerial student at Adriatic Union College in Maruševec, Croatia.

Sabbath Advice: Stop, Look, and Listen

Carlton P. Byrd

We carefully teach our little ones to stop, look, and listen before they cross the street. Ironically, the very same principle beautifully expresses why and how we can enjoy Sabbath.

Stop

Sabbath is, first and foremost, a day of stopping. "To stop" is built into the literal meaning of the Hebrew word *Shabbat*, which means "rest." Yet, most of us can't stop until we complete the tasks, the duties, and even the desires on our personal to-do lists. On the Sabbath, however, we can embrace our limits.

God is God. He is indispensable. We are His creatures. He continues to work when we stop—and when we stop, we honor Him.

Look

Every Sabbath reminds us to "be still, and know that [He is] God" (Psalm 46:10, NIV). God invites us to slow down, *look*, pay attention to who He is and what He has done. "The heavens declare the glory of God; the skies proclaim the work of his hands" (Psalm 19:1, NIV).

God also models the opportunity for us to delight in one another as His children. In the Gospels, whether it was a Samaritan woman, the widow at Nain, the rich young ruler, or Nicodemus, Jesus modeled a prayerful presence with people—He deliberately built relationships. Like Jesus, let's slow down and leave lots of free space and time on Sabbath to look for opportunities for unexpected conversations with neighbors, family, and friends. Let's ask God for the grace to leave the frenzied pace around us and be a contemplative, encouraging presence to others.

Listen

What does it mean to prepare ourselves to worship, *listen*, and receive the Word of God? What time do we need to go to bed the night before? When might we set aside moments of silence and solitude for prayer during the day—moments free from tasks, technology, and temptation to listen to God? King David declared, "I will listen to what God the LORD says; he promises peace to his people" (Psalm 85:8, NIV).

The result

Keeping the Sabbath is not a duty; it's an intentional opportunity to stop the hurried pace of life, look at the wonderful creation of our God, spend time in communion with His creation, and listen to our Creator's voice.

The phrase "Stop, look, and listen," then, is not just good advice for our children. It's a command from God Himself: "Remember the Sabbath day by keeping it holy. . . . For in six days the LORD made the heavens and the earth, the sea, and all that is in them, but he rested on the seventh day. Therefore the LORD blessed the Sabbath day and made it holy" (Exodus 20:8, 11, NIV).

Sabbath rest restores, refreshes, and revives our hearts.

Carlton P. Byrd is the president of the Southwest Region Conference of Seventh-day Adventists in Dallas, Texas, United States.

Sabbath: For My Sake

Mario Ceballos

The Sabbath was made for the purpose of fulfilling the needs of humankind. Our Creator knew what our needs would be. The first thing God did was create a space in time and set it aside for a specific purpose, to fulfill the needs of His creation. He fulfilled the need for rest, our communion with Him, a relationship with Him, and worship of Him. The space of time is for spiritual, moral, and character development.

We were not created to be subject to the Sabbath. Rather, it is a gift to be enjoyed by all humankind. In other words, the Sabbath is God's gift to us.

One of the greatest challenges a person can face is when the responsibilities and commitments of a job interfere with the time created and set aside by God for restoration. People can walk away from most jobs, but there are some jobs where it is not easy to do so. It is not easy to walk away from a job that one has been "drafted" into, such as the military, where one has affirmed allegiance to protect and defend. There are penalties for not obeying direct orders from superiors. What can be done when that happens?

As a young man, I enlisted in the army, not knowing all that it entailed. I was told that accommodations could be made for me to keep the Sabbath for the purpose God intended. What I was not told was that the accommodation would be at the discretion of my superiors. I was serving in the medical field in a military hospital in Texas as a pharmacy technician. I did not have a problem helping others in this capacity during the Sabbath hours. Besides my duties in the hospital, there were other duties not related to my medical work. Those monthly duties usually did not interfere with the Sabbath, but there was one time when they did. I was told that I could not switch with or pay anyone to take my place in completing the assigned duties scheduled for a Sabbath.

I spoke with the chaplain of my unit, and he told me, "My soul belongs to God, but my body belongs to the US Army, and I have to obey the order I was given." That day

I decided to become a chaplain to help others in the same situation. I asked to speak with my commanding officer and explained what the Sabbath meant to me and the importance of that day in my life. After attentively listening, he said, "Mario, I know and understand about the Sabbath. I was once an Adventist." He then asked my superior to allow me to make the necessary arrangements so that I could be off duty during Sabbath hours.

It is very important to carefully and prayerfully consider how the decisions we make may interfere with our primary responsibility to be loyal to God, our Creator. Making good decisions is good for our success on this earth and throughout eternity.

Mario Ceballos is the director of Adventist Chaplaincy Ministries for the General Conference of Seventh-day Adventists in Silver Spring, Maryland, United States.

The Sabbath Exhausts Me—but I Am Happy

Keith Chuumpu

I work on the Sabbath day. In fact, I work so hard that by the end of each Sabbath, I am so exhausted that I just want to throw myself into bed and sleep. Yet, the Sabbath is truly a delight to my soul. I prepare for it all week long so that by the time it comes, I am completely ready. And as one enjoys a roller-coaster ride, I enjoy my Sabbath day encounter. Then I look forward to another Sabbath day. And the cycle continues.

During the week, I have an encounter with God. I seek His face and glory. I seek His blessings and open myself up for God's infilling. There I absorb His glory. And once I am full, I look forward to the Sabbath. At about 11:00 A.M. on Sabbath, I am tense and anxious to convey God's Word to His people. At about 12:00 P.M., I sigh in relief because by then, I am done with my preaching and I get to freely mingle with God's children. We laugh, talk, and have lunch together. After that, we enjoy great Bible studies. Sometimes I go to visit some families with special needs—perhaps in the hospital or at a funeral home. Once in a while, I drive off alone with my family and we spend some special Sabbath moments together. By the end of the day, I am exhausted. Then I wait for God to bless me again so that I can bless others.

"Six days you shall labor," says the Lord, "and do all your work, but the seventh day is the Sabbath of the LORD your God. In it you shall do no work" (Exodus 20:9, 10). I guess my labor consists of coming close to the Lord. And my rest consists of emptying myself of God's blessings so that others may be blessed.

I am a pastor. That's what I do for a living. During the week, I study God's Word. And I walk with people in their daily lives in order to understand them more and then petition

God for their needs—material and spiritual. And when the Sabbath day comes, I am well prepared for it. Then I wait for the next Sabbath. And the cycle continues. I believe it will even be better when we are finally home with the Lord (Isaiah 66:23).

Keith Chuumpu is the stewardship and church development director for the Lusaka Conference of Seventh-day Adventists in Lusaka, Zambia.

The Sabbath and the Chief

Diói and Silvia Cruz

Our first Sabbath at Powa village of the Kissi tribe, Guinea Conakry, Guinea, West Africa, was awe inspiring. To reach our destination, we drove six hours to travel about ten miles through the rocky mountain pass and then walked for forty minutes. The view from the top was fabulous! It was a memorable day as all of the village people were baptized, and the church was organized. Four months before, they were all animists who practiced sorcery and sacrificed animals daily to appease the evil spirits they feared.

Two years earlier, a young man, Michel, left the village to study French in a nearby city. For the first time, he visited several churches and found a church that worshiped God on the seventh day. He received Bible studies and was baptized.

Returning home, he told his parents and his chief that he was now part of the seventh-day God's worshipers. They were very enthusiastic about it because in that region of the forest, nobody farms on Saturday since, for them, it is a resting day for the earth. Even the sorcerers could not help with their witchery because the evil spirits were resting in the forest on Saturdays. The chief appreciated Michel's ability to read the Bible, and he decided that all the people would join the church of the seventh-day God's worshipers.

The chief told me, "Jesus Christ is the best Protector and Savior we have, and we must adore God on His holy day, the Sabbath. Only the God of the Sabbath can protect us from all sorceries."

The chapel made of straw, standing at the side of a solid building, shows how eager the people were to have a church in their village. More than two hundred people praise God every Sabbath. The baptism and church inauguration ceremonies were breathtaking. The children's choir sang inspiring songs that the children composed. It was incredible for children who had never studied music. Now, years later, other villages around Powa have also been baptized and worship the God of the seventh day.

The word *Kissi* means "protector, savior, pacifier." The chief told me that the village existed for a few centuries, and others around often requested a good Kissi warrior to protect their people as they were the most courageous and powerful. Powa continues sending Kissi warriors to other villages, but now they are warriors of God who announce salvation in Jesus Christ and the God of the seventh day.

We are reminded in Exodus that keeping Sabbath holy is God's plan to protect our families from evil forces and diseases: "If you listen carefully to the LORD your God and do what is right in his eyes, if you pay attention to his commands and keep all his decrees, I will not bring on you any of the diseases I brought on the Egyptians, for I am the LORD, who heals you" (Exodus 15:26, NIV).

Diói and Silvia Cruz served as missionaries in West Africa from 1999 to 2008. Presently, they serve at Adventist International Institute of Advanced Studies in Silang, Cavite, Philippines.

Unexpected Sabbath Blessings

Ana Džuver

During our graduate theological studies in the United Kingdom, my husband and I were invited, along with a few other theology students, to join a Sabbath afternoon Bible study group led by one of our professors. A few of the families decided to meet every two weeks to enjoy a potluck after church and then deepen their knowledge and understanding of the Bible in the remaining hours of Sabbath. It seemed difficult to accept the invitation as, apart from studying, we worked many hours during the week in order to cover our tuition costs and living expenses. Sabbath was our only free day. Also, during the week, we would have to prepare for the Sabbath afternoon Bible study. Notwithstanding all these difficulties, we decided to participate. For us, the best Sabbaths had always been those combining fellowship and Bible study, so we gladly accepted the invitation. But we did not imagine just how rewarding it was going to be.

We met Sabbath after Sabbath, and, at the start, I was exhausted from working long hours sleeping very little during the week. Sometimes I felt so feeble that even my thoughts were scattered. On some occasions, I struggled to speak louder than a whisper. As the Bible study progressed, however, instead of feeling more tired, a transformation took place in me. My mental and physical strengths were gradually renewed, I could think clearly again, and my voice returned. Above all, people who used to be complete strangers became very dear friends. And even though we stayed late, each time we left the meeting refreshed and full of joy. We were prepared for the demands of the week ahead, and we looked forward to the next Sabbath afternoon fellowship and Bible study.

Whenever I remember these Sabbaths, the words from Psalm 19:8–10 come to my mind:

The statutes of the LORD are right, rejoicing the heart;
The commandment of the LORD is pure, enlightening the eyes;
The fear of the LORD is clean, enduring forever;
The judgments of the LORD are true and righteous altogether.
More to be desired are they than gold,
Yea, than much fine gold;
Sweeter also than honey and the honeycomb.

I experienced the truth of these verses. I learned that when Sabbath is united with fellowship and Bible study, I experience a three-fold blessing—physical regeneration, mental renewal, and a heart filled with joy.

Ana Džuver is an associate dean at Adriatic Union College in Maruševec, Croatia.

A More Rounded Perspective

Charles Eaton

The Sabbath has always meant more to me when I am under serious strain. In high school, the Sabbath seemed like an annoyance that needed to be planned around. At that point in my life, I did not have enough responsibilities to value Sabbath rest. As a student at Oakwood University, the Sabbath meant a lot of socialization that I mistakenly interpreted as rest. But by the time I went to law school, I had matured enough to have a more rounded perspective on the Sabbath.

I was told that, in order to succeed in law school, I needed to learn how to function on five and a half hours of sleep a night and I needed to plan to spend six to seven hours each day reading material for the next day. The Sabbath became essential—I felt that I kept my sanity *because* of the Sabbath.

I guarded the Sabbath as if I was paid to do so. I did not allow anything or anyone to interfere with it. My protection of the Sabbath, however, made me anxious even as it brought me peace. Classmates with red-rimmed eyes occasionally told me of all the Saturday hours they spent mired in the details of legal writing. I, on the other hand, told them which books I had been reading or which sermon I had been absorbing.

In law school, I feared being academically outperformed by my classmates, since they were putting in hours while I rested. I learned to trust that God would take care of me and honor the time I spent cultivating our relationship on the Sabbath. I wish I could say that, despite my Sabbath keeping, I ended up with the best grades in my class. I can't say that, not by a long shot—but I did end up employed, happy, and sane. Not compromising my beliefs in that situation gave me the strength to hold on to them for a lifetime. I'd rather have that strength—a strength that God gave me through the Sabbath.

Charles Eaton is an attorney in Riverside, California, United States.

Sabbath and Health—A Physician's Perspective

Laura Khandagle

Our mental and physical health can improve by taking the time to relax and reset our souls. God has provided us with a helpful guide in the Bible on how we can do this. Our day of rest, the Sabbath, is one of the most important gifts from God that allows us to rest and reflect on ourselves and our health. God felt it was so important that He placed the Sabbath in His top-ten list.

I remember Sabbaths of my childhood as a flurry of events. I got up and put on my finest clothes. When mom started to play the piano, I knew I needed to head toward the car to go to church. Church was a social event where I got to hang with friends, listen to the sermon, enjoy a potluck meal, and socialize into the late afternoon. In the afternoon, if not still at church, I listened to Aunt Sue and Uncle Dan on the radio as they told stories about Christians and their experiences with God. Vespers closed the Sabbath day, and then family game night started. The next day, I woke up feeling refreshed and ready to start the week.

As an adult, I now cherish the Sabbath. As a physician, caring for patients continues Sunday through Saturday. I do not get to take Sabbath off, but even so, I have learned how to take the time to reset my mind and body. Instead of looking at working with patients at the hospital or dealing with medical emergencies that arise in the day as a job on the Sabbath, I look at it as an outreach to others for the God I serve. God blesses me with the reward of seeing His healing power on the patients that I care for. God's teachings are a blueprint to help me comfort my patients who cannot be healed. His blueprint gives me hope in the future that Jesus will come again one day and reunite family and friends with their loved ones lost in this life.

Life is precious, and the Sabbath gives me time to reflect on how blessed we are in life. We can reflect on all that God has created. He has blessed us with the simplicity of breathing and the complexity of the human body. He has surrounded us with nature, music, family, and friends to give us the support we need to reset mind and body as preparation for our next week in life. Thank God for the Sabbath! "Then he said to them. 'The Sabbath was made for man, not man for the Sabbath' " (Mark 2:27, NIV).

Laura Khandagle is a physician in Silver Spring, Maryland, United States.

The Sabbath and Health

Peter N. Landless

One exclaimed, "A Seventh-day *Adventurer*—how exciting!" Another asked, "Seventh-day Inventor—what have you *invented*?" Such were the comments from my elementary school friends in South Africa when they asked me why I went to church on Saturday. I was a young and happy Sabbath keeper—blessed by a wonderful weekly church experience stretching from Friday's dawning, ushering in preparation day, to Sunday morning. Friday sunset to Saturday night was filled with vespers, services, Pathfinders (a youth club), and then Saturday night church socials, and even church picnics some Sundays! I was blessed with a rich and healthy experience.

What *did* we "invent," as one of my friends asked? We did not invent anything. We simply accepted the blessings of rest, reflection, refreshment, renewal, stress reduction, and focused time to strengthen our relationships—all this is revitalizing and health-promoting! This "sanctuary in time"—as Dan Buettner, author of *The Blue Zones*, describes the weekly Sabbath rest of Seventh-day Adventists—provides the time and opportunity to focus on God and family, friends and fellowship, and nature and nurture.[1]

Throughout school and university life, at times, I felt the Sabbath was a test—I missed some prize-giving ceremonies, graduations, and other "opportunities" because they were scheduled to take place on the Sabbath. But the peace, joy, and equanimity that celebration of the Sabbath rest and blessings brought always eclipsed the importance and significance of the event I "missed" in order to honor the Sabbath, and more importantly, the Lord of the Sabbath.

As a young physician in boot camp in the South African military, I refused to take my military driver's license exam on a Saturday. "You'll be the only noncommissioned physician in the force if you do not take the test." "So be it," was my response. I am convinced the training officer was ultimately moved to relent because of human intercession. At the last minute, on the last day of grace before graduation—he ordered me to take the test on a Friday at midday!

Patients waited until sunset on Saturday to call when I worked in practice (unless urgency demanded otherwise) and said, "We waited for your Sabbath to end before calling." Mischievously, I responded, "Not my Sabbath—God's Sabbath!" Many conversations ensued, as did decisions to "taste and see that the Lord is good" (Psalm 34:8, NIV).

Sabbath is a blessing to our health. It gives us a golden opportunity to meet the needs of others who may be struggling with health issues. That's what Jesus did when He reached out, touched, or spoke, and people were healed. Many of His healings were performed on the Sabbath. He gives us the opportunity to holistically relieve physical, mental, emotional, spiritual, and relational suffering today—even on Sabbath. Not only in the emergency room, urgent care, or operating room but also in the home, community, and even church.

Jesus came that we "may have life, and have it to the full" (John 10:10, NIV). It is also for this reason that He gave us the sanctuary in time, the Sabbath. Enter into that rest—and be deeply blessed!

Peter N. Landless is a physician and director at Adventist Health Ministries for the General Conference of Seventh-day Adventists in Silver Spring, Maryland, United States.

1. Dan Buettner, *The Blue Zones* (Washington, DC: National Geographic Society, 2008), 244.

Sabbath Blessing

Andrea Luxton

Growing up as a Sabbath keeper means the rhythm of your life is different and wonderful. The gift that it brings was never so clear as when I was a doctoral student. Up until then, for all but two years of my life, I had attended Seventh-day Adventist schools. Now I had four years ahead of me when I was the only Adventist in my program and possibly the university as a whole.

One of my first discoveries was that all the department social gatherings were scheduled for Friday night. I didn't say anything but chose not to attend the first couple. My peers asked me why. I shared, and their response was immediate: "Well, that is all right. Let's move all our gatherings to Saturday night instead!" And they did. Of course, I got some well-meaning teasing, such as a typical Friday morning question: "What time do you jump into your coffin tonight, Andrea?" But all was friendly, respectful, and playful.

However, a couple of years into my program, a significant event happened. One day, one of my friends called me. She told me that she and her husband always had date night every Friday night. He was going to be gone for the next six weeks, and she would be fine most of the time, but Friday evenings were going to be tough. Then she asked, "I know you don't do anything on Friday nights, so do you think I could spend the next six Friday evenings with you?"

So for the next six Friday nights, my friend came to my place. We ate supper together, listened to music, chatted, and relaxed. The fourth Friday, she arrived at the door laughing. "You will never guess what happened to me today." She explained that she was downtown shopping and looked at her watch. Then she said—a smile involuntarily came to her face—"I thought, *Oh good, only another hour until Sabbath!*" We laughed together as she told me her story. Then we spent some more serious time as she shared what she had gained from our Friday evenings together. While we had not done anything unusual and had not talked theology, she had sensed a calmness and received a Sabbath blessing by experiencing the peaceful presence of God each of those evenings.

It took someone who wasn't a Sabbath keeper to show me what a great gift I had been living with all my life.

Since that day, as Sabbath draws near, I take a deep breath and smile too, knowing that I am soon to experience God's particular and unique blessing of the Sabbath day.

Andrea Luxton is the president of Andrews University in Berrien Springs, Michigan, United States.

Sabbath Resistance

Michael Pearson

I don't keep the Sabbath—the Sabbath keeps me![1]

That's not just playing with words. It's the truth. The Sabbath keeps me from being on a treadmill of activity 24-7.

The Sabbath used to keep my mind off work for a day. Now that I am retired, I don't have to think so much about the problems of working and earning a living. But there is still a lot to be done to keep the show on the road: a home to be maintained, shopping to be done, arrangements to be made. Obligations. Expectations. Worries.

The Sabbath allows a reset.

That has an effect that keeps me from greedy consumerism. It keeps me away for a while from the lure of attractive websites and retail shops.

I realize that having more stuff may block my emotional aches and pains for a while, but it does not really make me happy. If my mind is not focused on acquiring more stuff, then it has some energy to think about other things. That could be the real needs of friends and family or my own priorities in life now.

It means healthier relationships and a reduced likelihood of stress in the family. As we slow down, we can have a little time to do that serious talking and caring that we may never otherwise quite get to.

If I consume less, I can do my small part in keeping this wonderful, fragile planet of ours in better condition. Every time we see the havoc caused by a freak weather event, we are reminded that we are spoiling the earth and need to consume less.

Taking a regular pause from the relentless cycle of life is a healthy thing to do. It helps us breathe. The Sabbath trickles into everything, every day of the week. Sabbath rest is part of the rhythm of a healthy life cycle.

And there inevitably comes a day, after we have been on the treadmill of life for a while, when we start to ask the question, What's it really all about? The Sabbath gives us a fresh perspective on where we are, where we've been, and where we're going. It's like a hilltop that allows us to see into the distance as we ponder the deep questions.

There's nothing clever about keeping the Sabbath. There are no brownie points on offer. You don't achieve anything. That's the whole point.

The Sabbath slowly builds up our inner strength, so that we can resist the strong pressures we are all under. It helps build resistance to diseases of the mind and spirit. Of course, it's not all straightforward. It's not magic. But each Sabbath is a step toward maintaining balance in life. It helps us filter all the false messages that bombard us daily.

So let the Sabbath keep you. Join the resistance movement!

Michael Pearson is lecturer emeritus at Newbold College of Higher Education in Binfield, Bracknell, United Kingdom.

---

1. This article was first published in vol. 42, no. 2., of *Focus Magazine*, a publication of the Stanborough Press.

An Unexpected Blessing for Sabbath Observance

Rolf J. Pöhler

At a special ceremony, a pastor offered Bible verses to serve as life mottos. The verses were selected by the pastor, who also happened to be my father. As I stood on the verge of adolescence, the following text left a deep impression on my youthful mind and has accompanied me ever since:

Trust in the LORD with all your heart,
    and do not lean on your own understanding.
In all your ways acknowledge him,
    and he will make straight your paths (Proverbs 3:5, 6, ESV).

Not long afterward, I decided to commit my life to God and be baptized.

A few years later, I faced a situation that tested my resolve to follow the Lord in all circumstances. One of my Abitur (baccalaureate) examinations was scheduled to take place on a Sabbath. I had never attended school on Sabbath and always managed to make up for the missed classes in the following week. But this was a different situation. Without this test, no Abitur. Without Abitur, no university education. After some reflection and prayer, I decided to ask my teacher for an alternative date for the Latin exam. To my relief, it was granted. I was also told that I would be given another text to translate to make sure I wasn't able to cheat and know what was to be translated beforehand.

On the examination date, I was in church, wondering how I would cope on test day. When the time came, I was sitting alone in a room with my teacher and began to translate the Latin text into German. After a while, I started wondering why the text seemed somehow familiar to me. It was not included in my workbook, nor had we translated it in class. But the longer I worked on the text, the more familiar it became to me.

Suddenly, it dawned on me. In preparation for the exam, I had translated some Latin texts that I had kept from the previous secondary school in Nuremberg. I had saved six of them with the intent of using them as tutorials for the Abitur. It was one of these texts that my Latin teacher had chosen as the substitute for the regular test. At that moment, I knew God had provided an extra blessing when I had made the right decision to honor the Sabbath.

When the exam period was over, I thanked God for making sure I got a Latin text I had studied before. This helped me pass an exam that was organized just for me, because I had followed my conscience regarding Sabbath keeping. God had fulfilled His promise:

Trust in the LORD with all your heart,
    and do not lean on your own understanding.
In all your ways acknowledge him,
    and he will make straight your paths (Proverbs 3:5, 6, ESV).

Rolf J. Pöhler is a professor of systematic theology at Friedensau Adventist University in Möckern-Friedensau, Germany.

The Sabbath Saved My Ministry

Anthony Michael Reid

I was burning out. I led a hectic life, implementing ministry programs without taking time for vacation. Pastoral visits, phone calls, Bible classes, church errands, engaging with community leaders, and numerous other activities governed my life. Even on Sabbaths, I was so engrossed in attending to members' needs that Sabbath responsibilities were more dutiful than beautiful. Yes, I enjoyed serving and seeing the beneficiaries of my ministry flourish. One day, I felt the joy of ministry—the only work I ever wanted to do—waning fast. Upon reflection, I recognized that I needed to do something to address the deteriorating situation.

Consequently, I decided to reduce my involvement by delegating more to other church leaders. I also committed to utilizing my Sabbath afternoons differently to renew my energy.

This plan of action yielded immediate benefits. My spirit was rebooted and renewed, and intimacy with my family increased. We spent the time reading, reflecting, and engaging in meaningful and personal discussions. We listened to our favorite music, played religious games, and took long drives so that we could be refreshed by nature. One of my favorite things to do on Sabbaths is enjoy the well-manicured, rainbow-colored parks and green spaces. Visiting the parks is now a regular Sabbath custom. Our daughter has often commented, "I love when we go to the park, because we get to see the birds, hear the breeze rustling through the leaves of the trees, hang out and have lunch, and communicate on a deeper level." It is a joy going by Lake Ontario, hearing the waves crashing on the shore, and feeling the sun on my skin.

Spiritually and mentally, I found this new emphasis renewing and reviving. The experience brought to mind what it truly means to "Come . . . apart . . . and rest a while" (Mark 6:31, KJV). The Sabbath now offers me time for reflection, meditation, and prayer that completely focuses on my Creator, who continues to give me extraordinary privileges and trusts me with His work (1 Timothy 1:12).

The result of changing my Sabbath practice saved me from full burnout, declining interest in ministry, and stress. It allowed me to refocus while bonding with my family. Indeed, the Sabbath saved me from losing my ministry.

Anthony Michael Reid is a pastor at the Mount Gilead Seventh-day Adventist Church in Toronto, Ontario, Canada.

The Sabbath—A Six-Decade Journey

Robert O. A. Samms

Moreover also I gave them my sabbaths, to be a sign between me and them, that they might know that I am the LORD that sanctify them.
—Ezekiel 20:12, KJV

After graduation from high school, I lived with my father in Spanish Town, Jamaica. I experienced a new freedom and decided to enjoy the world's allurements. I was attracted to music, dancing, and girls. It was the age of rock and roll, with singers like Elvis Presley, LaVern Baker, Little Richard, and Fats Domino. I said to myself, "World, here I come!"

One Saturday morning, unexpectedly, I saw Doug, a former schoolmate. We talked about many things, and even religion came up. As teenagers, we usually didn't think about religious matters seriously. But this day was different. We actually talked about becoming Christians. But how would we do that? We agreed to visit different churches and then decide what to do.

My friend said, "Seventh-day Adventists worship on Saturday. Let's visit them." We searched and found an Adventist church. The pastor was about to conduct a baptism and asked an elder to meet with us. We listened to him for about three hours as he revealed the biblical teaching on the sacredness of the Sabbath commandment and its history. The elder even talked about three angels and their messages as described in the book of Revelation. This was new to us. Both of us accepted Christ and the Sabbath. Amazingly, we decided then and there to become ministers to tell others about this message.

The following week, I obtained my first job as a bookkeeper in Kingston, Jamaica. The job required working until noon on Saturdays. After work, we traveled four miles back to the Seventh-day Adventist Church in Spanish Town. The following week, we heard about a closer Adventist church in Rollington Town, Kingston. We arrived at that church in the midafternoon and spent the rest of the day with the members. We had a wonderful experience that Sabbath, and I knew that I needed to talk to my employer. Monday morning, I told my boss that I could no longer work on Saturdays because it was the Sabbath. His response was immediate and final.

"Samms, it is either your job or your church." On Friday, I collected my pay and never returned. My decision was based on God's promised blessing: "Then you shall delight yourself in the LORD; and I will cause you to ride upon the high hills of the earth" (Isaiah 58:14).

For the next two years, I struggled to find a job, but eventually, the Lord blessed me. My friend, Doug, graduated from an Adventist university but tragically lost his life. I miss him, but I still remember some of the wonderful Sabbaths we spent together.

For me, the Sabbath is still a blessing, and I thank God for it.

Robert O. A. Samms is a former president of the Quebec Conference of Seventh-day Adventists in Longueuil, Quebec, Canada.

God's Grace and a Wonderful Wife

Bernard Sauvagnat

I grew up in France. My father was a Seventh-day Adventist pastor, and ever since I was three weeks old, I have happily gone to church every Sabbath with my family. I attended public schools, and my absences on Saturdays were tolerated as long as I remained up-to-date in my schoolwork.

When I was thirteen, I entered the ninth grade. When the weekly schedule was distributed, I noticed that Saturdays were not too heavy: two consecutive hours of English. But then the English teacher said all the tests of the year would be held on Saturdays. I went and spoke with her, explaining our Seventh-day Adventist faith, and told her that I would be grateful if she permitted me to be tested on other days. She refused very firmly and gave me a failing grade for the year.

At the end of the school year, I passed the state exam and was admitted into high school, but the English teacher convinced the other teachers that my failing grade in English prevented me from entering the upper grade. I was to repeat ninth grade.

As you can imagine, I was upset about having to repeat the ninth grade. But the Lord had a plan.

When I reached the twelfth grade, a new philosophy teacher arrived at our school. He was a very special man, a kind of genius in teaching. In class, he took apart the main schools of philosophy to show their system of thinking and their strengths and weaknesses. He did it with Christianity also. In spite of his unbelief, he was the one who made me understand clearly the centrality of God's grace in authentic Christianity. Thus, he pulled the trigger that made me decide to be baptized and devote my life to sharing this divine grace in Jesus. At the end of that school year, with my high school diploma, I was baptized and enrolled as a theology student to become a pastor.

Three years later, after I completed my theology degree, I went to a college in England to improve my English. Among the fantastic discoveries that I made in England was a precious young lady from Switzerland, who has been my wife since 1970. We planned to celebrate our fiftieth wedding anniversary in 2020 but could not because of the COVID-19 pandemic. But that does not prevent me from being grateful for the wonderful wife the Lord gave me.

These lifelong blessings would never have happened if that English teacher had not resisted the verdict of my state exam and convinced her colleagues that I had to repeat ninth grade.

But above all, I thank God for His Sabbath day, which brings the blessing of His grace into our lives.

_____

Bernard Sauvagnat is a retired pastor living in Paris, France.

What Sabbath Means in My Life

Jean Sequeira

As a North London teenager, I rode my bicycle home from work and passed Howard Hall, a community facility. Noticing an upcoming event, it never struck me that by attending the advertised meetings, my life would change forever.

During those meetings, Pastor Kenneth Gammon spoke on the Bible prophecy from Daniel 2 and immediately held my attention. Did God actually give Nebuchadnezzar a dream foretelling future events? How amazing! For an impressionable teen, it established an unwavering confidence in the Bible.

The two sermons that impacted me most were the biblical views regarding what happens after death and the seventh-day Sabbath. The former settled my mind against spiritualism; the latter created an awareness of the Creator and the importance of obeying Him.

The preacher's words warmed my heart. Why hadn't anyone shared this good news before? The Lord reached down, touched me, and rapidly changed a pleasure-seeking jazz-club enthusiast into a seeker of knowledge of a loving God.

How wonderful to devote an entire day to our Creator! What joy in taking time to "be still, and know that [He is] God" (Psalm 46:10, KJV). What an opportunity to attend church, fellowship with others, study the Bible, take nature walks, and visit the housebound.

The desire to keep Sabbath challenged my work as a librarian in a large greeting card company. Since Sabbath begins at sunset Friday, it meant leaving work before 3:00 P.M. during London's winter.

The Lord had blessed me with two wonderful bosses. In the main office, my immediate boss, Mr. Sawyer, was a Catholic who listened intently as I answered his numerous questions on "Why Saturday?"

My other boss, Ron, a practicing Jew, was fascinated that a Gentile worker wanted to keep the Sabbath (or Shabbat, as he called it). His endless questions reinforced my understanding of what it means to keep the Sabbath holy.

My interests centered on church and youth meetings. The youth in the Edmonton Seventh-day Adventist Church in London taught me what it means to belong to God's family (many of my old friends wanted nothing to do with a "religious fanatic").

I am so happy that the Lord provided a new outlook and a special day to devote to Him. It gave me a new focus, new friends, and countless opportunities to serve Him and His children around the world.

Now that I am an octogenarian, witnessing opportunities are fewer, but in our retirement home, neighbors often ask, "Why Saturday?" I relish sharing how Sabbath keeps me focused on my relationship with the Lord.

Since we currently face isolation and social distancing, I spend Sabbath hours with Hope Channel, listening to Dwight Nelson's sermons (preached from Pioneer Memorial Church on the campus of Andrews University) or Tanzania's Swahili choirs and inspirational nature videos on YouTube.

Sabbath blesses my soul, shutting away the cares and problems of every day and giving me time to draw closer to my Creator.

Jean Sequeira is a storyteller and writer living in Gladstone, Oregon, United States.

The Unhurried Gift

Ivan L. Williams Sr.

I grew up in the southern part of the United States. Sabbath never entered our home unannounced or unprepared. We welcomed the Sabbath by singing and reciting memory verses, especially Exodus 20:8–11. We shared our spiritual experiences and prayed. In our home, Father led our welcoming of the Sabbath, and Mother usually played the piano. Sabbath never sneaked in on Friday evening and never sneaked out on Saturday night. The Sabbath was recognized, cherished, and fondly remembered.

Reminiscing about Sabbaths as a child, it seems that food tasted better, sleep felt deeper, and fellowship was plentiful and unhurried. Long before the digital age of everyday access to the best in Christian music, Sabbath at my home was a haven of heavenly music played by an eight-track player or a turntable. The Sabbath had a different rhythm and was a time for childlike reflection. These experiences certainly helped me develop greater faith in the God of creation and shaped a positive outlook on life (Mark 2:27; Philippians 4:13).

Sabbath worship experiences blended home, school, and church. I learned to acknowledge the Lord, the Creator of this seventh day. Sabbath School classes and worship in church reinforced who the Author of the Sabbath is in my life. The Sabbath gave me meaning and purpose.

I must admit, however, that as a teenager, there were times I wished the Sabbath would rush by and fade into the new week. That happened, especially if I was anticipating something I thought was more exciting at school or in my playtime. But as I've grown older, I realize that running 24-7 without an acknowledgment, without a pause in the week, without worship of the Creator is out of harmony with God's plan for me. Like the apostle Paul, childish things in my life gave way to adult things, and the realization of the gift of time called the Sabbath became a precious unhurried blessing in these busy times. Now I want the Sabbath to linger all week.

I invite you to accept the Giver of the Sabbath, and Sabbath, the gift. You will declare, "What a Lord, what a Creator!"

Ivan L. Williams Sr. is the ministerial secretary for the North American Division of Seventh-day Adventists in Columbia, Maryland, United States.

Sabbath Blessings

Jesse Wilson

I was thirteen years old and excited about football tryouts. I had watched my neighborhood team dominate South Memphis, Tennessee, middle schools for years. And now, I was a wide-eyed seventh-grader vying for a precious spot on the squad.

Things went well, so well that I was chosen to play quarterback, the key position for the team of my dreams. But there was one problem. Our tryouts and practices were held weekdays after school. As a new Seventh-day Adventist, I was always aware of the "day dying in the west" on Fridays—in other words, the arrival of Sabbath. I would have to leave practice in time to shower and get home by sundown.

I was rarely missed at first, but as my role on the team grew, so did the complications. My teammates and coaches began to notice my early Friday exits. One day, the head coach pulled me aside and asked me about it. I explained that I was an Adventist, and he seemed to understand. In fact, all was well until the schedule was released and there were three Friday night games scheduled for that season. I broke out in a cold sweat.

What was I to do? Football was my passion, but I was also excited about my recent baptism. The doctrines were challenging, but my love for Jesus and the Sabbath was genuine. How would I explain this to the coach? How would I explain this to my father, who was not a Sabbath keeper and was very excited for me to follow in his athletic footsteps?

I prayed, wrestled, and made a decision. I spoke to my coach and explained that I would not play or practice from Friday night to Saturday night. He asked me if I could get a release from my pastor to play. He did not realize that in the Adventist church, the pastor does not have such authority. I explained to him that it was my decision, and I apologized for the inconvenience. He said he was sorry, but he understood. I was heartbroken, but I was satisfied.

A week later, that same coach called me into his office. He had consulted with the coaches of our Friday night opponents, and each one consented to reschedule the games to a Thursday night. What a wonderful surprise! Since then, I have had Sabbath conflicts that didn't quite turn out that way. But my school football experience was an early lesson in what the Lord of the Sabbath can do when we stand on our convictions.

Jesse Wilson is the director of the Bradford, Cleveland, Brooks Center at Oakwood University in Huntsville, Alabama, United States.

What the Sabbath Means to Me

Nancy Vollmer Wilson

Sabbath has always been my favorite part of the week. As a child, I looked forward to Sabbath, for it was such a special day. The housecleaning started at least the day before, on Thursday. By late afternoon on Friday, our Sabbath clothes were ironed, and the house was sparkling clean and accented with Mother's freshly cut flowers throughout. The amazing aromas coming from the kitchen promised a very special supper with traditions like homemade *schnecken* (a sweet roll passed down from my German Vollmer grandparents) and fruit salad, along with other traditions. As children, my brothers and I always had our baths taken and were in our pajamas in time for Friday evening worship. It was as though our family was preparing for something very special.

As the Sabbath hours approached, it seemed that heaven and our home came together to celebrate this very special day. In fact, the atmosphere in our home itself was different during those sacred Sabbath hours. It was a day to recognize that we were God's children, His creation whom He loved, and that He was our heavenly Father who met all of our needs and was the source of all that was good.

Even our worship was extra special on Friday night—an evening like no other. Daddy would lead out, and then all five of us would pray—Daddy, Mother, my two brothers, and I. Mother, who played the piano beautifully, often played hymns as we fell asleep that night. Growing up in my loving home, I never thought of the weekly observance of the Sabbath as being legalistic in any way. Instead, it was a beautiful experience.

I knew Jesus as my very personal Friend who loved me dearly and was interested in every aspect of my life. But it wasn't until I was an adult that I came to realize that the Sabbath was not only created to remind me of my Creator, who alone deserved my worship, but also of my Redeemer, who alone is able to restore me into His image. It was then that the Sabbath became not only a rest from my earthly labors but also a good weekly reminder that my salvation was in Christ, not in my human striving to do good works. As I surrendered to Him and walked with Him each day, He was the One doing the work in me. My part was to stay connected to Him; He would do the transforming.

The traditions of my childhood have continued in my husband's and my home. God knew we would need this very special day for physical, mental, social, and spiritual restoration. The Sabbath is one of God's most precious gifts, and it keeps us focused on our connection with Him. I'm so thankful we will be celebrating Sabbath throughout eternity!

Nancy Vollmer Wilson is a physical therapist and pastor's wife in Brookeville, Maryland, United States.

God's Gift to Me

Joy Woodbury

Just recently, at fifteen years old, I became a Seventh-day Adventist.

Although I grew up in an Adventist family, church, and school, for many years, I was not Adventist. The Sabbath was a day of rules dictating what I wasn't allowed to do. I believed the seventh day should not matter.

That was before I realized the Sabbath is Christ's gift to me.

Before accepting Christ as my Savior, my life was a mess. I thought I had resisted God too many times to be forgiven until I met the apostle Paul. Paul was a persecutor of Christians until Jesus, lovingly and mercifully, called him to a special mission (see Acts 9). From then on, he became a warrior for Jesus and a protector of His people, even to the point he was willing to suffer countless gory beatings, terrible hunger and thirst, cold, exposure, imprisonments, shipwrecks, and much more (2 Corinthians 11:23–28). Paul said that through his conversion, Jesus meant to reassure us that we can be saved too (1 Timothy 1:16).

Those words caused me to believe in Jesus' love and let Him bring joy into my life. As I continued reading about Paul, I noticed the dedication with which he followed God's commandments. Everything Jesus taught Paul he regarded as a gift; that was why he was willing to suffer so much (Philippians 3:7–11). I began to wonder: *If all Jesus' teachings are a gift, does that include the seventh-day Sabbath?*

I decided to study the seventh-day Sabbath in the Bible and was amazed by my findings. It turned out that the Sabbath was not a day dictating what I wasn't allowed to do, but a day of *freedom* to spend with God.

Six days of the week, there is always work to do. God Himself spent six days working to create our beautiful world and everything in it. He saw that His work was very good, so He rested on the seventh day and blessed it as a gift to us (Genesis 2:3). Through the Sabbath, God tells us, "You have done very good work for Me for six days! I am inviting you to come and rest with Me for a whole day on the Sabbath." The blessing God wants His people to experience is restated in the Ten Commandments (Exodus 20:8–11).

The prophet Isaiah tells us the Sabbath brings delight in the Lord (Isaiah 58:13, 14). The Sabbath matters because God desires to give us joy. Jesus told the religious leaders that the Sabbath is not a day of rules but is indeed a gift (Mark 2:27).

As a teenager, it is so liberating to know Jesus created the Sabbath to bring me delight. Longing to thank Him by honoring His day, I became an Adventist. Because of the Sabbath, I delight more in my friendship with Jesus.

Thank God for the gift of His seventh-day Sabbath!

Joy Woodbury is a tenth-grade student at La Sierra Academy in Riverside, California.

More About God's Gift of the Sabbath

Nikolaus Satelmajer

Would you like to study more about the Sabbath? In this section, we are sharing some helpful resources. This list is not exhaustive, but we believe you will find it helpful. In order to make this list more practical, it is divided into sections.

The Sabbath in the Bible

What does the Bible say about the Sabbath? To find out, use the subject index found in many Bibles. Or use an exhaustive print or online Bible concordance.

Books about the Sabbath

Andreasen, M. L. *The Sabbath*. Washington, DC: Review and Herald®, 1942.

Andrews, J. N. *History of the Sabbath and First Day of the Week*. Battle Creek, MI: Steam Press of the Seventh-day Adventist Publishing Association, 1862.

Bacchiocchi, Samuele. *Divine Rest for Human Restlessness: A Theological Study of the Good News of the Sabbath for Today*. Rome: Pontifical Gregorian University Press, 1980.

Bediako, Daniel, and Ekkehardt Mueller. *The Sabbath in the Old Testament and the Intertestamental Period*. Silver Spring, MD: Biblical Research Institute, 2021.

Brunt, John C. *A Day for Healing*. Nampa, ID: Pacific Press®, 2016.

Colon, Mary-Ellen. *From Sundown to Sundown: How to Keep the Sabbath . . . and Enjoy It!* Nampa, ID: Pacific Press®, 2008.

Davidson, Jo Ann. *Rediscovering the Glory of the Sabbath*. Nampa, ID: Pacific Press®, 2021.

MacCarty, Skip. *In Granite or Ingrained: What the Old and New Covenants Reveal About the Gospel, the Law, and the Sabbath*. Berrien Springs, MI: Andrews University Press, 2007.

Odom, Robert L. *Sabbath and Sunday in Early Christianity*. Washington, DC: Review and Herald®, 1977.

Strand, Kenneth A. "The Sabbath." In *Handbook of Seventh-day Adventist Theology*. Hagerstown, MD: Review and Herald®, 2000.

Strand, Kenneth A., ed. *The Sabbath in Scripture and History*. Washington, DC: Review and Herald®, 1982.

Tonstad, Sigve K. *The Lost Meaning of the Seventh Day.* Berrien Springs, MI: Andrews University Press, 2009.

Sabbath resources emphasizing a geographic area

Ball, Bryan W. *The Seventh-Day Men: Sabbatarians and Sabbatarianism in England and Wales, 1600–1800.* Cambridge, UK: James Clarke, 2009.

Bradford, Charles E. *Sabbath Roots: The African Connection.* Silver Spring, MD: Ministerial Association of the General Conference of Seventh-day Adventists, 1999.

Liechty, Daniel. *Andreas Fischer and the Sabbatarian Anabaptists: An Early Reformation Episode in East Central Europe.* Scottdale, PA: Herald Press, 1988.

Satelmajer, Nikolaus. "Theophilus Brabourne and the Sabbath." *Andrews University Seminary Studies* 26, no. 1 (Spring 1988).

Journals and magazines

The following publications often have articles on the Sabbath.

Adventist Review—www.adventistreview.org
Andrews University Seminary Studies—digitalcommons.andrews.edu/auss/
Message magazine—www.messagemagazine.com
Ministry—www.ministrymagazine.org
Signs of the Times—signsofthetimes.com

Media programs

These media ministries offer Bible study lessons that feature the Sabbath.

Breath of Life—www.breathoflifestudy.com
Faith for Today—faithfortoday.tv
It Is Written—www.itiswritten.study/home
It Is Written Canada—https://itiswrittencanada.ca
Jesus101—www.jesus101.tv
Voice of Prophecy—voiceofprophecy.com/bible-studies

Creation Sabbath resources

The fourth Sabbath of every October is set aside to celebrate God as our Creator. For resources to make Creation Sabbath special, visit creationsabbath.net. And for additional information, visit www.ministrymagazine.org/archive/2009/07/god-our-creator.

List of Contributors

The Gift